The Language of Exclusion

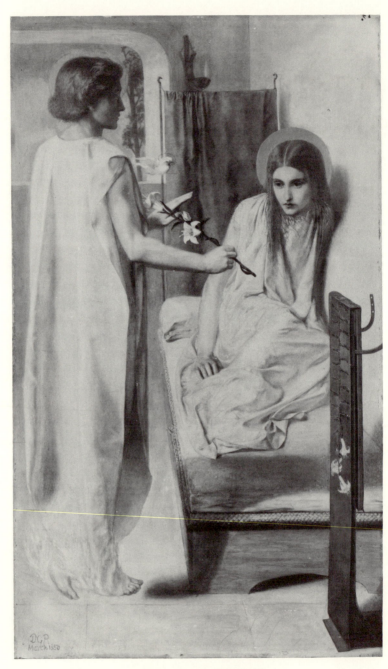

"Ecce Ancilla Domini"
("The Annunciation") by Dante Gabriel Rossetti, 1849-50.
The Tate Gallery, London.

THE LANGUAGE OF EXCLUSION

The Poetry of Emily Dickinson and Christina Rossetti

Sharon Leder with
Andrea Abbott

Contributions in Women's Studies, Number 83

Greenwood Press
New York • Westport, Connecticut • London

Library of Congress Cataloging-in-Publication Data

Leder, Sharon.
    The language of exclusion.

    (Contributions in women's studies, ISSN 0147-104X ;
no. 83)
    Bibliography: p.
    Includes index.
    1. Dickinson, Emily, 1830-1886—Criticism and
interpretation. 2. Rossetti, Christina Georgina,
1830-1894—Criticism and interpretation. 3. Women
and literature. 4. Feminism and literature. 5. Sex
role in literature. 6. Literature, Comparative—
American and English. 7. Literature, Comparative—
English and American. I. Abbott, Andrea. II. Title. III. Series.
PS1541.Z5L37 1987   811'.4'09   87-7519
ISBN 0-313-25629-2 (lib. bdg. : alk. paper)

British Library Cataloguing in Publication Data is available.

Library of Congress Catalog Card Number: 87-7519
ISBN: 0-313-25629-2
ISSN: 0147-104X

First published in 1987

Greenwood Press, Inc.
88 Post Road West, Westport, Connecticut 06881

Printed in the United States of America

∞™

The paper used in this book complies with the
Permanent Paper Standard issued by the National
Information Standards Organization (Z39.48-1984).

10 9 8 7 6 5 4 3 2

Contents

Illustrations

Preface

This book began with the perception that most biographies of nineteenth-century women poets written before 1960 portrayed the same stereotype: Nineteenth-century women poets were, for the most part, love-starved, frustrated spinster/recluses whose poetry sprang from torment. Reading Mary Ellmann's *Thinking About Women* (1968) helped us see that these biographies derived more from stereotypes about women than from the poets' lives themselves.[1] Kate Millett's *Sexual Politics* (1970) extended and developed Ellmann's idea of "phallic criticism" by uncovering sexist biases not only in traditional literary portraits of women, but also throughout the fields of literary history and literary criticism.[2] Other early feminist classics which gave rise to the present volume include Ellen Moers' *Literary Women* (1976) which established the early theory of a female literary tradition based on thematic and metaphoric patterns.[3] Elaine Showalter's early thesis of separate women's literary cultures which expressed different levels of feminist awareness, *A Literature of Their Own* (1977), inspired the meshings between women's literature and social history in this book.[4]

Showalter's new anthology, *The New Feminist Criticism: Essays on Women, Literature and Theory* (1985), has remained true to one of the early prescriptions for feminist literary criticism, that it examine the relationship of literature to life in order detect distortion and evaluate social impact.[5] Since those early days of feminist literary criticism, however, the field has come to focus more on women poets' use of language than on the relationship of language to life or on the conditions out of which literature is born.

Especially in Dickinson and Rossetti criticism this has been so, not only because poets are usually associated with art above life, but also because little of their actual lives has been uncovered by research. One recent trend applies psychoanalytic and linguistic theories to their poetry. This can be useful if the theories also aim at a fuller understanding of the writer's circumstances politically and historically. In Dickinson criticism, Shira Wolosky's *Emily Dickinson: A Voice of War* (1984) achieved this type of linguistic analysis and helped the reader to understand the way Dickinson used language to mediate her historical experience.[6]

However, there is a popular critical thrust to connect the linguistic techniques poets employ to certain universal aspects of women's psyches. This false-universalizing tends to reify old stereotypes of Dickinson and Rossetti as reclusive and as weakened by the dominant culture. Dolores Rosenblum's first article on Rossetti embodied this type of criticism in its emphasis on Rossetti's "inward pose"; Sandra Gilbert and Susan Gubar echoed this idea for Dickinson in their description of Dickinson's masks.[7] While these readings do indeed provide a sense of the layered complexity of Dickinson's and Rossetti's language, they also sustain limiting images of them as strange eccentrics whose language expressed fractured reactions against patriarchal linguistic structures. Margaret Homans has continued this trend in her comparison of Dickinson and Rossetti.[8]

We, on the other hand, follow the tradition of Showalter, Lillian Robinson, and Martha Vicinus. Robinson expressed one of the major goals of this tradition in *Sex, Class and Culture* (1978): "Only from an understanding of the mass experience that forces us to *become* heroes can we build a movement to make fundamental changes in social institutions or our own lives."[9] By focusing on the shared historical experience of these two most "private" poets, we reveal their public significance and demonstrate the inadequacy of the spinster/recluse model for studying their work.

We started to discuss the ideas for this book in 1978. In joy and pain, we wrote this book together, although the nature of our collaboration has changed over time. These changes have resulted in a book somewhat unusually described as authored by Sharon Leder with Andrea Abbott. The following explains the nature of our collaboration.

We composed the last chapter first. We wrote sentence by sentence together in one of our kitchens or living rooms. "War Poems" came next but with a different methodology. This suited our different living situations since we were now living in different cities. Often, we met to map out the book in coffee shops located at different midpoints between us. Leder wrote "Rossetti's War Poems," and Abbott followed with "Dickinson's War

Poems." Then we exchanged drafts and edited one another's work. We followed the same pattern for "The Market Is for Bankers, Burglars, and Goblins." To provide a background coherence for these thematic chapters, Leder wrote Rossetti's biography, and Abbott followed with Dickinson's, while Leder helped the babysitter mind Ian and Nicky, Abbott's children. "Women's Place/Women's Nature" was originally two separate chapters which Leder synthesized and condensed into one chapter. Then Leder composed the comparative "Overview" that justifies the linkages between the two poets and the chapter "Parallel Sketches" which establishes the methodology for composite biography. Leder revised and edited the entire manuscript and brought it through to publication.

Production can be a frustrating process when one is under time pressure and lacks adequate technological assistance. Fortunately, Leder was bailed out by her brother, a Decmate computer, and a laser printer. This book had a longer gestation period than a human birth, but it represents a new life nonetheless. Writing, producing, and publishing a book are all-engrossing, time-consuming endeavors around which it is not easy to arrange the vicissitudes of one's professional, social, and family life. We feel fortunate that we were able to change the nature of our working relationship and the extent of our co-authorship to meet the changing needs and priorities in our lives.

We have numerous people to thank: our readers Sue Tournour, Ruth Meyerowitz, Ellen Dubois, Michael Frisch, Mary Ann Ferguson, Martha Vicinus, Judith Fetterley, Moira Ferguson, Lillian Robinson, Berenice Fisher, Elaine Ognibene, John Dings, Claire Kahane, Theresa Morone, Virginia Cyrus, Marilyn Matis, Gisele Feal, Tucker Farley, and Milton Teichman. Technological assistance from Ron Leder and Pierre Hahn was invaluable, along with assistance from Rosario Enriquez. Angel Wahler put the first draft on disk. Women's Studies at the State University of New York at Buffalo and Elizabeth Kennedy, one of the program's founders, pushed this project at every stage. Endesha Ida Mae Holland stressed the need for a writing style in the active voice. Women's Studies at SUNY-New Paltz provided the context in which this project could be brought to completion. Special thanks go to Pat Clarke, Amy Kesselman, and Gale McGovern.

No set of acknowledgments would be complete without recognition of our roots and personal support networks. For Leder, the necessary encouragement came from family and friends. Harriet and Deborah Leder, Leder's mother and sister, who read the manuscript and offered criticisms of it, were always behind her, assuring her of the value of the project. Leder's friends, without whom the project could not have come to completion, include members of the National Women's Studies Association: Caryn Musil, Barbara Gerber, Nancy Osborne, Bonita Hampton, Wilma Beamon, the late Natalie Kazmierski, and many, many others. Members of the Buffalo community also must be remembered for their encouragement and support: Janet Chassmann, June Licence, Beverly Harrison, and many others. Leder's therapist, Bea Roth, had the "discerning eye" to affirm Leder's sense of reality.

Abbott acknowledges her father's memory, her husband, her children, her mother, and Women's Studies College at SUNY-Buffalo for making her ways of thinking possible.

PART I

LIVING IN THE WORLD

Chapter 1

Overview

Two geniuses, Emily Dickinson and Christina Rossetti, decided to write against the Victorian grain. "It's a weary life," Rossetti wrote in 1854:

> Doubly blank in a woman's lot:
> I wish and I wish I were a man:
> Or, better than any being, were
> not.[1]

A century of critical response misreads the poetry of Dickinson and Rossetti as the expression of neurotic madwomen. Critics forget Dickinson's words of 1862:

> Much Madness is divinest Sense—
> To a discerning Eye—
> Much Sense—the starkest Madness—
> 'Tis the Majority
> In this, as All, prevail—
> Assent—and you are sane—
> Demur—you're straightway dangerous—
> And handled with a Chain—[2]

Dickinson's and Rossetti's persistent image as neurotic women is a distortion, for they were not madwomen at all. Fueled with the temperature of their age, their poetry chronicles women's subordinate position in the dominant culture. Our new look at Dickinson's and Rossetti's poetry suggests an important, but neglected, feminist perspective on the nineteenth century. We need to adjust our readings of these two poets who were feminist gauges of their times to expand our vision of Victorian society.

Although Dickinson and Rossetti have signified neurosis for traditional critics from the Victorian period until the present, feminist critics have begun to rescue the two poets from the stereotype of spinster/recluse.[3] Despite many feminist interpretations of Dickinson, only Shira Wolosky's *Emily Dickinson: A Voice of War* convincingly places her in historical context. Even less work has been done on Rossetti, who has commonly been stereotyped as a religious recluse in the shadow of her more famous brother.

Traditional critics view the private worlds of Dickinson and Rossetti as neurotic and their departures from linguistic convention as pathological. Feminist critics have argued that Dickinson's and Rossetti's awareness of gender inequities led them to *select* privacy as a mode of filtering their experience. The feminist view evaluates their privacy as a valid, legitimate, and active way to mediate their experience of a hostile, larger world.

We need to readjust our view of Dickinson and Rossetti as purely private poets and begin to see them as public poets seriously engaging the major issues of their day. We need to see more fully and specifically how they expressed their gender exclusion in historical, economic, and political terms and how their poetry, by subtle use of complex linguistic figures and tones, embeds a radical, feminist critique of society industrializing around them.

In our study, the larger issue is to understand how women writers are involved in the world and how historical movements are reflected in their poetry, even when not explicit. The usual tendency is to read women's poetry in private, psychological terms. We argue that the poetry of Dickinson and Rossetti reflects an interest in current events and issues from a peculiarly feminist and feminine perspective. If we leave Dickinson's and Rossetti's personal and poetic images without this further exploration, we fail to understand important, social/historical dimensions of their poetry and the depth of their connection to the movements and events that shaped their lives, such as the rise of industrialism, changes in women's work and the privatization of women's sphere, the growth of nationalism and outbreak of European and American wars, evangelical reform and women's role in the spread of Puritan and Anglican ideology, and the beginnings of radical feminism.

Dickinson's familiar poem, #441, is a relevant example of poetry which comments indirectly on a major historical event, the Civil War:

> This is my letter to the World
> That never wrote to Me–
> The simple News that Nature told–
> With tender Majesty
>
> Her message is committed
> To Hands I cannot see–
> For love of Her–Sweet–countrymen–
> Judge tenderly–of Me

According to Dickinson's biographer, Richard Sewall, this poem is "too often regarded as a tearful complaint about being neglected." However, even for Sewall, Dickinson had "no social or political program," just the poet's desire to communicate the simple truth, a message no "more precise than Nature's."[4]

We suggest a different reading which reflects its historical context. The poem was written in early 1862 when the Civil War had already taken the lives of young men whom Dickinson knew from her home town in Amherst, Massachusetts. In late 1862, she included this poem, along with nineteen others, in a packet of poems she collected known as fascicle twenty-four. Indeed, two of the poems in the same fascicle, #444 and #596, are explicit critiques of the Civil War; #596 is actually copied onto the same manuscript sheet on which #441 appears.[5] Poem #596 is a well-known tribute to the mother of a brave soldier who died, and poem #444 is a meditation questioning the value of sacrificing lives in war for those who remain alive. Both these poems are discussed at length in our chapter "War Poems." The fact that Dickinson placed poem #441 in a fascicle with these two poems clearly moves us to consider #441 as a Civil War poem, though its treatment is more oblique than the other two.

The opening line of #441 establishes the "letter" as a metonym for the poem itself. The poem is immediately identified with a form of popular writing appropriate for women. Feminist social historians have documented the importance of correspondence to nineteenth-century middle-class women as a means of establishing bonds and maintaining friendships and a sense of community.[6] The world of letters was especially vital for Dickinson who consciously began to narrow her public activities during the Civil War.

At the same time, however, a tension is introduced because the poem/letter is boldly sent across the gender boundary into the public, male sphere which is the "World." The tension grows, not only because in line two, the "World" is accused of never writing, but also because in line three, the public but routine world of "News" is uniquely linked with the serene "Majesty" of "Nature."

Dickinson's linking of "News" with "Nature" exemplifies her complex system of signification. She employs "News" and "Nature" simultaneously as opposites and as equivalents. They are opposites in that they occupy entirely different temporal realms. "News," signifying the daily press, is episodic and historical. "Nature," signifying organic life and the natural world, is cyclic and suprahistorical. Following this reading, the historical "News" is incongruously invested with an oracular message which seems too vast for it to contain. However, if historical time is to be redeemed, especially during a period of civil war, Dickinson suggests the boundaries between "News" and "Nature" must be broken.

Dickinson yokes the two words together in the same poetic line and sets them up as parallel. By capitalizing both and stressing their alliteration, she miraculously forges an equivalency. Indeed, if "Nature" does her own reporting, the mediation process which "News" signifies becomes redundant. Our attention is drawn to "Nature" directly. Holding only transparent status, "News" denies that it is being differentiated from "Nature" at all. "Nature" becomes what is *really* new. Dickinson has–through metaphoric equivalency–transformed the very significance of news and history. However, the power of this transformation resides precisely in the different levels on which "News" and "Nature" signify.

This tension between nature and history, which is only implicit in the text of the poem itself, is foregrounded by introducing the historical dimension of the Civil War and applying it to the interpretation of poem #441. Dickinson leads us to the public realm by the historicity of the words she capitalized: World, News, Majesty. The world of daily "News" was as vital and familiar to Dickinson as the world of letters. Dickinson's own letters show she read *The Springfield Republican* every day, and letters were regularly published in the paper.[7] The "News" from "Nature" which Dickinson's letter/poem conveys concerns "Majesty" which is "tender." But the actual news of the day, in *The Springfield Republican*, was about the violence of power.

In "From Missouri," on January 1, 1862, *The Springfield Republican* reported that rebel forces under General Price took over Springfield. "With 8,000 men," he "had taken all the homes in Springfield for his troops, turning the children into the streets."[8] On the same day, Federal Brigadier-General W.S. Rosencrans stated in the paper: "Remember, you are fighting for your country, for your flag, for your homes. Your enemies are implacable in their hatred of you."[9]

Whether victories or defeats, Civil War battles led to deaths. In "From Fortress Monroe," on January 3, 1862, the paper reported that "Captain McQuade . . . died at Richmond on the 26th."[10] On the same day, in "The Upper Potomac," news came that "the rebels . . . attacked the railroad workmen 11 miles east of Hancock . . . with the loss of 20 killed."[11]

In stanza two, Dickinson capitalized "Hands." They hold a double meaning, depending on one's interpretation of "committed / To." If one reads "committed / To" as signifying "entrusted to," then "Hands" become a synecdoche for God. Although God's hands are invisible, they are committed to an ineluctable plan for which the poet can not be held responsible. At the same time, the synecdoche "Hands" also signifies the new class of laborers generated by the factory system. In this context, God's hands become God's workers or agents of God. The poet, committed for "love" of "Nature" to conveying the "News," also becomes identified as one of God's hands. The poet's apprehension about being judged suggests that God's plan, Nature's message which the poet conveys, is at variance with what the poet's "countrymen" do. Dickinson's countrymen were then waging war, having forgotten nature's message of how to temper "Majesty" with tenderness.

One can also read "committed / To" as signifying "carried out by." "Hands" then become a synecdoche for "countrymen" who wage a war Dickinson cannot see. In this reading, Nature's message remains the same, but it is Nature's message alone, not God's. Nature, "Sweet" and love-eliciting, is the supreme, commanding authority, and the audience for her "message" is targeted–the "countrymen"–rather than the creator of it, God.

By using this historical and ideological model, we show that the initiative for Dickinson's and Rossetti's linguistic innovation lies not only in their desire to reconstruct language, but also in their visions for reforming the public realm. It will help to look at Dickinson and Rossetti–the most interior women poets of the nineteenth century–to develop a broader method for understanding the woman writer's way of living in the world. By looking at both Dickinson and Rossetti, parallel in some ways, different in others, both exemplars of the problem at hand, we argue that the relationship between women writers and their larger society, so hidden in the usual approach to individual biography, can be unfolded. This approach is in dramatic contrast to the feminist critics who understand Dickinson and Rossetti's remarkable power as writers according to the critical model of phallogocentrism in which female creativity stems from primal rage over male domination.[12] By showing these poets' engagement with the world, our model connects their creativity to their positive desire to reconstruct social conditions.

When we look at the lives and poetry of Emily Dickinson and Christina Rossetti more closely through historical frameworks, we note how their development marks a somewhat parallel trajectory. They both began writing poetry in their youth and became most productive and prolific in the decade before and during the American Civil War when women were emerging as a political force.

They lived at exactly the same period of time in societies that were inextricably linked economically, politically, and culturally. Although Rossetti was not as secure in her class or financial position as Dickinson, they were both white women born into relatively comfortable circumstances within five days of each other in December 1830. Dickinson came from a socially prominent, Puritan family concerned with its public image in Amherst, a relatively small American college town, while Rossetti came from an Anglo-Italian family intensely involved in European arts and revolutionary ideas in the London metropolis. They occupied similar positions in their families, and later in society at large, as single women with poetic vocations. They shared some favorite poetic foremothers, like Letitia Landon and Elizabeth Barrett Browning. In the contemporary poetic marketplace, they read and were measured against the same women poets, such as Adelaide Procter and Helen Hunt Jackson. It is likely Dickinson knew Rossetti's poetry; her "goblin" images echo Rossetti's after the publication of Rossetti's first volume, *Goblin Market and Other Poems* (1862). It is less likely Rossetti knew Dickinson's work until after Dickinson's death.

However, whether they knew one another or not is less germane to our study than the fact that they both occupied similar positions in the dominant culture as "redundant," seemingly useless, women. Their "redundancy" spurred their identification with the women's rights movement, and in their poetic critiques, they developed different visions for a better, future world. Although they developed very different poetic styles, the function of style in their aesthetic was similar. Their self-fashioned styles were the means by which their visionary messages could be conveyed to the world in order to awaken consciousness.

Dickinson and Rossetti emerged as women writers in the context of evangelical revival, economic transformation, and a new cult of womanhood. They chose to remain single daughters throughout their lifetimes, despite the lack of social status and the economic dependency connected with this role. It was a difficult decision, considering the tremendous pressure on women in the 1840s, 1850s and 1860s to conform to the dominant cults of romance, marriage, and motherhood. "A girl in the upper and middle classes could go on being somebody's daughter only so long as her father was alive," according to feminist historian Ray Strachey:

> And after that, if she had not succeeded in becoming
> somebody's wife, she was adrift. Without money, or the
> possibility of earning for herself, she was reduced to
> being dependent on her male relatives; and the position
> of being somebody's unmarried sister, or somebody's
> maiden aunt was far from agreeable. . . . With the
> laws of inheritance as they were, the single woman
> nearly always had narrow means; and her life was passed
> in trying to be as little in the way as could be
> managed. Through all the literature of the first half
> of the nineteenth century the pathetic figure of the
> old maid is found, a "proper sport" for comedy and
> satire.[13]

The Saturday Review reported the general opinion for 1859:

> Married life is woman's profession; and to this life
> her training—that of dependence—is modelled. Of course
> by not getting a husband, or losing him, she may find
> that she is without resources. All that can be said of
> her is, she has failed in business; and no social
> reform can prevent such failures.[14]

There *were* heroic women, such as Florence Nightingale, Emily Davies, Susan B. Anthony, Clara Barton—and Christina Rossetti and Emily Dickinson—who, by defying the conventional push toward marriage, risked being stigmatized. But the paths of these "independent women" who pursued "the cult of single blessedness" were minority patterns within the dominant culture.[15]

Dickinson's and Rossetti's decisions to remain unmarried were among the most compelling forces behind their poetic visions. It was also a primary way for each to resolve the tension which surfaces throughout their poetry between the idealized domesticity of married life, on the one hand, and the few opportunities for economic independence on the other.

One of Rossetti's poems, "The Lowest Room," illustrates this tension.

Written in 1856, when feminists were agitating for reform in marriage laws, the poem is a deceptively simple, long dialogue between two sisters. It is written as a parlor debate in four-line, iambic tetrameter stanzas, with the first and third lines rhyming. This rhythmic, lilting structure, while appropriate for the decorum of a parlor, diverts attention from the public import of the poem's subject matter. The sisters debate over women's role in several areas. What positions should women take on the issues of economic independence, war, slavery, and religious and marriage reform?

One sister is a poet who is less conventionally feminine than her counterpart. She complains that the contemporary age lacks heroic material for her writing, and that women, especially wives, lead meaningless lives in Victorian society. According to her, classical Greeks worshipped slaves more than Victorians worship their wives:

> "So yesterday I read the acts
>   of Hector and each clangorous king
> With wrathful great Aeacides:–
>   Old Homer leaves a sting.

> . . . .

> "He stirs my sluggish pulse like wine,
>   He melts me like the wind of spice,
> Strong as strong Ajax' red right hand,
>   And grand like Juno's eyes.

> "I cannot melt the sons of men,
>   I cannot fire and tempest-toss:–
> Besides, those days were golden days,
>   Whilst these are days of dross.

> . . . .

> "Then men were men of might and right,
>   Sheer might, at least, and weighty swords;
> Then men in open blood and fire
>   Bore witness to their words,

> . . . .

> "Then hand to hand, then foot to foot,

Stern to the death-grip grappling then,
Whoever thought of gunpowder
   Amongst these men of men?

. . . .

"Then heavenly beauty could allay
   As heavenly beauty stirred the strife:
By them a slave was worshipped more
   Than is by us a wife."[16]

The more conventional, feminine sister maintains that the real issues for women are protection and security. She argues that in pagan days, women were just the spoils of war. Now, in the Christian era, if women wish to achieve meaning in life, they possess the free will to do so:

She laughed again, my sister laughed;
   Made answer o'er the laboured cloth:
"I rather would be one of us
   Than wife, or slave, or both.

. . . .

"Then captive in an alien house,
   Hungering on exiles' bitter bread,—
They happy, they who won the lot
   Of sacrifice," she said.

. . . .

"But life is in our hands," she said:
   "In our own hands for gain or loss:
Shall not the Sevenfold Sacred Fire
   Suffice to purge our dross?

. . . .

"Our life is given us as a blank;
   Ourselves must make it blest or curst:
Who dooms me I shall only be
   The second, not the first?"

The supreme irony in the poem is that the sister who advocates the potentialities of free will for women chooses—for herself—the most conventional role:

> Well, twenty years have passed since then:
> My sister now, a stately wife
> Still fair, looks back in peace and sees
> The longer half of life—
>
> . . . .
>
> A husband honourable, brave,
> Is her main wealth in all the world:
> And next to him one like herself,
> One daughter golden-curled.

The narrator of the poem, however, remains unconvinced there are meaningful alternatives for women and chooses for herself the independent life instead:

> While I? I sat alone and watched:
> My lot in life, to live alone
> In mine own world of interests,
> Much felt but little shown.

In the critical decade before and during the American Civil War, when the women's rights movement was becoming visible in England and America, Dickinson's and Rossetti's themes of self-assertion and the urgency to realize themselves as poets—even at the expense of an idealized domestic life—dominate in their poetry as they never will again. Not only do their poetic voices defend the autonomy and strength of women alone, they take responsibility for "self" in an age when conventional literature prescribed exactly the opposite roles for women.

Although both poets reached poetic heights in originality, productivity, and political relevance during this period, they also encountered resistance from the traditional, critical establishment. In Rossetti's case, the critic John Ruskin objected to what he called "quaintnesses and offences" in her poetic form. "I sate [sic] up till late last night reading poems," Ruskin wrote to Christina's brother, Dante Gabriel:

They are full of beauty and power. But no publisher—I
am deeply grieved to know this—would take them, so full
are they of quaintnesses and offences. . . . Your
sister should exercise herself in the severest
commonplace of metre until she can write as the public
like. Then if she puts in her observation and passion
all will become precious. But she must have the Form
first.[17]

However incorrect Ruskin's judgment was about the popularity of
Rossetti's style, it did reflect dominant assumptions about women's
inferiority. Women were purported to have the same lack of intellectual
range and self-discipline as children. Rossetti had to struggle to find an
editor who would view her poetic style as innovative instead of untamed or
undisciplined. Alexander Macmillan was the visionary editor who published
Rossetti's first two major volumes in 1862 and 1866. The volumes, and
especially the poem "Goblin Market," won Rossetti public acclaim. The
public liked Rossetti's untraditional use of French "feminine" rhyme.[18]

At the same time Rossetti began to publish with Macmillan, she also
became an active social reformer. Her activities drew her to create
increasingly dramatic characterizations and intricate, narrative lines.
Dickinson, on the other hand, was more brilliant and innovative as a
dramatic lyricist than Rossetti. Her poems are spoken by a poetic voice or
persona she identified as "a supposed person."[19] However, during
Dickinson's lifetime, she only published seven of her almost two thousand
poems.

At the same time Rossetti was publishing, Dickinson's poetry received
lackluster response from Thomas Wentworth Higginson, a well-known man of
letters who was also a feminist and suffragist. Dickinson wrote to
Higginson after reading two of his articles in *The Atlantic Monthly* which
encouraged young authors to find markets for their writing.[20] However,
Higginson simply did not understand Dickinson's work. He pleaded with her
to regularize her form, while recommending Whitman. She replied that she
had not read Whitman because she heard he was "disgraceful." As to her own
poetry, she stated, "You think my gait 'spasmodic'—I am in danger—Sir—" and
further, "when I try to organize—my little Force explodes—and leaves me
bare and charred—."[21] She sought, and ignored, his advice throughout her
life, while he steadfastly advised her against publication.

Actually, Higginson held a dual evaluation of Dickinson's poetry.
Whereas he confided in others about Dickinson's genius and lauded her work
to them, he focused on the problems in her writing when he spoke to her

directly.[22]

This rejection of her work must have weighed heavily. After all, Higginson was publicly receptive to innovation in young writers, and he showed concern for the development of women writers in particular. Moreover, his political background appealed to Dickinson who wanted to rebel against Amherst. Dickinson's refusal to publish may be linked to Higginson's discouraging reception of her poetry, especially since this was generally a flourishing period for the publication of women's writing.

Before Dickinson received Higginson's feedback, she published three poems in *The Springfield Republican* edited by Samuel Bowles.[23] Bowles published her poems anonymously with manufactured titles and regularized them to conform to conventional patterns. Although Dickinson agonized over her decision not to publish again, it did free her from sentimental convention to develop a sharp, social criticism in her own, extraordinary style. A published poet, Rossetti remained tied to poetic convention more than Dickinson, although Rossetti drew on conventions from a diversity of cultures—French, Italian, and German, as well as English and American.

The years from 1858 to 1866 represent the period of Dickinson's greatest output. Although it is clear that Dickinson probably wrote most of her life, she did not consciously begin to gather poems together until 1858. She began thinking of herself as an artist and put together her first fascicle—a group of poems she collected, organized, and bound with string. In 1862, her peak writing year, she averaged a poem a day. It was also the year she wrote to Higginson, whose "Letter to a Young Contributor" in *The Atlantic Monthly* elicited many responses from young writers who were just beginning to market their work.

Most of Dickinson's critics, including many feminist critics, are too glib about Dickinson's refusal to publish. Often, Dickinson's position is presented as too positive a decision in her life, which implies she had foreknowledge that one day her poems would be important.[24] However, the three poems she wrote on the subject of fame between 1862 and 1863 (#406, #709, #713) do not express confidence about becoming famous to later generations. Instead, they claim that being famous to oneself, and living by one's own standards, provide enough reward. Coupled with Dickinson's request that her sister Lavinia burn all her papers, this evidence certainly suggests that Dickinson had little faith in her work being accepted by future critics.

Despite Dickinson's poor reception by these editors, from 1862 on, the syntax and structure of her poetry display the flourishing of her unique style. Feverishly, she continued to write poems, assemble fascicles, and refine her original form. Her familiar 1863 renunciation—"Publication—is the Auction / Of the Mind of Man—"—shows how, by way of extended metaphor and ironic toning, Dickinson minimizes the value of writing for publication. By figuring "Publication" as an "Auction," Dickinson claims publication sells "the Mind of Man" short, for it reduces the thought process to a completely material, economic exchange. Economic relations, in her view, were essentially at odds with creativity in that they were driven by naked self-interest. The creative process, on the other hand, involved the writer's spiritual interchange with God. As in Dickinson's earlier poem, #441, the poet's communication was actually the message of God and nature, the incarnation, the word made flesh, and not merely the extension or expression of the self:

> Thought belong to Him who gave it—
> Then—to Him Who bear
> Its Corporeal illustration—

In an ironic twist in tone, Dickinson shows how absurd and evil publication is to "reduce" the "Human Spirit / To Disgrace of Price—." First, she compares publication to an absurdity: "Sell / The Royal Air—." Then, she compares it to the evil of selling grace: "Be the Merchant / Of the Heavenly Grace—." No reader would be foolish enough to enter either exchange.

Dickinson's aesthetic as a poet was to make the world new, to address the complicated and dazzling truth, but in ways that could be received. This involved a kind of hermeneutics, a telling of the truth "slant," in metaphor and linguistic figures. This aesthetic is articulated in the familiar poem of 1868, #1129:

> Tell all the Truth but tell it slant—
> Success in Circuit lies
>
> . . . .
>
> The Truth must dazzle gradually
> Or every man be blind—

Because she refused to devalue the legitimacy of her perceptions, Dickinson became more aware of the complexity of historical experience and natural and spiritual phenomena. Even her nature poems reflect this increased awareness, and her themes extend to the Civil War, the increasing dominance of the market relation, the contradictions for women in institutionalized religion, her relationships with other women, and speculations on women's nature.

Unlike Dickinson, Rossetti was well-published and well-known during her lifetime. Yet, as a single woman and daughter, she was acutely sensitive to and sharply critical of the push to exclude women from public life. In the 1850s and 1860s, she created her major dramatic heroines, all of whom express a common ruling passion to "do" something with their lives. They are mainly women alone, especially rebellious daughters, who identify their lives as single women with a larger cause or purpose that often expresses no less than the pulse of their age. The increasing dramatic development of Rossetti's characters, and the psychological realism of her themes, reflect not only her widening experiences after 1854, when the more isolating roles she played—reluctant companion for her sick father, closet poet, and potential wife and mother—no longer applied to the changing conditions of her life. They also evince her greater feminist awareness due to her work as a High Church reformer. By the time *Goblin Market* and *The Prince's Progress* were published, Rossetti had learned to encode radical ideas about the commercialization of the marriage market, the bonds of sisterhood, illegitimate children, and war and peace, as well as women's autonomy within the newest and most innovative poetic structures of the day. Rather than use the satiric, didactic, heroic couplet, the conventional poetic form for social criticism, Rossetti adhered to an early Pre-Raphaelite rule of aesthetics: If the artist attempts too forcefully to "teach" morals, or to achieve fame, the artist will fail. This recalls Dickinson's maxim: "The Truth must dazzle gradually / Or every man be blind—." Thus, when Rossetti brought brutal aspects of women's lives to the public consciousness, she appealed to the emotions and to the heart as well as to the intellect and logical faculties.[25]

From one perspective, the lifestyle Rossetti chose was determined by her desire to write and to develop intellectually. She rejected governessing as an unsuitable long-term career, despite her training for the role. She rejected marriage in 1850, and again in 1866, to men who were inappropriate for different reasons. Like the duties of marriage, the responsibilities of governessing were too demanding for a poet. She began an involvement with social work in 1854 that would mushroom into a lifelong commitment after 1860, and she took two continental trips. She preferred remaining single, doing volunteer social work, and sharing household management with her sister and mother, since this lifestyle facilitated, rather than hindered, her writing.

The peaks of creativity both Dickinson and Rossetti achieved in the 1850s and 1860s have been attributed to unnecessarily narrow causes—

romance or the lack of it, considered seclusion, ill health, ecentricity, fanaticism, madness. The political and economic ferment over women's issues in the decade from 1856 to 1865 provides a more adequate context for understanding Dickinson's and Rossetti's emergence as poets. These connections become clearer if we examine the different kinds of formal communities for single, middle-class women that Martha Vicinus and Nina Auerbach studied, as well as the informal networks that Carroll Smith-Rosenberg and Nancy Cott identified.[26] In these groups and relationships, women developed an awareness of the condition of their sex. To different extents, Dickinson and Rossetti were involved in these networks and communities, from the chains of correspondence among female friends, to the women's colleges, the social work settlements, and the religious sisterhoods. The impact of these women-centered activities appears throughout their poetry.

We are not the first to note parallels between Dickinson and Rossetti in terms of their status as single daughters. The tradition began with their nineteenth-century critics. However, the first contemporary expression of this focus on spinsterhood appeared around 1930, Dickinson and Rossetti's centenary year, when critics interpreted their single state as seclusion and forged parallels between the two poets as unmarried and as, therefore, sexually unfulfilled. Since their single state was assumed to be a sign of withdrawal rather than of their movement toward autonomy and self-expression, they were both approached essentially as poets of the tortured, inner self.

Responding to these treatments, Allen Tate was one of the first critics to identify the bias against single women operating in this kind of critical presentation of Dickinson's work:

> Miss Dickinson was a recluse; but her poetry is rich
> with profound and varied experience. Where did she get
> it? Now some of the biographers, nervous in the
> presence of this discrepancy, are eager to find her a
> love affair, and I think this search is due to a modern
> prejudice: we believe that no virgin can know enough
> to write poetry. . . . The moral image that we have of
> Miss Dickinson . . . is that of a dominating spinster
> whose very sweetness must have been formidable.[27]

Most studies of Rossetti and Dickinson are "eager to find love affairs" for them. The 1960s produced Lona Mosk Packer's literary biography of Christina Rossetti which used the entire body of Rossetti's poetry to prove the identity of her missing lover as the already married freethinker, William Bell Scott. One of the "newest" approaches to Dickinson, by William Shurr, is based on a reading of Dickinson's forty fascicles as they have been reconstructed by R. W. Franklin. It yields yet another variation on the same theme, as its title implies—*The Marriage of Emily Dickinson.*[28] We do well to recall Conrad Aiken's point that "Miss Dickinson became a hermit by deliberate and conscious choice."[29] Allen Tate reminded us that "we cannot repeat" Aiken's "sensible remark . . . too often."[30]

Except for Shira Wolosky's recent book *Emily Dickinson: A Voice of War*, literary criticism accepted as a given that both poets were recluses. Wolosky shows how the Civil War appears through Dickinson's martial imagery and how it influenced her metaphysical relationship to history. However, because of this stress on Dickinson's metaphysical use of history, Wolosky does not develop how the actual conditions of the war changed the direction of Dickinson's writing.

While Richard B. Sewall's *The Life of Emily Dickinson* (1974) laid to rest old myths and misperceptions about the poet's eccentricities, it did not place Dickinson within broader social and historical contexts. Eleanor Thomas' *Christina Georgina Rossetti* (1931) is still considered the best biography of Rossetti, though it, too, focuses on Rossetti's poetry in literary contexts divorced from historical and political influences.

Many recent anthologies, articles, new editions of poems, literary biographies and critical surveys of nineteenth-century women writers argue for the complexity of Dickinson's and Rossetti's methods of composition. Representatives of the scholarship published within the last six years are Cheryl Walker's *The Nightingale's Burden*, which places Dickinson within an aesthetics-of-pain tradition of women poets; Barbara Antonina Mossberg's *Emily Dickinson: When a Writer Is a Daughter*, which undercuts sentimental images of Dickinson and constructs instead a mature poet who used poetry in part to challenge conventional ideas of femininity; Georgina Battiscombe's *Christina Rossetti: A Divided Life*, which connects Rossetti's themes of spiritual and psychic suffering to her poor physical condition, her religious commitment, and the cultural division between English and Italian in her family background; and Dolores Rosenblum's "Christina Rossetti's Religious Poetry: Watching, Looking, Keeping Vigil," which demonstrates the self-affirming ways Rossetti subverted the Anglican message for women in her poems. Each work represents these women as internal poets, or poets of the mind, whether confessional, psychological, or devotional, and as outsiders, estranged from political issues and reform movements of their day. Nowhere in the literature is there a serious and coherent study of the various political and economic forces that shaped the content and the style of their poetry. This book goes beyond the current criticism by releasing the poets from the prison of their private selves and by demonstrating their poetic responses to public events in their age.

We develop and demonstrate these ideas in several stages. First we chart their parallel trajectories as emerging writers by presenting biographical sketches. The sketches treat family relations insofar as they provide necessary background for understanding references in subsequent chapters. We highlight certain aspects of their lives: that is, their worldly activities as opposed to their seclusion, domesticity, virginity, and so on. We place them in the context of the major events and movements of their times—growing urbanization, religious reform, nationalistic wars, and changing roles for women. We compare what they were able to accomplish, their decisions to remain single, their struggles to achieve a sense of autonomy and faith, their modern-day reputations, and their very different poetic styles.

"The Victorian World" applies these historical and ideological contexts to literary interpretations of their poetry on war, industrialism, marriage, feminism, and sisterhood. Through subtle irony and metaphor, their war poems embed a radical feminist critique of male heroism and the high human price of the Crimean War and the American Civil War. Within this historical framework, well-known poems are treated in a new light and lesser-known poems on the themes of sacrifice, victory, and defeat assume greater significance. In "The Market Is for Bankers, Burglars, and Goblins," we show how their imagery and dramatic characterizations question the stability of the market relation and its increasing dominance over the texture of social interchange. In "Woman's Place/Woman's Nature," we draw together the different strands from the previous chapters to form a coherent picture of the two women in relation to the dominant society, and we compare their different poetic visions for an alternative social order based on the model of sisterhood. We show how their poems of sisterhood express some of the boldest, most strongminded ideas about women in nineteenth century poetry. Moreover, we examine distinctions between their positions and those of other women poets on the issues of women's rights and women's nature, considering how poets' opinions related to the social context for all women at that time. Finally, in our conclusion, we consider their place in literary history, their influence, and their inclusion in the literary canon.

The Victorian age has been re-examined from many perspectives over the last two decades: The sexuality of the period has been discovered and we have a new vision of the different traditions of women writers of the age. We need to place Emily Dickinson and Christina Rossetti in the forefront of these developments and to show how their gender and literary activity placed them in the major historical movements. Our study demonstrates how their writing reflects a significant grappling with the social, political, and economic, as well as the psychological, realities of mid-Victorian women's lives and thoughts.

Chapter 2

Parallel Sketches

For each extatic instant
We must an anguish pay
In keen and quivering ratio
To the extasy.

Dickinson, #125

I have desired, and I have been desired,
   But now the days are over of desire,
   Now the dust and dying embers mock my fire;
Where is the hire for which my life was hired?
   Oh vanity of vanity, desire!

Rossetti, "Soeur Louise de la Miséricorde (1674)"[1]

We move into parallel sketches of Emily Dickinson and Christina Rossetti. Although they both displayed rare aesthetic sensitivity and talent as children within their well-educated families, the constraints on them as younger daughters taught them to be unsure of their creative gifts and doubtful about putting themselves forward. To find adequate support, space, and time for intellectual development and writing, they each had to overcome the patriarchal structure of their families, to negotiate an acceptance of themselves as dependent daughters, and to identify with a network of supportive, literary women. With their mothers and sisters, they arranged a division of household and nursing responsibilities, though Dickinson's family maintained servants, while Rossetti's family did not.

As poets, they resisted domestic drudgery as antithetical to the poetic frame of mind.

Along with their sisters, Emily Dickinson and Christina Rossetti were socialized to be married, and they both had opportunities to enter matrimony. However, they chose to remain single. Their sisters, Lavinia Dickinson and Maria Francesca Rossetti, had shortlived romances that did not result in marriage. Dickinson's father could afford to keep his daughters close, while Christina and Maria Francesca Rossetti followed the model set by their widowed mother and three maiden aunts, all of whom were trained to work outside the home. When Christina Rossetti's father died, after not having worked because of illness for ten or eleven years, she and her sister were in their mid-twenties. Thus, as young women, the Rossetti sisters were forced to rely on themselves, their brothers, and their mother for economic survival. Emily Dickinson and Christina Rossetti looked to their sisters and to a network and tradition of literary women for unqualified support for the life of their minds. Their sisters lived with them and were supportive of their poetic vocations.

Both Emily Dickinson and Christina Rossetti developed stronger bonds with their brothers than their sisters did. When their brothers were away at school or living apart from the rest of the family, Emily and Christina both functioned like family scribes by maintaining correspondence with them.

However, Dickinson and Rossetti played subordinate roles in relation to their brothers. When they were sparring, the Yankee Dickinson challenged her older brother, Austin, much more overtly than the European Rossetti ever challenged her older brothers, Dante Gabriel and William Michael. Within the Anglo-Italian structure of Rossetti's family, she was compelled, by the force of a longer, more established tradition, to defer to her brothers' authority. They were men of letters in their own right who offered her access to the literary and artistic society of London. Dante Gabriel especially gave Christina regular advice about what her literary and artistic pursuits should be. Christina would listen to this advice, the way Dickinson listened to her mentor Higginson's criticisms or the feedback of her best friend and sister-in-law, Sue Gilbert Dickinson. Rossetti and Dickinson followed their *own* judgments. Dickinson's brother married Emily's best friend. Until the 1860s, Sue Gilbert Dickinson was Emily's most intimate literary confidant. Rossetti's brothers, on the other hand, married women who did not become intimates of their sister.

Both of their fathers were deeply involved in politics, although Rossetti's father was a radical, while Dickinson's father was a Republican. A great deal of the family discourse in both households was dominated by controversial public issues. When Dickinson's and Rossetti's mothers and sisters took part in these discussions, it was as supportive commentators, but they were not expected to play active political roles. Dickinson's and Rossetti's fathers and brothers, on the other hand, viewed political involvement as part of their manly responsibilities, however reluctantly Austin Dickinson may have assumed them.

Christina's father, Gabriele Rossetti, was an Italian revolutionary and poet in exile in London. He strongly believed in individual freedom and national liberation and generally endorsed the wave of liberal reforms coming before Parliament during the first half of the nineteenth century. Women should support men in these ideas, but in Gabriele's experience, men were the agents of history. When in 1832 he began as professor of Italian at the newly opened King's College, and the First Reform Bill was coming up for review, he compared his two-year-old daughter Christina's stubbornness to the House of Lords' conservative opposition.[2] In metaphor, as well as in practice, Christina Rossetti was introduced to radical thought, not only in politics, but also in art and religion, by her father and later by her brothers.

Rossetti's early poetic speakers express a warning to society about excluding women from progressive reforms. One poem, the monodramatic narrative, "Shut Out" (1856), illustrates some psychological consequences of exclusion, namely dimmed social expectations and alienation. The poem was written after Rossetti had a number of personal disappointments and had developed contact with "penitents," or women prisoners. It is titled in manuscript, "What happened to me." Yet the speaker, an imprisoned woman, represents her entrapment in such generalized imagery–shut doors, iron bars–that her condition expresses a metaphor for woman's position in society in general, that is, her "outcast state":

> The door was shut. I looked between
> Its iron bars; and saw it lie,
> My garden, mine, beneath the sky,
> Pied with all flowers bedewed and green:
>
> . . . .
>
> A shadowless spirit kept the gate,
> Blank and unchanging like the grave.
> I peering thro' said: "Let me have
> Some buds to cheer my outcast state."

. . . .

> The spirit was silent; but he took
> Mortar and stone to build a wall;
> He left no loophole great or small
> Thro' which my straining eyes might look:
> So now I sit here quite alone
> Blinded with tears; nor grieve for that,
> For nought is left worth looking at
> Since my delightful land is gone.
> A violet bed is budding near,
> Wherein a lark has made her nest:
> And good they are, but not the best;
> And dear they are, but not so dear.[3]

Presenting an ironic shift in a speaker's tone and mood in a closing quatrain or couplet is one of Rossetti's typical poetic techniques. Here, the speaker's psychological shift from disappointment to alienation offers the audience a signal. If women penitents, like those Rossetti encountered, are excluded from the "delightful land" and left without hope, they will no longer value the society that has rejected them. The insight can also be applied more generally to other social outcasts.

Emily Dickinson's father, Edward, was not a college professor, but rather a lawyer who became treasurer of Amherst College. He then entered the political arena and was elected to the House of Representatives, supplying Emily Dickinson with a trip to Washington. Active in the Republican Party, he was at one time mentioned as a choice for Lieutenant Governor. Although Edward enjoyed the life of a politician, and indeed, died after giving a speech before the General Court in Boston, Edward Dickinson's family, especially his wife and eldest daughter, did not enjoy the life of a politician's helpmeets.[4] From some of Emily Dickinson's letters and poems, it is clear she resented playing a subordinate role in relation to political events of national importance at a critical time. One letter to Sue Gilbert (later married to Emily's brother Austin), shows how deeply politics influenced the Dickinson dinner table and parlor. Written in June 1852, when her father was a delegate to the national Whig convention in Baltimore where Sue was teaching, Emily's letter suggests that she experienced women's exclusion much like Christina Rossetti did. At this early date, she was quick to exaggerate and to turn against the society that rejected her:

Why cant *I* be a Delegate to the great Whig Convention?–
dont I know all about Daniel Webster, and the Tariff,
and the Law? Then, Susie I could see you, during a
pause in the session–but I dont like this country at
all, and I shant stay here any longer!⁵

Women like Emily Dickinson knew as much as men to qualify for political
roles. Moreover, if women like Dickinson held political positions, they
would find ways to combine friendship *with* public responsibility. Since
women were not considered for political office, however, the twenty-two
year-old Dickinson rejects the "country" that prevents this possibility.

Dickinson struggled against the ideology of separate spheres and the
appropriation of social roles along gender lines because the serving roles
traditional domesticity demanded of women desiccated their minds. Her
familiar proclamation, "God keep me from what they call *households*,"
captures her view.⁶

Dickinson's connection to Amherst College provided her with a broader
ranging educational background than Rossetti had. Dickinson had more
training, for example, in the natural sciences. Rossetti, on the other
hand, who never attended school, was more steeped in artistic and religious
subjects. She was trained by her mother.

Dickinson was introduced to feminism through her involvement in the
intellectual debate over women's education. She was educated initially at
Amherst Academy, a progressive, co-ed institution founded by her family,
then later, for a year (1847-1848), at Mount Holyoke, a newly established
women's institution. At Mount Holyoke, women were taught to become
efficient and productive in the domestic sphere–as housewives and mothers–
and to shed a civilizing influence over an increasingly corrupt patriarchal
society. Moreover, there was an emphasis on soul-saving and accepting
Christ encouraged by the seminary's founder, Mary Lyon. Dickinson
resisted this explicitly religious purpose. She understood acceptance of
Christ to mean a traditional renunciatory posture that she could not accept
for herself. She honestly loved the world too much to renounce it.

Her father summoned her home from Mount Holyoke after just two
terms, probably because it was Lavinia's turn to attend school. Emily was
needed to share responsibility for the household with her mother while
Lavinia was away. For the winter term in 1850, Lavinia attended Ipswich
Female Seminary. At home, Emily realized how completely domestic
responsibilities threatened the development of her intellectual work. She
committed herself more fervently to the unholy and unwomanly task of
becoming a poet. Her letter of January 23, 1850, to her friend Jane

Humphrey complains about the pressure on women to follow the conventional path of duty, with its implications of meekness, patience, and submissiveness. She asserts that she inclines to other paths which "Satan covers . . . up with flowers":

> I reach out to pick them. The path of duty looks very
> ugly indeed—and the place where *I* want to go more
> amiable—a great deal—it is so much easier to do wrong
> than right—so much pleasanter to be evil than good. I
> dont wonder that good angels weep—and bad ones sing
> songs.[7]

When Lavinia returned, she resumed the major responsibility for the household. This allowed Emily to cultivate her intellect and imagination and to develop her poetic craft. In 1856, Sue Gilbert married Austin Dickinson and settled in the Evergreens, built alongside the Dickinson home; Sue encouraged Emily's talent as a poet. Together Sue and Emily read feminist classics, such as Tennyson's *The Princess* (1847) and Elizabeth Barrett Browning's *Aurora Leigh* (1857), about intellectual women who were viewed as unwomanly for their educational and vocational endeavors. Women writers who portrayed strongminded heroines and who were favorites of Dickinson's included Emily and Charlotte Brontë, George Eliot, and the poet, Adelaide Ann Procter.[8] According to Dickinson's niece, Martha Dickinson Bianchi, Dickinson was an "instinctive feminist."[9]

Christina Rossetti came to the feminism of reform and the cult of single blessedness through her mother, sister, and maiden aunts and to progressive, intellectual feminism through the Langham Place Group. She and her sister were educated at home by their mother, who had been a professional governess. She gained her ideas on women's moral superiority from her mother, ideas that can be traced to the reformist theory of separate spheres. However, she later came to see, in her contact with the Langham Place Group, that power in the political sphere was necessary for women to gain equality.

These two poets, whose lives began a few days apart and whose experiences as younger daughters and single women exposed them to similar social pressures, never recorded knowing one another's work in their formative years, nor did they carry on any literary exchange. They both attempted to publish their poetry in the 1860s. Rossetti's mentor, Alexander Macmillan, was, however, more receptive to her innovation than either Bowles or Higginson was to Dickinson's. Rossetti published her two leading volumes of poetry in 1862 and 1866 with Macmillan, while Dickinson, unpublished, continued to organize poetic gems in her self-styled fascicles until 1872. Well-educated and intelligent, they responded positively in their poetry to the changing roles for women that reformers and radicals were advancing in the 1850s and 1860s, and their themes of independent strongmindedness for women are clearer in this period than they are at any other time. In supporting strongminded women in their poetry, they opened themselves to the same criticisms levelled at Elizabeth Barrett Browning and her heroine Aurora Leigh, namely that would-be independent women poets were unmanly for not fuliflling women's natural roles of marriage and motherhood.

In the 1870s, Dickinson's childhood friend, Helen Hunt Jackson, took a profound interest in Dickinson's work and encouraged her to publish. Through constant pressure, Jackson convinced Dickinson not to object to having her poem "Success is counted sweetest" (#67) appear in the last volume of Roberts Brothers' No Name Series, *A Masque of Poets* (1878). All the stories and poems in the series were published anonymously, but each story was advertised as authored by "a great unknown." Only the last volume was of poetry, with the advertisement suggesting that authors like H. H. (Helen Hunt Jackson) and Christina Rossetti would be represented. Jackson coaxed Dickinson to publish by arguing persistently that such a publication would spare Dickinson the seemingly unwanted publicity. In August 1876, she wrote to Dickinson:

> I enclose to you a circular which may interest you.
> When the volume of Verse is published in this series, I
> shall contribute to it: and I want to persuade you to.
> Surely, in the shelter of such *double* anonymousness as
> that will be, you need not shrink. I want to see some
> of your verses in print. Unless you forbid me, I will
> send some that I have.[10]

Although Dickinson did actually consult with Thomas Wentworth Higginson about this publication, she gave no answer to Jackson directly. Undaunted, Jackson tried again in late April 1878:

> Would it be of any use to ask you once more for one or
> two of your poems, to come out in the volume of "no
> name" poetry which is to be published before long by
> Roberts Bros.? If you will give me permission I will
> copy them–sending them in my own handwriting–and
> promise never to tell anyone, not even the publishers,

whose the poems are. Could you not bear this much of
publicity? Only you and I would recognize the poems.
I wish very much you would do this–and I think you
would have much amusement in seeing to whom the
critics, those shrewd guessers would ascribe your
verses.[11]

It is ironic, of course, that once Dickinson's masterpiece was finally
printed in the volume, it was attributed to the giant Emerson.

Although "Success is counted sweetest" (1859) is a pre-war poem
employing martial imagery which treats the war dead in a rather idealized
fashion, Dickinson included the poem in her fourth letter to Higginson in
July 1862, just five months after her brother's friend, Frazar Stearns, was
killed in action. In the poem, she treats defeat, for all its agony, as
having redeeming value:

> Not one of all the purple Host
> Who took the Flag today
> Can tell the definition
> So clear of Victory
>
> As he defeated–dying–
> On whose forbidden ear
> The distant strains of triumph
> Burst agonized and clear!

Like the heroines of so many Victorian novels who die martyrs' deaths,
Dickinson's defeated, dying soldier is somewhat elevated to a position of
glory. The poem's assumptions betray Dickinson's socialization as a woman
to ennoble self-sacrifice.

Dickinson's actual experience of the Civil War, however, changed her
abstract, romantic formulation of defeat. A parallel poem of 1862, #639,
which we examine in our chapter "War Poems," stresses instead the waste of
defeat, the loss, and the preference for heroic victory, even at the risk
of death:

> There's somewhat prouder, over there–
> The Trumpets tell it to the Air–
> How different Victory
> To Him who has it–and the One
> Who to have had it, would have been

Contenteder– to die–

Ironically, the American Civil War also changed Rossetti's poetry. She was then clearly writing for publication, and her female speakers became more outspoken than earlier in their defense of liberty. Like Dickinson's speaker in poem #639, Rossetti's heroines prepared to die heroically for their views.

Rossetti did not record an awareness of Dickinson's work until 1890 when, after Dickinson's death, her poems were published in collected form for the first time. In a letter to William Michael Rossetti, written a day after her sixtieth birthday, Rossetti recorded that a volume, "Poems by Emily Dickinson," was "lately sent" her "from America." Her comment is that Dickinson had "a wonderfully Blakean gift, but therewithal a startling recklessness of poetic ways and means."[12] It was a telling comment, for Rossetti herself had been accused by Ruskin of having reckless poetic ways and means. Even her poem "Husband and Wife," which was published alongside Dickinson's in *A Masque of Poets*, displays her as a maverick by virtue of its social criticism.

In Rossetti's poem, written in 1865 when feminists were organizing around legal equity for women and children in the family, the speaker is a woman married "by might and right / And forsworn marriage vow" to a sailor who has forced her "will" and marred her "life." "Marring" suggests sexual abuse. They have a baby, but the sailor leaves her with child and expects that, despite his mistreatment, she will act lovingly and forgivingly to him– because he is her husband:

> "And I was wrong to force your
>   will,
> And wrong to mar your life:
> But kiss me once before we part
> Because you are my wife."

> . . . .

> "Though I'm your wife by might
>   and right
> And forsworn marriage vow,
> I never loved you yet," said she,
>   "And I don't love you now."

The wife is dying in the last stanza. She is willing to give her husband sexual affection on demand if he will provide proper care for their child after she is gone:

> "And tell him, not for might or right
> or forsworn marriage vow,
> But for the helpless baby's sake,
> I would have kissed him now."[13]

The fact that the wife, driven by maternal love, must employ her sexuality as currency for the child's care, throws criticism on society. Social institutions should enforce fathers' responsibility for their children.

After 1866, the direction of Rossetti's and Dickinson's poetry noticeably shifted. Dickinson's poetic output dropped off after 1865, and she became increasingly isolated. The pressures of reconstruction and the antagonism to women's suffrage reinforced the fragmentation of the women's rights movement. In this broader context, Dickinson's estrangement from her sister-in-law, Sue, who was her link to feminism, signifies a certain disaffiliation with any organized position. This, combined with increasing responsibility for nursing her invalid mother, drove Dickinson to a less active posture. Dickinson's father died when she was forty-three, and her mother suffered a severe stroke when she was forty-four. Dickinson then became a mother to her mother. Unlike Rossetti, Dickinson found no comfort in any religious sect, though she fashioned her own kind of faith. Her poetry repeats themes and techniques she used earlier. While she eventually became the recluse of legend, we will show how the legend has been mistakenly extended backward to encompass all of her life.

After Dickinson rejected publication, she used poems primarily in traditional women's ways. She would give them as gifts, like quilts or food, linking them with other forms of women's handiwork. Though she was unconcerned about publication, the fascicles make it clear that at least until 1872, when she assembled her last fascicle, she made conscious decisions about her poems.

Rossetti's poetry also declines after the 1860s in that it demonstrates none of the earlier innovative qualities. After 1866, Rossetti stopped recording poems regularly in notebooks and abandoned the kind of subtle social realism upon which her poetic reputation was based. Her themes and poetic voices gradually transform from narrative and dramatic social criticisms to more lyrical, spiritual visions. Although she continued as a social reformer, actively involved in such issues as antivivisection and minors' protection, and as a mentor for young women writers, she devoted less time to public work due to increased nursing responsibilities at home. Her voice as a poetic visionary subsumed her earlier voice as a social/political critic. Chapter four explores how this shift in Rossetti's poetic form and voice reflects a broader change in her views about the role art played in creating changes for women.

PART II

LIVES

Emily Dickinson.
From the daguerrotype, Amherst College Library

Chapter 3

Emily Dickinson

What we offer in this brief biographical sketch of Emily Dickinson is a corrective to the view that her later reclusiveness extended backwards to include her entire life. We show that she. like Christina Rossetti, was interested in the major social, religious. economic, and political movements of her day, although women who expressed these interests, and especially poets, were considered manly. Even in childhood and youth, and especially in contrast to the privileges afforded her older brother Austin, Emily Dickinson expressed frustration at the limitations placed on women. She became involved in aesthetic and political ramifications of women's rights through her intimate friendship with Sue Gilbert Dickinson, and her deep desire for excellent education brought her in close touch with the debates over the nature of what women's education should be. She became most productive and assertive as a poet when women in America and England were politically advancing their cause, and she found her best support for becoming a poet from the "sisterhood." Her gradual withdrawal was a reasonable response to a society that had already rejected single, middle class women as redundant. She used her time to develop her genius. Her later reclusiveness was not so much an expression of eccentricity as it was a common life mode for single daughters. despite the fact that single daughters were somewhat of an anomaly. since "natural" women married and had children.

Emily Dickinson said, "My life has been too simple and stern to embarrass any."[1] After reading Richard Sewall. few biographers can disagree. The incredible outpouring of speculation on Dickinson's life looks like the result of myriad detectives on the trail of red herrings in a Peter Sellers comedy. The poems point in a million directions; the letters imply many things and state none simply. She is a person who lived much more in her own mind than in life, as if by limiting her actual physical existence she had room and time for more lives.

Since Emily Dickinson was clearly one of the most remarkable poets of all time, we want to see her life as equally remarkable, as vastly different from other women's lives around her. Yet, there is no one blueprint for a poet's life. Had her younger sister, Lavinia, obeyed her instructions and burned her poems, she would hardly have survived in family annals, unlike Margaret Fuller or Madame de Staël whose dynamic lives are remembered along with their writing.

In one way, Dickinson's "private" character was standard New England fare. The familiar figure who laments the inroads of urban life into rural New England began to appear in book after book from the early nineteenth century. Hosts of village eccentrics were portrayed with stranger sets of behavior than becoming reclusive and wearing white. In the second half of the century, Mary Wilkins Freeman stories were laced with women determined to live as they felt was best, regardless of public opinion.[2]

The active events of Emily Dickinson's life were few and were mainly a series of renunciations. In considering these renunciations, however, it is necessary to remind ourselves that we are not discussing a consumer society, or even an urban society like mid-nineteenth-century London, with hosts of different lifestyles. In Amherst, Massachusetts, of the 1840s through 1870s, there usually was only one game in town. One played or one did not play. One did not choose another option. There was one church, one school, one small set of "acceptable" people, the number of which diminished as one went up the social ladder. Choices were more limited for women than for men, and were, again, further circumscribed by gentility. For a woman to travel, she had better either be able to withstand ridicule or become a missionary (or marry one). For a woman to work, she had better have a poor family, as did most of the early women schoolteachers, including Emma Willard, founder of Troy Seminary, and Emily Dickinson's sister-in-law, Sue Gilbert, or again, be willing to withstand tremendous censure. Then, as now, most women worked because they had to, but then, it was more to the shame of their families. Since it was believed the writing process for women poets was natural, spontaneous, and effortless, to actually *work* at a profession, such as writing, was much more odd than locking oneself in a room and wearing white.

When Emily Dickinson was born, on December 10, 1830, Amherst was no frontier village, no new Jerusalem, no wilderness, if it ever had been

the Puritan Eden so often fantasized by her biographers. In his novels,
Hawthorne would prove how far the self-conscious New England artist had
moved from those days.[3] Already "those days" were myths, and the Pilgrims'
descendants were more remote in time and circumstance from their ancestors
than we are from the Transcendentalists. Amherst was comfortable, already
beginning to dedicate itself to piety and learning. These endeavors were
to remain its stock in trade, its most important resources, although not
everyone in town was employed by the college or the academy.

While Amherst never became an industrial center like Lowell, it too
was touched by the Industrial Revolution. There were several small mills in
or near the town, and one principal industry—the making of straw hats. The
hats were made from straw imported from Cuba, and the finished product
returned there for sale, thereby giving Amherst a toehold in the
development of mercantile imperialism.[4]   However, as far as Emily
Dickinson's family was concerned, the academy and the college were the
principal features on Amherst's landscape.

The Dickinson family's class position gave them the option of being
endlessly protective toward all their children. It is important to
remember this as a family pattern, not as a pattern devised by her family
to protect their one problem child. Within the family, Emily occupied the
position of perpetual daughter, until, in her forty-third year, her father
died. Had she been left fatherless at an earlier age, clearly her ability
to engage in renunciation as a positive choice would have been more
limited.

Edward Dickinson's overprotectiveness worked against the rugged
individualism he inherited from his father, Samuel Dickinson. Samuel
Dickinson played an important part in the establishment of Amherst College.
The role of the college was not to be that of providing knowledge to the
male youth of western Massachusetts simply for the vain pleasure of
acquiring knowledge. Antipapism, antihumanism, were real causes for the
Congregationalists who saw the beast of Catholicism rearing its seven heads
in the West with the advent of European immigration, while the Unitarians
threatened Harvard and the rest of the East with well-heeled heresies. The
Puritan tradition relied on a literate—primarily Bible-literate—clergy and
congregation; its purpose was to train young men for the ministry and
missionary work. There is a strong egalitarian impulse in the intent of
the more Puritan churches. In addition to the necessity for universal
literacy, there is also the desire to open the possibility of church
leadership to the hard-working and worthy, not to make it a refuge of the
upper classes. It was perhaps this impulse that kept Amherst College
tuition low. The only colleges or seminaries with lower fees were the

early women's institutions, Mount Holyoke and the Troy Seminary.[5] Perhaps Samuel Dickinson's own financial troubles influenced the desire of the college to be relatively inexpensive. He lost or gave away his fortune and the family home to establish the college. He died a poor man in Ohio, where he had gone to manage a small college and to try to restore his reputation.

The Dickinsons, by Emily's father's time, occupied an interesting role in a Puritan town torn between admiration for her grandfather's selflessness and scorn at its results. Single-minded devotion is often translated "fanaticism." Whatever the neighbors thought, Edward Dickinson was clear in his mission. He was to be the perfect Puritan and recoup the family's fortunes through his law practice. When Emily was in her twenties, he rebought the family Homestead, the house in which Emily Dickinson was born and lived briefly as a young child. The house in which she did most of her growing up, and which was the source of her metaphors of home and house, does not survive; it was torn down years ago. Only the Homestead, with its added Victorian cupola, remains a shrine for Dickinson worshippers. Although Edward spent much energy restoring the Dickinsons' worldly position, he did not neglect his community duties. He was said to have never lost a penny and to have improved the College's fortunes through astute management, rather than personal sacrifice. His law practice, of course, was concerned with the very real and theoretical events surrounding the town.

Emily Dickinson's mother, Emily Norcross Dickinson, appears to have been the "ideal" Victorian woman: sickly, retiring, devoted to her housekeeping. She hardly emerges from the letters or biographies, except as an encumbrance. She performed minimally the functions of the wife of a prominent citizen, but did not seek them out. The picture of Edward Dickinson as stern paterfamilias, feared in his domestic circle, may have referred more to his role as a husband than as a father. Sewall's portrait of Edward's relationship with his children implies more affection and tolerance than fear, but something certainly made Mrs. Dickinson nervous. In her dealings with her husband, she was the paradigm of Victorian frailty. She was the homebody, in need of protection and support, just what every man seemed to want. Yet, having secured such a wife, or rather molded her, since Edward Dickinson's early letters to Emily Norcross express more the Puritan promise of partnership than the desire for a submissive wife, no Victorian man knew quite what to do with this helpless bit of nonsense. Her son and older daughter regarded her with some contempt. It is more difficult to discern how Lavinia, less clever than her siblings by most reports, felt about her mother. Despite the children's ambivalences, in many ways all three of them, by remaining either close to or at home, became more like their mother than like their decisive, stern father. Emily nursed her mother briefly when she took ill in 1850, and her mother's "long illness" began in November 1855. According to Lavinia, her mother's poor health and all the extra work it involved were the most decisive influences on Emily Dickinson's reclusiveness in later life.[6]

If Emily Dickinson's mother and father move from the ideal of early New England working partnership to Victorian male tyranny and female submission, as if we watch American Gothic dissolve into a domestic steel engraving–father seated, mother anxiously standing behind him, children on rug–then Austin Dickinson's life takes us into an Aubrey Beardsley illustration. As the eldest child and a boy, he assumed the outward appearance of his father but had trouble fitting his own personality into the narrow lines his father managed to impose around himself. He, too, became a lawyer, but not immediately. He taught young Irish children for a while in Boston and developed a disdain for them and for teaching. Teaching was a rather conventional choice for a young man of his day, quite common for a year or two between college and preparing for a profession. Austin chose law only because he disliked teaching so much. Moreover, his father made it easy for him to follow in his footsteps. He had no particular interest in politics or religion, yet he joined the church and took on his father's duties as treasurer of Amherst College.

Austin's engagement to Sue Gilbert, one of Emily's best friends, was a stormy, interrupted one, and there is some indication that she married him as an escape from teaching in Baltimore. Their marriage was far from happy. He eventually had a long affair with a young faculty wife, Mabel Loomis Todd, the woman who saw Emily Dickinson's poems through to publication. In his later years, he wore an improbably red wig and a slouch hat. His real interests were in collecting paintings and landscaping the town of Amherst. These activities hint at suppressed aestheticism, to which Emily Dickinson refers in her early letters to him. One wonders if Austin dabbled at painting or writing, avocations that, as the eldest child and only son, he could never have developed. Certainly, his periodic attempts at escape ended in failure. At one point, he proposed going west with his new wife, but his father instead had a large house in the latest Italianate style built for his family, next to the Dickinson Homestead. That, and a partnership with his father, kept him in Amherst for life, a strange successor to his father's position.

Lavinia, too, made ineffectual gestures to end her dependence on the Homestead. She was the youngest Dickinson, inheritor of a certain amount of the Dickinson sharpness, if not of Emily's brand of intellect. Her birth left Mrs. Dickinson ill for some time and sent two-year-old Emily to stay with her Aunt Lavinia Norcross, thereby engendering a relationship that lasted for two generations as Emily Dickinson became the protector and inspiration of the elder Lavinia's two daughters, the "Little Cousins."

Since the Dickinson family was comfortable, but not extremely wealthy, Emily and her sister were expected to do some household tasks, probably as a way of training them for managing a house of their own as well as distributing the difficult work of housekeeping. The Dickinsons kept servants, a series of Irish immigrant women, considered "natural" servants then, but Emily's early letters, and later ones too, complain about the amount of housework she was expected to do. In the following letter of May 1853 to Austin who was then attending Harvard Law School, Emily complained that domestic work even prevented her from maintaining their correspondence:

> "Strikes me" just so, dear Austin, but somehow I have
> to work a good deal more than I used to, and harder,
> and I feel so tired when night comes, that I'm afraid
> if I write you, 'twill be something rather bluer than
> you'll be glad to see—so I sew with all my might, and
> hope when work is done to be with you much oftener than
> I have lately been.[7]

She had no early affinity with what a woman of her time was expected to do. As time went on, Lavinia did not mind domestic tasks as much as Emily did or, at least, did not complain as much.

Unlike Austin or Emily, who seem to have been the "clever ones," Lavinia is portrayed, somewhat incongruously, as the pretty, vain, and empty-headed social butterfly who did much of the domestic drudgery. Though she was the younger sister, as they grew older and Emily became more reclusive, Lavinia began to assume more of the responsibility of fronting for Emily in the outside world and became her link to public interactions. She was even fitted for Emily Dickinson's dresses.

Emily and Lavinia Dickinson were not immune from the pervasive socialization of women towards marriage. However, they avoided the pressures of the marriage market not only because their father could afford to keep them, but also because, like the fathers of many women who became well-known writers (Charlotte and Emily Brontë, Elizabeth Barrett Browning, Rebecca Harding Davis, George Eliot), he preferred to keep them close. They avoided becoming wives because they were allowed to remain daughters.

Nevertheless, Lavinia wanted to marry, but she did not have to take anyone who came along. She was forward with at least one suitor who described the pleasant sensation of her soft arms around him and her long hair. Like Emily, however, she never did marry, and the one serious involvement she had, with a remote Lyman cousin, was not as serious on his part as it was on hers; he married an old girlfriend when he returned to the south. Lavinia became increasingly strange, sharp, and hard to get along with as she grew older. Interestingly enough, Lavinia responded crisply to the mythmakers who asserted that romantic disappointments had drawn Emily Dickinson to reclusiveness. In a letter dated January 29, 1895 which Sewall reproduced in his biography, Lavinia wrote to one of the mythmakers, Mrs. Dall, that there was not one particular incident, much less a romance, that made Emily Dickinson reclusive–it "'was only a happen.'"[8]

Despite Lavinia's closeness to Emily throughout their lives, Lavinia was not included in the Emily-Austin grouping. She did not write Austin, nor did her mother; they always added their greetings to Emily's long, impassioned letters. Austin was annoyed by this at times, but, coupled with the division of housework, which seems to have been satisfactory to both Emily and Lavinia, it is easy to postulate the kind of situation in which Lavinia dusts while Emily writes. Lavinia certainly felt that Emily was worth the protection she gave her, even without knowledge of Emily's prolific writing. It was Lavinia, of course, who saved the poems, in defiance of Emily's wishes, and who bullied, entreated, and wheedled others to help her in getting them published.

Dickinson's earliest writing described the activities of the chickens and horses, dogs and cats, to her absent brother who had been sent to boarding school at Williston Seminary when he was thirteen (18 April 1842):

My dear Brother

As father was going to Northampton and thought of coming over to see you I thought I would improve the opportunity and write you a few lines–We miss you very much indeed you cannot think how odd it seems without you there was always such a Hurrah wherever that you was I miss My bedfellow very much for it is rare that I can get any now for Aunt Elizabeth is afraid to sleep alone and Vinnie has to sleep with her but I have the

privilege of looking under the bed every night which I
improve as you may suppose the Hens get along nicely
the chickens grow very fast I am afraid they will be so
large that you cannot perceive them with the naked Eye
when you get home.[9]

The letter reveals the intimacy of their early relationship, and the last few lines also show Dickinson's unique perspective and sense of humor. Throughout Emily's correspondence to Austin, she stresses his obligation to return and understand her. Though her mother, sister, and father were still with her, she craved the dyad of Austin and Emily, the clever ones, the ones who flouted her father's austerity, their mother's wooliness, their sister's flightiness, away from the rest of the family.

There is no hint that Lavinia was included in the Emily-Austin dyad. When Emily was seventeen and at school at Mount Holyoke, for example, she wrote to Austin, not to Lavinia, although both siblings were at home. She corresponded with Austin as with an equal counterpart, addressing him as someone with whom she could freely discuss the male world of politics. He was the one man whom she need not reverence–not a teacher, "master," lover, father, but one of her generation and her family. She could say to *him* that they were like no other people. Her first letter to Austin from Mount Holyoke is typical of those she wrote during her entire stay there (21 October 1847):

My dear Brother. Austin.

I have not really a moment of time in which to
write you & am taking time from "silent study hours,"
but I am determined not to break my promise again & I
generally carry my resolutions into effect. . . . I
had a great mind to be homesick after you went home,
but I concluded not to & therefore gave up all homesick
feelings. Was not that a wise determination? How have
you all been at home since last week? I suppose
nothing of serious importance has occurred, or I should
have heard of it, before this time. . . . I want to
know when you are coming to see me again, for I wish to
see you as much as I did before. . . . Wont you please
tell me when you answer my letter who the candidate for
President is? I have been trying to find out ever
since I came here & have not yet succeeded. . . . Has

the Mexican war terminated yet & how? Are we beat? Do
you know of any nation about to besiege South Hadley?
If so, inform me of it, for I would be glad of a chance
to escape, if we are to be stormed. . . .
Be a good boy & mind me.[10]

Victorian convention did not mean for brother-sister relationships to
last except in a very attenuated form. Emily was, in the natural course of
time, intended to belong to another man's family. She might have been
expected to love her brother, to be his good angel, but she was also
expected to give up this sort of relationship in deference to his wife.

Within her dyad with Austin, however, Emily was also anxious to exert
the opposing force of competition. She joked with Austin about the danger
of his becoming too exalted, too above her. In what she knew was a loaded
battle, she desired to compete on equal terms and win in the acquisition of
intellectual skills. When Austin entered Harvard Law School, for example,
she challenged his attempts at writing poetry although she had published
only one poem by this time, March 1853:

And Austin is a Poet, Austin writes a psalm. Out of
the way, Pegasus, Olympus enough "to him," and just say
to those "nine muses" that we have done with them!. . .
Now Brother Pegasus, I'll tell you what it is–I've
been in the habit *myself* of writing some few things,
and it rather appears to me that you're getting away my
patent, so you'd better be somewhat careful, or I'll
call the police![11]

She is often angry at him for being puffed up or for feeling more
important than she is. There is a great deal of competition in these
letters, a male sort of camaraderie and teasing, wit and originality of
phrase that she does not use with her girlfriends.

How to keep the brother-sister relationship one of equals then, into
maturity? The easiest way would be to marry him herself, and one thinks of
the literary flirtations with incest, with brother-sister pairs, with
foster brother-sister pairs, as in *Wuthering Heights*, where the man with
whom a woman is raised is her male equivalent, not her lord and master.
Clearly, this sort of flirtation could not be consummated outside the pages
of a book. What, then, would be more natural than to marry Austin off to
her best friend and alter ego, the woman she believed understood her more
than any other?

Sue Gilbert was the daughter of the town drunk, the hotelkeeper. She and her sisters seem not to have suffered from their father's reputation since they were accepted and popular with their peers. Of course, unlike the Dickinson sisters, they had their livings to make, but they were not sent out unprovided. Sue was educated in Geneva, lived with a married sister, but maintained her contacts with Amherst, especially with Emily.

It is possible to misunderstand the violence of Emily Dickinson's feelings for Sue if one reads her removed from the perspective of her times. Here, she wrote to Sue while Sue was away teaching in Baltimore (27 June 1852):

> Susie, will you indeed come home next Saturday, and
> be my own again, and kiss me as you used to? Shall I
> indeed behold you, not "darkly, but face to face" or am
> I *fancying* so, and dreaming blessed dreams from which
> the day will wake me? I hope for you so much, and feel
> so eager for you, feel that I *cannot* wait, feel that
> *now* I must have you–that the expectation once more to
> see your face again, makes me feel hot and feverish,
> and my heart beats so fast–I go to sleep at night, and
> the first thing I know, I am sitting there wide awake,
> and clasping my hands tightly, and thinking of next
> Saturday, and "never a bit" of you.[12]

Violent, passionate friendships between young girls were expected. Girls were supposed to be attached to family members, to brothers, and they were given encouragement to exhibit their feelings in exalted language. Some of the sentiment is undoubtedly real.

Emily Dickinson encouraged Sue's romance with Austin. Though she must have received the confidences of both parties, her letters do not reveal any tendency to gush over the young lovers. The letters are more concerned with confidences Sue and she have exchanged, philosophical speculations, and poems. Emily Dickinson consistently presents Sue as the one person who shares her taste in literature, and the one person who can understand her feminine sensibility. The same day Austin left Amherst for Harvard Law School, Emily wrote to Sue (5 March 1853):

> I know dear Susie is busy, or she would not forget
> her lone little Emilie, who wrote her just as soon as
> she'd gone to Manchester, and has waited so patiently
> till she can wait no more, and the credulous little

heart, fond even tho' forsaken, will get it's big black
inkstand, and tell her once again how well it loves
her. . . .

Why dont you write me, Darling? Did I in that quick
letter say anything which grieved you, or made it hard
for you to take your usual pen and trace affection for
your bad, sad Emilie?

Then Susie, you must forgive me before you sleep
tonight, for I will not shut my eyes until you have
kissed my cheek, and told me you would love me.[13]

Again, lacking Sue's letters, it is difficult to say how much of this
desire expressed the standard school talk among young girls in the 1840s
and 1850s, how much Emily's faith in Sue was justified, or whether Emily
was expressing unusual desire. Then, as now, female adolescents valued
their peer group and found understanding with others of their own age that
"dear mamma or pappa" could not provide.

The form of competition between Emily Dickinson and her friends sets
them apart from their mothers' generation. Earlier, girls might have
competed with fancywork or butter churned. Dickinson and her peers were
more concerned with what they have learned or will learn. They are
academically competitive, not for grades or honors, but in terms of what
subjects each has mastered. Education for girls– how much, what kind–was
hotly debated.

During Emily Dickinson's first semester at Mount Holyoke, she wrote
to Abiah Root, one of her closest girlfriends (6 November 1847):

My dear Abiah,

I am really at Mt Holyoke Seminary & this is to be my
home for a long year. Your affectionate letter was
joyfully received & I wish that this might make you as
happy as your's did me. . . . I find no Abby, or
Abiah, or Mary, but I love many of the girls. Austin
came to see me when I had been here about two weeks &
brought Viny & Abby. I need not tell you how delighted
I was to see them all, nor how happy it made me to hear
them say that "they were *so lonely.*" It is a sweet
feeling to know that you are missed & that your memory
is precious at home. . . . Only to think Abiah, that
in 2 1/2 weeks I shall be at my *own dear home* again.

> You will probably go home at Thanksgiving time & we can
> rejoice with each other. . . .
>
> From your aff
> Emily E. D– [14]

Young girls were supposed to be in love with each other. It was supposed
to teach them how to love their husbands. In reality, it must also have
been the one chance women had for a mutually fulfilling relationship in a
society that regarded men and women as distinct species with some
unbridgeable biological and cultural gulfs between them. In the same
letter to Abiah:

> I will tell you my order of time for the day, as you
> were so kind as to give me your's. At 6. oclock, we
> all rise. We breakfast at 7. Our study hours begin at
> 8. At 9. we all meet in seminary Hall, for devotions.
> At 10 1/4. I recite a review of Ancient History, in
> connection with which we read Goldsmith & Grimshaw. At
> .11. I recite a lesson in "Pope's Essay on Man," which
> is merely transposition. . . .

Education in Emily Dickinson's day began and ended at arbitrary
levels.[15] People began their schooling at different ages and left at
different times. Learning was an activity which, at least for the middle
class and below, was fitted in and around family needs. Students might
take one or four years to complete the same curriculum. The academies
which sprang up in America to meet the needs for local education recognized
the needs of a predominantly rural population. Students came and left as
they were needed on the farm. Many acquired a year or so of education but
left without receiving a certificate or diploma. The lack of a diploma or
certificate did not mean, however, exclusion from the job market. Higher
education was a rare commodity then. Someone in Emily Dickinson's
position, of course, had no need to train for wage labor.

What was important to Dickinson was the acquisition of knowledge.
Her poems reflect a vast number of facts–facts used creatively, combined
in strange ways–but facts. They are samplers of her education–geology,
geography, astronomy, zoology, botany. Poem #70 (1859), for example,
reflects her sitting in on the open lectures held at all-male Amherst
College:

> "Arcturus" is his other name–

I'd rather call him "Star."
It's very mean of Science
To go and interfere!

I slew a worm the other day–
A "Savant" passing by
Murmured "Resurgam"–"Centipede"!
"Oh Lord–how frail are we"!

I pull a flower from the woods–
A monster with a glass
Computes the stamens in a breath–
And has her in a "class"!

Critics who have diligently discovered Dickinson's domestic metaphors have passed in silence over her scientific terms.[16]

The necessity for literacy in the service of piety opened debates on women's education.[17] If women could read the Bible, they could read other books as well. The hard-pressed small farmers of western Massachusetts needed daughters to work as mill girls or as schoolmarms. These working daughters may have written poems, stories, and essays in the process, like Lucy Larcom, a mill girl later turned poet who was a popular writer and contemporary of Dickinson. But the wife or daughter of a leading citizen often had time for study which had no particular end. Was there really a need for women's education? If so, what was the need, and what shape should the education take?

Emily Dickinson arrived at school age in the middle of these debates and found different answers waiting for her. These answers introduced her to the major issues in the women's rights movement. One view, Margaret Fuller's, was to study the same subjects as men. Like most women, Dickinson acquired a good deal of education second-hand, through her father and brother. The former she admired; the latter she admired and envied in a way that makes the reader see the query between the lines–"Why aren't I a boy?" One way to acquire knowledge, through the backdoor, was for women to sit in on the open lectures at Amherst College. Dickinson's circumspect peeking in on male education seemed immensely satisfying to her. Neither in her letters nor in her poems does the reader sense any unease with her ability to learn any of this material, although as in the poem "Arcturus," there is some humorous criticism of the material itself. This criticism was probably aimed at Edward Hitchcock, noted geologist and president of Amherst College, whose obsession was to reconcile God and science.[18]

If these were her interests and preoccupations, she must have found the other solution to the need for women's education an abrupt turn away from these concerns. The all women's academies, such as Mount Holyoke and the Troy Seminary, stressed the usefulness of education for women for producing better mothers and citizens, whether out of real conviction, or as a strategy for bringing education to them. The women who founded the women's academies–Emma Willard, Mary Lyon, and others–were themselves impoverished, hardworking, self-sacrificing. Are women fundamentally different from men? Who is going to define the difference? Most will recognize these debates as closely aligned to the debates over women's rights in general, and as with these controversies, there is a good deal of unresolved ambiguity in them. The answer was that women were different, even superior, but only morally. Intellectually, they were inferior. Education for them would improve their calling as mothers in the home and mothers in the world. As Catherine Beecher was arguing, this was women's "natural" calling. Women were to make homes and havens for the wilder and more uncivilized male workers. They would do this, in part, because of their natural, Protestant piety. These were givens, even before education began. There is no evidence that Emily Dickinson ever saw her mission in the world in these terms, and for her, relating to God was a constant series of frustrations, not an acceptance of grace.

Dickinson has been criticized for snobbishness, and there is certainly a degree of exclusiveness in her letters, but there is also a great deal of agony about being different, not fitting in, and especially about not being able to "accept Christ." It is as if she mocks, and at the same time, wants very much to be that which she mocks. She regards other people's lives as infinitely easier than hers and fluctuates between envy and contempt.

Through her early correspondence with girlfriends, like Abiah Root and Jane Humphrey, Dickinson's spiritual struggle is revealed. Eight revivals shook Amherst from 1840 to 1862. On January 31, 1846, Dickinson confessed with terror to Abiah that she could not become a Christian during the revival of 1845: "Perhaps you will not beleive it Dear A. but I attended none of the meetings last winter. I felt that I was so easily excited that I might again be deceived and I dared not trust myself."[19] Self-reliance *was* one of the Puritan axioms Dickinson incorporated in her own life, and she did not trust the mass experience that characterized revivalism. Although Dickinson expresses nervousness to Abiah about "her decision not to accept Christ–she had seen "many who felt there was nothing in religion . . . melted at once,"–she later became surer of her independent stance. Concerning the fervent 1850 revival in Amherst, Dickinson wrote to Jane

Humphrey: "Christ is calling everyone here, all my companions have answered, even my darling Vinnie believes she loves and trusts him, and I am standing alone in my rebellion, and growing very careless."[20] Dickinson showed few signs of aptitude for the future that Mary Lyon wanted for her alumnae. Dickinson was one of the "no-hopers" at Mount Holyoke–the others being the "Hopers" and the "established Christians." She was not interested in serving, either as missionary, teacher, mother, or wife. She was interested in acquiring knowledge, for the simple reason that she was inquisitive and interested and wanted to use her knowledge and apply it creatively, rather than as a commodity. She came from a home in which learning was commonplace and must have found many of the other girls naive. She could not glibly accept the price that was being asked for her learning.

It was her father's decision that Dickinson leave Mount Holyoke. Dickinson herself expressed ambivalence. She was glad to be home, but sad about leaving friends and possibilities for learning. Significantly, she wrote that while she was at home on vacation, she "had a feast in the reading line," which implies she preferred self-directed study.[21] Dickinson's important world was not that of Mary Lyon nor her disciples, and, for the rest of her life, Dickinson searched for *her* mentor, *her* school. Unfortunately, it had not yet been built for women.

Unlike the daughters of the impoverished or genteel poor farmers and small merchants who found the female academies heaven on earth and their founders visible saints, Emily had already had some taste of higher education at Amherst College. This education, though anxiously laced with Christianity, had been designed for men, and therefore may not have been as self-conscious in its mission. Amherst College may have been intended for the male counterparts of Mount Holyoke and Troy Seminary in terms of class, but it had in its faculty noted scholars and a serious commitment to scholarship and science. Although Amherst College educated many ministers and missionaries, it also turned out men who entered other professions, such as law, education, journalism, and business. Amherst did not feel it had to provide only one sort of education to prove its worth, unlike the beleaguered and anxious early women's institutions.

After one year at Mount Holyoke, Emily came home and, to all intents and purposes, ended her separation from her family. Events of change, benchmarks to use in a timeline of her life, became rarer. This seeming lack of change may also be exaggerated by a modern need to see external activity as indispensable for a public figure. She had no hope of being a public figure in her lifetime, and many nineteenth-century men, or women, never left the boundaries set by a day's carriage ride.

What is known is that she and her sister went to Washington, in 1855, to be with their father who was then serving a term in the House of Representatives. On the way home from this trip, after a social round, the sisters visited Philadelphia to see their friends, the Colemans, and there Emily Dickinson met the eminent minister, Charles Wadsworth.

Emily Dickinson's niece, Martha Dickinson Bianchi, asserted that it was on this famous trip to Philadelphia that Emily Dickinson "met" her "fate."[22] Again, the assumption is that this "fate" is Wadsworth. Many books have been written which promote the idea that the Philadelphia preacher and the unknown Amherst poet maintained some sort of long distance, hopeless affair–he was married as well as famous.[23] While many possibilities are conjectured for rendezvous, only two meetings after Emily Dickinson's Philadelphia trip are verified. Wadsworth came to visit Emily Dickinson in 1880, twenty years after his first visit. After years of casual acquaintanceship and letters, this meeting reinforced the idea that here must be the man whose inaccessibility drove Emily Dickinson into seclusion.

There is equal evidence that this was not the case. The idea that there was a man at all is due to the "Master Letters," drafts of three letters (1858, 1861, 1862) written to a man addressed only as "master" with whom Emily Dickinson was deeply in love. The only physical point of description is the man's beard. The pictures of Wadsworth show mutton-chop sideburns but no beard. The existence of the beard has not stopped the artists from many camps from explaining it away in a number of ingenious ways–from the letters being a sort of double blind to a metaphorical beard. It seems difficult to know why this sort of concealment would have been necessary or why it would have focused on one hirsute detail. What becomes annoying is that the game of "who was Emily Dickinson's lover" is very infectious, and it is only with great self-discipline that one turns aside from it to move on to, if not more important, at least more documentable matters.

No one seems to have ever listened to Lavinia. She, who lived intimately with her sister and adored her, protested when the storm of speculation about her sister's affairs broke and asserted that Emily Dickinson's withdrawal from the world had been due to no mystery lover but just, as we have seen, "a happen."

One popular theory is that the letters are written to Christ. However, the letters are very detailed and physical, even for Emily Dickinson's imagination. If they are based on her actual experience, then at some time in her early thirties, Emily Dickinson may have been passionately, but hopelessly, in love with a man. He was possibly married and possibly unaware of her love for him. On the other hand, he could have been very aware and interested in pursuing the relationship as well. Whether or not this romance was consummated, the poems of this period reflect personal upheaval in emotions from ecstasy to betrayal. It is a mistake, however, to ascribe them all to the same object. Emily Dickinson felt all her relationships keenly, and there is also evidence that the betrayal poems are aimed at Kate Scott Anthon, a friend of Sue's from Utica Female Seminary, who began to visit Amherst in 1859 and formed an intimate romantic friendship with Emily. Moreover, evidence also points to Sue as the object of these poems. Problems in Emily's relationship to Sue began to surface after Sue's engagement to Austin in 1853. Sue's neglect became one theme in Emily's letters and poems. The relationship became more tense and strained during the period of the Master letters when Sue became a mother. Ned's birth and Sue's seeming preoccupation with her new baby exacerbated Emily's sense of betrayal.

Sue moved from a certain amount of high spirits and intellectual pretension and snobbery, which she shared with and encouraged in Emily both before and after her marriage, to something much more sinister in her later years. In her early years as a new wife, she outraged the Puritan town by the New York custom of putting wreaths in her windows at Christmas. Beauty before sober contemplation was a late-Victorian slide into decadence. Other legends about her include supposed abortions, because of her fear of childbirth, persistent nagging of her husband, who already was father-pecked, and vague and unspecified psychological torture of both Emily and Lavinia.[24]

Sue also played a prominent role in Emily Dickinson's development as an intellectual, a poet, and a feminist. Sue hosted local literary lions and even entertained Emerson himself at the Evergreens. She and Emily read Coventry Patmore's *The Angel in the House*, the same angel whose murder Virginia Woolf plotted years later. There is evidence that Sue herself did a good deal of angel-bashing.

A symbol of Sue's estrangement from Austin and the wifely role is her signing her maiden name in 1859 to a newly acquired translation by Margaret Fuller of German feminist Bettina von Armin's work. Moreover, in Sue's copy of *The Princess*, she marked Princess Ida's proposal to do away with love:

> Love is it? Would this same mock-love,
>   and this
> Mock-Hymen were laid up like winter-bats,
> Till all men grew to rate us at our worth,

> Not vassals to be beat, nor pretty babes
> To be dandled, no, but living wills, and
>   sphered
> Whole in ourselves and owed to none.
>   Enough![25]

In late 1858, Sue introduced Emily to Elizabeth Barrett Browning's *Aurora Leigh*, a verse-novel about a successful woman poet, and this encouraged Emily to become "whole" in herself as a poet and "owed to none."[26]

Emily pursued autonomy through the development of her imaginative and intellectual faculties. To do this, she carefully narrowed the numbers of people whom she had to serve. At the time she decided upon this course, the late 1850s, the path of singleness for some women had become a mark of female independence, despite the stigma it also held.

In early August 1860, Dickinson wrote to Samuel Bowles that her "friends are a very few," that she was aware that she "smiled at women," and that she revered "the holy ones"–Mrs. Fry and Miss Nightingale–the two leaders in the professionalization of nursing for women.[27] Though Elizabeth Fry, the Quaker, was married, her establishment of the Institution for Nursing Sisters in 1840 began a movement for advancing women's position through service work which ultimately elevated the social status primarily of unmarried, middle-class women.[28] Florence Nightingale, of course, epitomizes the figure of the heroic, single woman, and she was, as we will see in the next chapter, a role model for Christina Rossetti as well. Perhaps Emily Dickinson even began calling herself "Daisy" in poems and letters beginning in late 1859 as a way of identifying herself with the popular spinster heroine, Ethel May, in Charlotte Yonge's *The Daisy Chain, or Aspirations* (1856).[29]

Emily Dickinson's poems and letters discuss the cultivation of her female self in terms of her search for autonomy and meaningful work and her thirst for education. After the death of Elizabeth Barrett Browning, in June 1861, Emily wrote to the Norcross cousins that both Elizabeth Barrett Browning and George Sand had achieved the status of "queens" as women writers–despite their seeming weaknesses in childhood–and that she fashioned herself and her cousins as "little stars from the same night."[30]

Her poem #789, of 1863, is her culminating expression of self-confidence and self-reliance as an intellectual female. The poem freshly employs the language of architecture as a metaphor for self-development to create an image of the self in construction:

On a Columnar Self–

How ample to rely
In Tumult– or Extremity–
How good the Certainty

That Lever cannot pry–
And Wedge cannot divide
Conviction– That Granite Base–
Though None be on our Side–

Suffice Us– for a Crowd–
Ourself– and Rectitude–
And that Assembly– not far off
From furthest Spirit– God–

Sue, on the other hand, remained a passionate but thwarted woman. If she had the taste to recognize the worth of her sister-in-law's poems, and the daring to send at least one off for publication without its author's permission, she lacked the will to flout public opinion, or the desire to see her sister-in-law's work through to publication after Emily's death.

The one documented example we have of Sue's exchange with Emily over a poem occurs in the summer of 1861, when, in letters and packets, Emily revised the second stanza of "Safe in Their Alabaster Chambers" three times to meet Sue's criticisms. Usually, this exchange is used to show the fruitfulness of Emily's literary relationship with Sue; and indeed, many of her letters describe Sue as a muse. In fact, however, Emily never quite followed Sue's advice, but used Sue's comments as a way of becoming her own best critic. Sue's ideas would spur Emily to revise as she thought best.

Sue thought "Safe in Their Alabaster Chambers," originally composed in 1859 with two stanzas, should exist as one stanza alone. Sue thought that since "the first verse is complete in itself it needs no other, and can't be coupled– Strange things always go alone– as there is only one Gabriel and one Sun– You never made a peer for that verse, and I *guess* you[r] kingdom does'nt hold one–."[31] However, the version of this poem which Samuel Bowles published in *The Springfield Republican* (March 1862) is the original version, minus any of the revisions, with, of course, Bowles's own bowdlerizing.[32]

It is about this time that Emily Dickinson engaged in her most fervent attempt to publish. Just six weeks after the 1859 version of "Safe in Their Alabaster Chambers" appeared in *The Springfield Republican* as "The Sleeping," Dickinson sent the second, 1861 version, also unacceptable to Sue, along with three other poems to Thomas Wentworth Higginson, in her famed, first correspondence to him. This letter began a relationship which may have retarded any hope Emily Dickinson had for being published in her lifetime, but her choice of contact person may not have been as misguided as is sometimes suggested. It is easy to make a butt of Higginson at this distance: how conventional, how misguided of him, how criminally philistine. We forget how much we are prisoners of our own time's taste, and, if we pride ourselves on our greater range of vision, it is still a range that has limits. After all, Thomas Wentworth Higginson asked Dickinson if she had read Whitman. She did choose an advisor who was kindly to her as a person, if not helpful as a literatus. She chose a man who had a good deal of sympathy for women. And she chose a man whose range of enthusiasms would have appalled her immediate family. Her father would have had scant sympathy for a man who was an abolitionist and women's rights activist, not so much for his ideas as for his vehemence in carrying them out. If one discards Wadsworth as "the lover," and substitutes "spiritual advisor" as his role, then she chose two liberal clergymen for mentors, men whose theological ideas were far more tolerant than Emily Dickinson's Calvinist training.

In the rest of Dickinson's adult life, which was dramatically punctuated by the Civil War and the changes brought to an increasingly developed college community, there was an increasing withdrawal from community life to a life lived within the confines of "her father's house." Yet, the years 1858-1865 represent her greatest output. By spring 1862, when she wrote to Higginson, she had written three hundred poems. In Part III, "The Victorian World," we demonstrate the marked ways in which the important economic and political events of this period–the war, industrialization, and the women's movement–permeated her thinking and appear throughout her poetry.

Even as she withdrew physically, she kept up her correspondence, a controlled measure of participation. Letters were sent to people whose lives she obviously knew well, though she may have not seen them in ten, fifteen, or twenty years, if she had ever met them at all.[33] She left her home again only twice, for eye treatments in Boston, in 1864 and 1865, during which time she stayed with the Norcross cousins. After these trips, she never left Amherst. Traditional biographers identified only one breach in this isolation, her friendship and romance with Judge Lord, a man many years her senior. They are supposed to have considered marriage, but he died before this could be carried out.

Besides the Amherst friendships which she maintained by notes and gifts of flowers or jams, accompanied by poems, she carried on a voluminous correspondence with many people in New England and across the country.

Though some of these people, such as Josiah Holland, Samuel Bowles (another strong candidate for the recipient of the Master Letters), and Helen Hunt Jackson, were, like Thomas Wentworth Higginson, important literary figures of the time, Josiah Holland made no move to help her attain prominence as a poet. Samuel Bowles, as we have seen, published her, but only after regularizing her work. Only Helen Hunt Jackson championed her as a poet. Insistently, she beseeched Emily Dickinson to publish and to allow Jackson to act as her agent. While Karl Keller finds sinister motivation in Jackson's partisanship, reducing it to the unhelpful levels of Bowles or Higginson, it is on a very different level.[34] Jackson does not seek to change a word, only to get Dickinson into print. Like Higginson, her own verse and taste were conventional, but, unlike him, she was able to accept what she did not understand. Again, like Higginson, she spent the last part of her life in defense of victims of injustice, Native Americans in this case. For a person who was reputed to be determinedly anti-political, Emily Dickinson had some strange friends.

Besides hopeless love, disenchantment with the confines of small-town, conventional life, or her own desire to find time for herself, away from nursing her mother, the other forces that may have sent Emily Dickinson to her seclusion were the stormy relationships between her brother and his wife and his wife and the rest of the family. Never a happy marriage, Austin and Sue's relationship became increasingly upsetting. Sue began to pursue her own career as local arts patron, while Austin found a mistress in a newly arrived faculty wife whose husband was subject to bouts of insanity. This story, worthy of a Gothic writer, is of particular interest to Dickinson scholars since it was Austin's mistress who, after Sue dallied too long with the poems Lavinia gave her, undertook to get them published.

Sue and Austin's marital problems ended the relationship between Sue and Emily, who sided with her brother. Emily also became an active aunt to his three children and continued what was left of her relationship with Sue vicariously through the children. Indeed, it was the death of their youngest son which brought Emily out of seclusion for the last time.

Deaths became increasingly frequent during these later years and fed Emily's speculations on life after death. Always heretical, she seems to have found comfort in no one sect, neither in the harsher doctrines of the Congregationalists nor through her liberal clergymen. Her father's death in 1874, followed a year later by her mother's incapacitating stroke, ended her status as daughter since, as she remarked, she then became a mother to her mother.[35] Whether the end of this relatively privileged status affected her creative ability, or her belated debut as an adult left her with no time, as she complained, she wrote less and less, generally on themes she had explored during the fruitful 1860s when she often wrote more than a poem a day.

When she died after a short illness in 1886, she had written almost two thousand poems. She had instructed Lavinia to burn all her papers, but Lavinia followed her wishes only in regard to the letters she had saved. She was amazed at the amount her sister had written and, though she herself had no interest in poetry, she had great faith in Emily's ability. Stubbornly, persistently, she cajoled, threatened, and prodded people until, feeling unable to do the actual work herself, she managed to convince Mabel Loomis Todd to look at them. Whether to please Austin or because she was bored or intrigued, Mabel Loomis Todd looked at the poems and became convinced of their worth. It was she, modern, attractive, young, energetic, and sophisticated, who finally persuaded Thomas Wentworth Higginson to publish at least a small edition, and finally to give them the publication that they deserved. This was the edition, "Poems by Emily Dickinson," Christina Rossetti perused on her sixtieth birthday.

Meanwhile, Sue refused to part with those poems which Emily Dickinson had sent her, as well as those Lavinia had given her after Emily Dickinson's death. The fight to get all the poems published took two generations, with Martha Dickinson Bianchi, Sue's daughter, and Millicent Todd Bingham inheriting the war from their mothers.

The story of Emily Dickinson's life was subject to mythologizing, bowdlerizing, censorship, and enlargement, some of this in order to keep the family scandal of Austin and Mabel from surfacing. A moralist might say that Emily Dickinson remained a victim of her overpowering family to the end. That would be too neat, however. Whatever impulse kept her sister from obeying her wishes set in motion events that transcended one small-town family's reputation. She who had come to be the most private of beings became the most public property, the blank page on which to write one's own fears and wishes. Because of the sparse record of her life, what we are left with is what she found ultimately more satisfying than the acting out of events, her imaginings of the significance and order of all phenomena, from the smallest bee to the shape of God.

In this chapter, we have shown that the distortions of Emily Dickinson as withdrawn, reclusive, and uninvolved in her age represent incomplete views. We turn in our next chapter to Christina Rossetti who, despite family, class, cultural, and religious differences from Emily Dickinson, was also a woman poet thought to be primarily subjective, but who, like Dickinson, was concerned with the public issues of her times. By examining both poets in tandem, we see more clearly the public nature of their poetic visions during the period of women's activism and the forces which have obfuscated our ability to see them in relation to their times.

"Goblin Market."
Reproduced by Special Permission
of PLAYBOY Magazine: Copyright © 1973 by PLAYBOY.
Illustration by Kinuko Craft.

Chapter 4

Christina Rossetti

Although the traditional view of Christina Rossetti presents her as unsympathetic to the women's movement, there is biographical and poetic evidence to suggest that this was not the case. In addition to volunteering to be one of Nightingale's nurses, Rossetti was involved with one of the most radical experiments for women of the day: the Anglican Sisterhoods. Moreover, she was influenced by the progressive Langham Place Group, although she ultimately did not affiliate herself with them. Like Dickinson's "supposed person," Rossetti's poetic speakers often express the desire for independence, self-reliance, and autonomy, and these characters and themes surface most prominently in Rossetti's work in the 1850s and 1860s, when the women's rights movement was becoming visible. In this biographical sketch, Christina Rossetti's development as a poet and her struggle against redundancy as an unmarried woman will be presented in the context of the emerging women's movement.

Christina Rossetti was born on December 5, 1830–just five days before Emily Dickinson–at 38 Charlotte Street near Portland Place in London. Like Dickinson, she was raised by a politically active father, but in addition, her mother, Frances Lavinia Polidori Rossetti, provided her with intellectual stimulation and a model for social reform Dickinson's mother could not.

Frances Lavinia had been intellectually inspired by her own mother. She was one of eight children born to Anna Louise Pierce, an English governess, and Gaetano Polidori, an Italian émigré. After Anna Louise bore eight children, she adopted the role of invalid, completely retired from the duties of domesticity, which she handed down to her youngest daughter Eliza, and spent the remainder of her energy on an intellectual pursuit, namely training Frances Lavinia and two other daughters to be governesses. Frances Lavinia's training was conducted from her mother's invalid chamber, and she learned all the necessary accomplishments, except dancing. Thus, Frances Lavinia acquired a passion for intellect not only from her father, who was a political exile and teacher of Italian, and her favorite brother John, who authored a Gothic novel and was Lord Byron's traveling physician, but also from her mother who had retired to her chamber to preserve her mind.

Although Frances' passion for intellect did not manifest itself in her own literary accomplishments, it did greatly influence her choice of husband. Frances Lavinia Polidori met Christina's father Gabriele Rossetti while she worked as a governess. Gabriele Rossetti was especially known for his ode to liberty, the "Sei pur bella," which became the theme song of the constitutional movement in Naples. After the fall of Napoleon, when the Bourbons regained control, Gabriele was exiled for his republican enthusiasm, and he fled to Malta in 1821. With the financial help of a few of his English patrons, he came to London in 1824. Once in London, Gabriele became a teacher of Italian and befriended other Italian émigrés, including Gaetano Polidori. He was attracted to Polidori's second daughter, Frances Lavinia, and they married in 1826. As we will see in our chapter "War Poems," Christina learned about her father's revolutionary background when she was a young child, and this influenced her thoughts and poetry on the subject of war.

Although Gabriele described his relationship with Frances as ideal, their class and religious differences were as deep as their different conceptions of romantic and platonic love. Gabriele Rossetti's background was working-class, and in London, even with private students, he earned only about £300 a year. In contrast to Christina's father's meager, working-class earnings, her grandfather achieved professional status as a teacher and was able, when he died, to leave Christina's mother with a small annual income. Thus, Christina Rossetti grew up in a household in which her mother was well educated and capable of economic independence, and her father was intellectually and politically stimulating but not especially ambitious.

Gabriele was loved for his warmth and affection and criticized for being a doting and overly sentimental father and husband. His radical, religious ideas led him to Freemasonry, while Frances began as an Evangelical and became, in the 1840s, an active High Church supporter, which, in effect, made her something of a social reformer. She resisted

Catholic exaltation of the Virgin Mary as perverse mariolatry, and she perhaps sensed an unfortunate dependence–emotional, economic, and ideological–in Gabriele on the feminine.

In early childhood, Christina was influenced by her mother in not favoring her father's sentimentalizing of the feminine, and she clearly preferred the more professional, detached Italian grandfather Polidori to the exuberant father who fussed over his daughters to excess; and the father preferred Maria, the eldest daughter, for she reminded him of his own peasant-stock Italian mother in manner and appearance. Although there was never an argument between Gabriele and Frances to speak of, Frances was so thoroughly opposed to Gabriele's obsession for connecting Dante's spiritual love for Beatrice to Petrarch's physical love for Laura that immediately upon Gabriele's death in 1854, she burned his *Amors Platonica.*[1]

The complex, psycho-sexual dimensions of their children's lives reflect the unexpressed intensity of the parents' differences.   Dante Gabriel–his father's favored son–vainly attempted in his lifetime, through his painting and poetry, to make manifest his father's circuitous, patriarchal ideas on love by elevating his physical attraction for Elizabeth Siddall to spiritual levels.   Indeed, the Pre-Raphaelite ethos of spiritualized eroticism, which eventually led through figures like Algernon Swinburne, Edward Burne-Jones, and Walter Pater to the decadent aestheticism of the 1880s and 1890s, derives a great deal from Gabriele's abstruse researches into Dante's conception of romantic/spiritual love.   In Christina's life and work, romantic love and marriage lead to disaster.   As Nina Auerbach observed, in relationship to Christina's novella *Commonplace*, "Rossetti allows no doubts that friendship ranks higher on the spiritual scale than heterosexual love."[2]

Gabriele's favorite children were the two eldest–Maria Francesca, born in 1827, and Dante Gabriel, born in 1828.   As the first son, Dante Gabriel became the dominating personality.   The two younger children were William Michael, born in 1829, and Christina, born a year later.   Talented, sensitive, and beautiful, Christina Rossetti found learning "not to be first" particularly difficult.   Rossetti wrote to the critic Sir Edmund Gosse: "'Besides the clever and cultivated parents who headed us all, I in particular beheld far ahead of myself the clever sister and two clever brothers who were little (though but a little) my seniors.   As to acquirements, I lagged out of all proportion behind them, and have never overtaken them to this day.'"[3]

Yet family, friends, and acquaintances noticed a strange, exaggerated quality in the way this accomplished poet yielded to authority.   The

Italian "deference" she displayed for the "'head of the family.'" according to William Michael, had "a rather unusual feeling" about it. She was overly or "punctiliously polite." "Some persons who knew her intellectual and literary standing in the eye of the world," he continued, "fancied that there was something of affectation or even sarcasm in this."[4]

At a year and a half, Christina was "skittish." She was an angelic demon at three and insistent on her share of the cakes at four. When she was six, she and Dante Gabriel were the two storms, while Maria and William Michael were the two calms. Once, in response to a rebuke of her mother's, Christina ripped up her own arm with a pair of scissors.[5]

Maria and Dante Gabriel were both critical of their younger sister's literary strides and considered her the "least bookish." Thus, as a child, Christina frequently sought to avoid the criticisms of her two older siblings. "I, Maria and William know several scenes" of Richard III "by heart," Dante Gabriel boasted to his Aunt Margaret when he was seven. He had been writing blank verse dialogue since he was five. Maria was reading English and Italian at five. William Michael was so embarrassed he had not learned to read before he was six that his Aunt Margaret had to be called in to tutor him.[6] In mutual self-defense, he and Christina became "chiefest chums." If Emily Dickinson shared a bond with her brother, Austin, which reinforced their superiority in the face of the rest of the world, then Christina Rossetti's parallel confidant was William Michael; he helped her rebuff the criticisms of their older siblings. Precisely because William Michael was exceptionally loyal and responsible as a brother and supported her financially from 1854 to 1876, it is difficult to criticize the biases he exercised later as Christina Rossetti's editor and biographer.

Christina Rossetti's maternal grandfather, Gaetano Polidori, adored her. He believed Christina had "more wit than any of the others." Rossetti told Gosse: "'If any one thing schooled me in the direction of poetry, it was perhaps the delightful idle liberty to prowl all alone about my grandfather's cottage-grounds.'"[7] Polidori privately printed Christina's first volume, *Verses* (1847), on his own press.

Throughout childhood, Rossetti sought to unleash her creativity, as one of her dreams about the canaries at the Regents Park Zoo illustrates; but as a daughter and sister, she received contradictory messages about developing her creative talent. When she visited the Zoological Gardens with Dante Gabriel for the first time, she wanted to write verses celebrating the captive birds. In her dream, she was in the park at dawn; just as the sun rose, she saw "a wave of yellow light sweep from the trees." A multitude of canaries "had met, and were now going back to captivity."[8]

If, as psychologists say, animals in our dreams manifest aspects of ourselves, the birds in flight presaged the flowering of Rossetti's poetic talent. But the canaries dutifully returned to captivity even in her dreams, just as Rossetti sensed that her muse was expected to adhere to a female posture. The image of captivity was a common one in women's poetry.

Although Rossetti shared this symbolic poetic vision with Dante Gabriel, he never made the picture of it he promised. Dante Gabriel's frequent slowness to respond, his failure to follow through, characterized the lifetime relationship of the two poets and siblings. It was not until the late 1850s, when Rossetti settled into her identity as a single woman and had established her own circle of literary acquaintances and supporters, that she was in a position to consider herself a serious poet and take an active role in marketing her writing.

One recurring issue in Rossetti's biography is how the tempestuous and buoyant child became transformed into a reticent youth. A series of mysterious illnesses are usually offered by way of explanation. The first lasted approximately five years, if we trust Dante Gabriel's memory that by the time his sister was twelve, she had become melancholy.[9] Battiscombe is the most recent biographer to offer the view that in early adolescence, Rossetti's "melancholy" consisted of a nervous breakdown, brought on by having to adjust to puberty under too stressful conditions.

Battiscombe cites as evidence for the nervous breakdown theory that Rossetti had already been seen by three doctors by the time she was fifteen for her illness, whatever it was. Then she points to Kohl's discovery of an inscription by Godfrey Bilchett. On the back of Bilchett's copy of the Rossetti biography written by Bilchett's friend Mackenzie Bell, Bilchett wrote: "The doctor who attended on Christina Rossetti when she was about 16-18 said she was then more or less out of her mind (suffering, in fact, from a form of insanity, I believe a kind of religious mania)."[10]

However, it is incorrect to think that Rossetti's "melancholy," to use Dante Gabriel's term, resulted from religious fanaticism. Instead, the work of feminist historians strongly suggests that hysteria of the sort Christina may have been exhibiting was a common symptom of women who did not wish to conform to oppressive roles. In Rossetti's case, she developed melancolia when she was given the responsiblity of nursing her invalid father, a chore against which it is understandable she would want to rebel. Moreover, she needed a shield to protect the privacy she required for writing poetry. In addition, the poetry she was writing, which reflected her involvement with the High Church Movement, was highly critical of self-denial as a virtue for women.

In 1843, Gabriele's illness and partial blindness caused him to abandon his post at King's College. This forced his forty-three-year-old wife to seek employment as a teacher of languages and two of his children to find work for the first time. Frances relied on all the children to contribute to the family income, except for Dante Gabriel. Considered the most talented, attractive, and brilliant child, he continued his art studies at Mr. Cary's and went on to study at the Academy School of the Royal Academy. William Michael took a post as a clerk with the Board of Excise and earned a moderate stipend. It was not until 1850, however, that he began to get paid for literary employment. Maria became a governess for the children of Lord Thynne, but afterwards, she instructed pupils in her home.

Someone had to nurse the aging Gabriele, and as the youngest, Christina was hardly fit for outside employment. She was the closest daily witness to her father's physical decline; he was sixty years old, slowly withering from extreme bronchitis, later consumption, and continued blindness. It seems likely that Rossetti's melancholy had at least a good deal to do with her internalization of and reaction against the family's troubles, since the time noted by Dante Gabriele corresponds closely to the time of Gabriele's physical breakdown.

Feminist historians, like Barbara Ehrenreich and Deirdre English, have shown how the nineteenth-century doctors' view of middle-class women as "innately sick" provided a "powerful rationale against allowing women to act in any other way." Victorian women appropriated the epidemic of hysteria and the cult of invalidism to turn the sick role to their own advantage. In the epidemic of hysteria, for example, "women were both accepting their inherent 'sickness' *and* finding a way to rebel against an intolerable social role. Sickness having become a way of life, became a way of rebellion."[11] Perhaps Christina learned this form of rebellion from the English women on her maternal side. After all, her maternal grandmother retired to her invalid chamber after her eighth child in order to gain greater control over her time and to free her intellectual imagination for training her daughters to be governesses. In this way, she used illness as a strategy for her own advantage. Christina's Aunt Margaret, the one who tutored William Michael in reading, would erratically break out into fits of hysteria, conveniently preventing Margaret from having to secure *permanent* employment as a governess.

Since Christina's bouts with "insanity" occurred when her father had become so ill he could no longer work, and everyone except Christina and Dante Gabriel was obliged to find employment, Christina may have felt pressure to justify her absorption with writing. This absorption began, ironically, when she was twelve, the same year Dante Gabriel noticied she became melancholy.[12]

Rossetti participated in the High Church Movement (otherwise known as the Oxford, or Tractarian, Movement) with her mother, sister, and maiden aunts. However, as her early poetry illustrates, she was no simple true believer. The movement, led by John Henry Newman and Edward Pusey, attempted to strengthen the spiritual fiber of society by building the Anglican Church as a bulwark against growing scientific rationalism and utilitarianism. Practically, this meant separation of church and state and opposition to increasing state encroachment in religious matters. Rossetti was active in Christ's Church, which was one of the leading Tractarian centers. Pusey himself helped to establish Christ's Church and often took the pulpit from its vicar, Reverend William Dodsworth. Dodsworth eventually followed Newman's lead, abandoned the movement, and converted to Roman Catholicism. Leaders like Pusey, William Wilberforce, and John Mason Neale supported unity within the Anglican Church, especially given several accomplishments of the movement, including an enormous increase in parish memberships and the development of schools under the auspices of the newly developing Anglican Sisterhoods. The women in Rossetti's family supported Pusey's position that the Church of England needed to be maintained and that state intervention should be resisted as Anglicans, not as Roman Catholics.

Rossetti's early poems reflect her growing critical awareness of the contradictory roles assigned women in the movement and, more broadly, within the church. Many poems explore the psychology of nuns, while others examine potential, self-destructive consequences of seemingly virtuous behavior, such as renunciation. Feminist artist Anna Howitt, daughter of literary celebrity and reformer Mary Howitt, appreciated Rossetti's ironic examination of female stereotypes. She was particularly struck by one of Rossetti's early poems, "The Ruined Cross" (1847). Rossetti's biographer, Eleanor Thomas, tells us this poem was published only once in Rossetti's lifetime in *Verses* (1847). Howitt probably found the Rossetti poem in this volume which Rossetti's grandfather privately printed and which Dante Gabriel had circulated among his literary friends. Dante Gabriel's letter to Christina of 1852 informs her that Miss Howitt had "a drawing . . . she calls *The End of The Pilgrimage* . . . which furnishes an exact illustration of your *Ruined Cross.*"[13] Christina's poem, which Thomas found in a 1906 reprint of *Verses*, depicts a conventional heroine in "slow decline" on a long pilgrimage to the ruined cross. However, the ending displays the ironic twist Rossetti had perfected by this time. As quoted in Thomas:

" 'The ancient cross is standing yet, / The youthful wanderer died.' "[14]

More than any other member of the immediate family, Rossetti's mother encouraged her to develop her poetic talent. Rossetti explored the mother-daughter relationship in her juvenilia and other early poems, as well as in her later valentines. Mother and daughter lived together as long as Frances Lavinia was alive, though always with others around them—whether it was the whole family or just Christina's father, her sister and brother William, William and his wife, Lucy, or the Polidori maiden aunts. In the poems of the middle period, however, from 1856 through 1866, daughters strike out against parental and other forms of hierarchical authority in order to assert their independence as single women.

Like Dickinson, Rossetti came forth slowly as a poet. Before the *Goblin Market* volume was published in 1862, she had only published ten poems in popular journals (1848-1861) and seven poems in the shortlived Pre-Raphaelite journal *The Germ* (1848-1850).

The variety of themes on which she was writing–from the war with China (1842) to Tasso, the Italian epic poet (1846)–reflected the lively conversations being held in the Rossetti front parlor on Charlotte Street. According to William Michael Rossetti's familiar account:

> The children were constantly with their parents; there
> was no separate nursery, and no rigid line drawn
> between the big ones and the little ones. Of English
> society there was extremely little . . . but of Italian
> society. . . . There were exiles, patriots,
> politicians, literary men, musicians, and some of
> inferior standing; fleshy good-natured Neapolitans,
> keen Tuscans, emphatic Romans. As we children were
> habituated from our earliest years to speaking Italian
> with our father, we were able to follow all or most of
> the speech of these "natives"; and a conspirator or a
> semi-brigand might present himself, and open out on his
> topics of predilection, without being told to leave the
> room. All this–even apart from our chiefly Italian
> blood–made us, no doubt, not a little different from
> British children in habit of thought and standard of
> association; and when Dante, and Christina proved, as
> poetic writers, somewhat devious from the British
> tradition and the insular mind, we may say, if not "so
> much the better," at any rate, "no wonder."[15]

Outside of these informal, intellectual gatherings, and a few private lessons in German, music, and art, all the schooling Christina and her sister Maria Francesca received was administered by their mother, Frances Lavinia. The two sons, however, attended day-schools; Dante Gabriel went off to school in 1836, and William Michael followed the next year.[16]

Frances applied herself assiduously to her daughters' education. Frances' "commonplace book," a lesson book with literary examples, provides a sense of the depth and range of her reading and a sampling of authors who influenced the young Christina. As described by Battiscombe, the book comprises extracts, some of them in Christina's hand, from a wide variety of authors, "including poets from Sappho (in translation) to Herbert, Crashaw and Dryden, Wordsworth, Southey, Crabbe, Tennyson, Poe, Tom Moore, Lamartine and Camille Desmoulins."[17] However, for all the support Christina Rossetti received from her literary family for becoming a poet, she still ' internalized a patriarchal pattern. "She could not have been very old," Packer observed, "before becoming aware that she was regarded . . . as almost as beautiful, almost as talented and . . . almost as clever as Dante Gabriel–but not quite."[18] Her brothers, of course, held traditional views of women's roles. As Pre-Raphaelite poets and artists, they exalted Christina for embodying a meek, saint-like, feminine ideal, and in their biographical treatments of her and in their art, they idealized that image. Perhaps William Michael overconfidently asserted that "in a roomful of mediocrities," Christina "consented to seem the most unobtrusive of all."[19]

Maria Rossetti, Christina's older sister, was Christina's almost constant companion. Like Christina, Maria also pursued the single life and applied herself intellectually to liturgical studies and to scholarship on Dante. Christina commented that had Maria been the younger instead of the older sister, she would have had more of an opportunity to develop her intellectual interests. As the oldest, Maria had to begin work as a paid governess when her father took ill. She was sixteen when she began working, and she continued this type of employment until she was twenty-seven. Domestic cares and religious scruples kept her from becoming more "celebrated." Christina Rossetti's poems on sisterhood, which we discuss in chapter seven, appear as early as her juvenilia (1842-1847) and continue into her activist period (1856-1870).

From 1854 until 1873, Maria, Christina, and their mother resided together, and they shared interests in literature, culture, and social reform. Christina said she shared a bond of duty with Maria, but the sisterhood poems of the 1850s and 1860s also express the kind of violent passion we found in Dickinson's letters to Sue Gilbert Dickinson. The clearest articulation of the physical intimacy of sisterhood is expressed between Lizzie and Laura, the sisters in "Goblin Market":

> "Eat me, drink me, love me;
> Laura, make much of me:
> For your sake I have braved the glen
> And had to do with goblin merchant men."

. . . .

> She clung about her sister,
> Kissed and kissed and kissed her:
> Tears once again
> Refreshed her shrunken eyes,
> Dropping like rain
> After long sultry drouth;
> Shaking with aguish fear, and pain,
> She kissed and kissed her with a hungry mouth.[20]

Playboy Magazine presented the first sexualized version of "Goblin Market" in 1973. *Playboy*'s illustrated version highlighted the erotic dimension of the sisterly love theme. The sisters' physical intimacy is portrayed as an unconscious sexual fantasy to act out a forbidden, titillating desire for lesbian incest.[21] We will show in chapters six and seven that in addition to exploring new dimensions of sisterhood, "Goblin Market" expresses a radical reaction against patriarchal market relations.

However, traditional critics still stress Rossetti's religious devotion and her reclusiveness, especially in later life. Feminist critics such as Sandra Gilbert, Susan Gubar, and Adrienne Rich establish that Rossetti's mode of existence, as a single daughter, was a conscious choice—the best alternative for attaining the leisure necessary to write.[22] We need to go even further to examine with depth the other forces tugging on Rossetti, such as her economic and emotional dependence on family, or her social and political responsibilities related to social work, antivivisection, and antislavery, about which biographers and critics have uncovered little new information. Volumes One and Two of R.W. Crump's variorum edition of Rossetti's complete poems have finally established the extent and seriousness of Rossetti's craft and skill as a poet. This has already occasioned a revaluation of the quality of Rossetti's poetry. The 1970s and 1980s have seen a flourishing of new interpretations of her most popular poem, "Goblin Market." However, Rossetti as the active agent—the woman who circulated antivivisection petitions and was asked to be director of a home for wayward girls—has not yet greeted the public.

Only two of Rossetti's poems with social/political messages were published in these early years: "Repining" (1847), published in *The Germ*, and "Behold, I Stand at the Door and Knock" (1851), published in *Aiken's Year* (1854), a progressive journal.[23]

The Germ, which lasted from 1848 to 1850, was the journal of the Pre-Raphaelite Brotherhood. It presented poetry, short stories, reviews, and articles. Although "Repining" is subtle in its criticism, it does express Rossetti's early pacifist ideas just months before the European revolutions of 1848. The poem will be discussed at length in chapter five.

"Behold, I Stand at the Door and Knock" was written when Rossetti assisted her mother in the management of a private day-school, and it condemns liberal reliance on state forms of charity like the workhouse as ungenerous and unChristian. In the poem, a woman of comfortable means is initially approached by God in the form of a homeless, hungry widow who asks for shelter. The lady declines to help, but sends the widow to the clergyman instead. Next, God visits the lady in the shape of a "way-worn and pale" old man who knocks on the lady's door:

> "Kind lady, I have journeyed far,
>   and fail
>   Through weariness; for I have
>   begged in vain
> Some shelter, and can find no
>   lodging-place."—
>   She answered: "There's the work-
>   house very near;
>   Go, for they'll certainly receive
>   you there"—
> Then shut the door against his
>   pleading face.

In the final instance, a "stunted child" with "sunken eyes" asks the lady for help and guidance. Again, the lady refuses and calls the child an imposter who should work instead of cry. Because the lady proves herself completely lacking in generosity, God visits her directly and admonishes her that she will lose her wealth:

> Who standeth at the gate, and will
>   be heard?

> Arise, O woman, from thy comforts
> now:
>
> . . . .
>
> "Thou wast as a princess rich and at
> ease—
> Now sit in dust and howl for
> poverty.
> Three times I stood beseeching at
> thy gate,
> Three times I came to bless thy
> soul and save:
> But now I come to judge for what
> I gave,
> And now at length thy sorrow is too
> late."

Although Rossetti was clearly writing poems with political themes, they were not the ones singled out for publication by male editors. "The first verses" of Christina's "which got into print after the cessation of *The Germ* in 1850" were "Behold, I Stand at the Door and Knock," but it was no accident the reformer Mary Howitt was connected with the journal which printed the poem.[24]

It is interesting to note that Rossetti objected to having her melancholy poems of frustrated love totally define her poetic image. In April 1849, she implored William Michael not to circulate any of her "love personals" to the Pre-Raphaelite sculptor, Thomas Woolner, who had expressed interest in seeing her poetry. Georgina Battiscombe tells us Rossetti wrote that it would be "'more than intolerable'" for her verses to be "'regarded as outpourings of a wounded spirit,'" especially since she suspected her reputation was already being formed on that basis: "that something like this has been the case I have good reason to know."[25] Two of her poems, written in 1847, which focused on the woman-as-forsaken-lover theme had already been published in *The Athenaeum*: "Heart's Chill Between" and "Death's Chill Between." The speaker in the first poem breaks her relationship to a lover who has been false, but she is left distraught and obsessed. The speaker in the second poem is haunted by her young husband who has just died.[26] Since women's poetry, like their journal writing, was viewed as a way of revealing the self to God, it was often read as synonymous with lyric confession.[27]   When Dante Gabriel changed the original title "Anne of Warwick" to "Death's Chill Between," he changed a character's speech in a dramatic monologue into a lyric expression by Rossetti herself.[28]

Despite Rossetti's clear distaste for having these "love personals" totally define her image, poems falling into the "morbid" category were the ones selected for publication.   Even six of the poems published in the *The Germ*, which was edited primarily by Dante Gabriel and William Michael with Christina handling the correspondence, belong in the "morbid" category and express themes of frustrated love and life's vanity.   These poems elicited praise; however, she published them either under a pseudonym, Ellen Alleyn, or anonymously.   The pseudonym not only protected her from being identified with "love personals," it also shielded her from personal embarrassment.   She did not want her poems of frustrated love to point to her own failing relationship with the Pre-Raphaelite painter, James Collinson.

Rossetti became engaged to James Collinson in November 1848, shortly after the Pre-Raphaelite Brotherhood was formed.   The engagement lasted until 1850, when the last number of *The Germ* was issued.   On account of his rather dull personality, his poor financial prospects, and Catholic religious views, Collinson was considered a poor match for Rossetti.   However, as one of the original members of the Pre-Raphaelite Brotherhood, Collinson was favored by Dante Gabriel.   By August 1849, when Rossetti visited Collinson's mother and sister at Pleasely Hill for the first time, it was apparent the engagement was not going well.   Collinson himself did not attend.   Instead, he went on a short holiday with William Michael to the Isle of Wight.   Moreover, during the engagement, Collinson's financial prospects dwindled, thus making the marriage enterprise less likely for him.   In January 1850 he pawned a watch and begged money from his friend Stephens.[29]

Whatever attraction Collinson held for Rossetti dissipated when Collinson left the Anglican Church and reconverted to Catholicism over the Gorham case.   Rossetti, who was loyal to the Church of England, opposed the resolution of this case which gave power to the state.   Collinson's conversion to Rome must have seemed like a betrayal since it came when the church needed support and was, in fact, losing ground.   It was not until Collinson actually reconverted to Catholicism in 1850, however, that Rossetti broke the engagement, probably following her mother's High Church urgings.   There is no extant correspondence between them during their engagement, much less love letters. Rossetti's family letters from this period contain only a few rather formal references to Collinson as well as to uncomfortable conversation between herself and Collinson's mother and sister over "beaux" at Pleasely Hill.[30]

Thomas was the first Rossetti scholar to connect Rossetti's "morbid" poetry with the popular literary conventions for women's poetry and not with Rossetti's own, personal melancholy. Poems on the same melancholy themes as Rossetti's—frustrated romance, destroyed hopes, and the heroine's slow decline to an early grave—appeared in such popular British journals as *The Keepsake*, edited by Caroline Norton, and *The Athenaeum*, and such annuals, gift books, and individual volumes as *Scrap Book*, *The Drawing Room*, *Heath's Book of Beauty*, and *Friendship's Offering*. Letitia Landon, the Countess of Blessington, and Felicia Hemans were some of the popular women poets. The image of the melancholy woman poet was imported to America and appeared throughout women's poetry of the mid-nineteenth century, as Cheryl Walker has shown in *The Nightingale's Burden*.[31]

The short novel *Maude*, which Rossetti began "sometime toward or during 1850," presents her ironic criticism of the melancholy woman poet and her own detachment from the stereotype. Maude Foster is the melancholy, self-preoccupied young poet who becomes increasingly isolated from family and friends. Her seemingly effortless and spontaneous melodramatic verse expresses the conventional world-weariness and sentimental ennui. However, according to a careful reading of the story, it is Maude's excessive guilt and not her poetic talent which sets her apart and becomes a sinful indulgence. After a carriage accident, Maude is consumed with guilt—until she dies. Her resignation to death represents a nihilism which self-renunciation can foster in the extreme, a lack of enabling faith.

The omniscient narrator in *Maude* exposes the pose of the melancholy poet as a facade and shows the vanity of renunciation. Somber Maude is alone in her room. She turns out a lyric in record speed about the appeal of suffering through life compared to dying. By focusing on the boredom that produces the poem, the nonchalant speed of its composition, and the yawn which culminates Maude's effort, the narrator mocks the seriousness of Maude's brooding.[32]

Cousin Agnes, the only character in the story who is centered in who she is rather than in any imposed role, carries the practical voice of reason. She says to Maude: "You . . . put up with me as I am."[33] Agnes helps the reader see through Maude's melancholy guilt as another side of vanity. Maude tells Agnes she will not take communion on account of her sinful display of verses. But the reader is reminded that "deep-rooted indeed was that vanity which made Maude take pleasure, on such an occasion, in proving the force of arguments directed against herself. Still Agnes would not yield; but resolutely did battle for the truth."[34] Critics like Battiscombe and Gilbert and Gubar have too quickly and totally identified Rossetti with Maude. However, we should also identify Rossetti with Agnes, the more realistic, reliable character who survives "to perform the task imposed upon her" of "burning Maude's manuscripts." By viewing Agnes a reliable narrator, we can see Rossetti's criticisms of Maude's excesses more clearly. Diane D'Amico has convincingly shown the connections between Rossetti's perspective and that of cousin Agnes:

> In assessing the importance of Maude and its place in the Rossetti canon, we must keep the figure of Agnes before us. . . . Both thematically and structurally the work outlines Maude's struggle to possess at least some of her cousin's wisdom. . . . Rossetti was attempting to encourage the Agnes part of her own personality while keeping the despairing poet under control.[35]

Other pieces written at this time also explore the destructive aspects of moral renunciation with similar subtlety. For example, the impeccable saintliness of St. Elizabeth of Hungary is treated ironically in a sonnet Rossetti wrote in November 1850: "The Portrait." The usual source given for this poem is Charles Kingsley's *The Saint's Tragedy*, a drama which Collinson showed Rossetti in 1849. However, there are also echoes of Charlotte Brontë's description of her sister, Emily.[36]

In the poem, Rossetti illustrated how the Christian doctrine of self-sacrifice, or passionlessness, could be turned to its extreme: self-flagellation. A deceased woman has been "full of ruth" towards others, but "towards herself" she has been "harsh." Although she gains sympathy for her exemplary life of humble service–she was "servant of servants" and "little known" to "praise"–she suffered unnecessarily, like her modern male counterparts, Richard Cory and J. Alfred Prufrock, in the regimen of her self-repression. After cataloguing additional examples of self-abuse–"She schooled herself to sights and sounds uncouth"–Rossetti uncovers her theme: "her own self learned she to forsake." The final irony is achieved with wrenching clarity in the closing couplet: "So with calm will she chose and bore the cross / And hated all for love of Jesus Christ."[37]   Image and detail culminate in the successful, single effect: she *hated* all for love of Jesus.

The irony of the sonnet is paralleled by an irony in Rossetti's life at the time.   Before Rossetti wrote her poem, Collinson completed a painting whose subject was the same St. Elizabeth.   Despite the fact that their engagement was broken, Collinson modeled all the women's heads on Rossetti.   He must have assumed she favored the saint's character. However, judging from the severe irony of her sonnet, it is clear Rossetti rejected the renunciation St. Elizabeth signified.

Like other members of the Pre-Raphaelite circle, including Rossetti's own brothers, Collinson perceived Rossetti more as a stereotype than as a woman.   Although Rossetti clearly shared the Pre-Raphaelite aesthetic with members of the Brotherhood, her formal relationship to the group was as a model, not a member.   Dante Gabriel may have originally proposed that she join the Brotherhood in its early stages, but he clarified, in a letter to William Holman Hunt, that he "never meant that she should attend the meetings."   Instead, he "merely" meant "that she should entrust her productions" to his "reading."[38]

Rossetti was emerging as a poet in the context of a middle class women's reform movement–the "revolt of the idle woman"–that was just becoming visible in the 1850s.   A liberal wave increased the middle class woman's consciousness of moral obligations due one's fellow human beings, although visiting homes of the poor became no more than a fashionable habit for some.   Women brought books of inspiration, like Charlotte Yonge's novels and the Tracts for the Times, to the poor and assumed that vice and starvation would be cured by religion and beef-tea.   Many ladies nursed the sick.   In some cases, this made them feel morally superior.   Not only was their work a symbol of their charity, but it also reinforced the idea that illness had morally delinquent origins.[39]

At the same time, more radical women who were friends of Dante Gabriel's, such as Anna Howitt, Barbara Leigh Smith, and Bessie Rayner Parkes, saw clear deficiencies in women's opportunities as the causes of their poverty and their poor condition legally and educationally.   From Waterloo to the First Reform Bill and after, the economic and social pressures on middle class women to marry were increasing, as their legal and economic position in society was becoming more limited.   For women, marriage meant loss of property rights, their own earnings, their rights to enter a contract, child custody, and other deprivations.   Fewer women in England, in fact, were marrying, owing to a complex set of factors which converged after the Napoleonic Wars. These created an increasing number of single women who were, in most cases, economically dependent. M. Jeanne Peterson summarized the causes for the increased number of single women at this time:

> From the research of twentieth-century historians it is clear that the number of single middle-class women in need of employment was a product not only of the unstable 'conditions of business in those years but also arose out of the emigration of single men from England to the colonies, from the differential mortality rate which favored women, and from the tendency for men in the middle classes to marry later.[40]

One widely read critic of the day was William Rathbone Greg who introduced a new use for the term "redundant" in his frequently reprinted article "Why Are Women Redundant?"[41] According to Greg, redundant women were those who had missed their opportunity to fulfill their natural, serving role in relation to men due to the large male emigration. Greg showed how, according to the population statistics of 1851, out of "every 100 women over twenty, 57 were married, 12 were widows and 30 were spinsters." According to Helene E. Roberts, Greg also estimated that "there must be 1,248,000 women in England and Wales 'unnaturally' single. What these women should do with their lives, especially when they needed some means of support, was discussed much in books, periodicals and newspapers."[42] Because it was considered "unnatural" for women to support themselves economically, Greg promoted the idea of female emigration to the colonies where competition for husbands, he surmised, would not be as stiff. This would, at least, rid England of the so-called surplus women who threatened the defeat of the family and the mutation of the race.

The largest group of redundant women Greg identified, according to A. James Hammerton, were among the lower middle classes. As daughters of poor teachers and sisters of a struggling civil clerk, both Christina and Maria Rossetti belonged to this class: "immediately above the laboring poor, 'the daughters of unfortunate tradesmen, of poor clerks, or poorer curates.'"[43] Yet women from the middle classes had the fewest alternatives. Working for money diminished the middle-class lady's moral status and honor. According to Roberts, the middle-class woman "could be a governess and not much else. Though the governess might be immune from physical maltreatment, her position had its own kind of degradation."[44] The salary was low, from £30 to £60 per year, and her social role or class was problematic, vague, undefined.

While there were about 25,000 single governesses from the middle classes in England in 1851, there were over 750,000 female domestic servants, not to mention women employed in industry. Indeed, the working-class woman, whose status was already diminished by her class as well as by her sex, had a wider range of narrow options. In addition to domestic service or factory work, she could also find employment in a shop or become a seamstress. But "in all of these," according to Roberts, "the work was hard and tedious, the hours painfully long, the pay pitifully low, the treatment frequently harsh."[45] When employed, the female domestic servant earned about £12 per year; but in 1850 alone, ten thousand female servants were unemployed. Given the lack of opportunity, many women were simply resigned to life on the streets. According to police records for 1850, there were 8,000 prostitutes in London and more than 50,000 in England and Wales:

> The double standard and the stern unforgiving attitudes
> toward unwed motherhood frequently left no other choice
> to a woman than to sell herself on the street. Using
> the census figure of 42,000 illegitimate children born
> in the year 1851, William Acton estimated that
> one-twelfth of the unmarried women in England and Wales
> must have "strayed from the path of virtue."[46]

To these conditions, women had a wide range of responses. Before demanding the right to vote, reformers and radicals alike tried to improve women's educational, economic, and legal position. Many women's activities–like sick nursing, teaching, and governessing–became professionalized. Sick nursing, of course, became professionalized through the impetus of Florence Nightingale whose reputation as a strongminded, unmarried, independent woman caused critics like Greg to bristle. Nightingale's career took off during the Crimean War, and it intersected with Rossetti's just when the poet was facing her father's death. While the death freed Rossetti from the role of private sick nurse she had played for over a decade, it also forced her to redefine herself.

The year before her father died, both Polidori grandparents had died. The day-schools in which she worked as her mother's assistant had both failed, and she had lost her primary status in the Pre-Raphaelite circle as a model and poet to Dante Gabriel's mistress and later wife, the milliner's apprentice, Elizabeth Siddall. Her failed relationship with Collinson soured her to the commercialization of marriage, as the social pressures to become a wife and mother receded in her mind. No longer a granddaughter, father's daughter, potential wife and mother, or much of a published poet, Rossetti needed desperately to find new definition and meaning for her life. Slowly, she was becoming redundant, if examined from Greg's point of view. It was at this critical juncture that Rossetti identified with the independent image of Florence Nightingale. For Rossetti, the ascent of adulthood began with what Nina Auerbach identified as the "descent of spinsterhood," following the example of Florence Nightingale.[47]

An institution for training nurses started in Fitzroy Square in 1850 with four ladies facing training that year. Then, with the Crimean War, the image of Florence Nightingale, as conveyed by war correspondents, firmly created sick nursing as a new outlet for feminine energy: "It became impossible to regard any longer the purely domestic as a woman's only suitable sphere. As a sick nurse she appeared to be more successful than as a mother, and the notion arose that possibly she might do equally well in other directions."[48] Just a few doors north of Christ's Church, Albany Street, in the parish of St. Pancras where the Rossetti and Polidori women attended church, Pusey founded the Park Village Sisterhood. The Sisterhood was not far, in fact, from the Polidori residence.

The Sisterhood was established as "a novel experiment" according to Packer. Pusey "had discussed" it "as early as 1838 with Tractarian leaders." Still "the religious community of women caused amazement and consternation even in a parish as radical as Dodsworth's."[49] Their force in the London community quickly became apparent, and the Rossetti sisters were attracted to their work. After Park Village merged with the Devonport Sisterhood at St. Saviour's Home, Florence Nightingale found her best nurses for the war in that group. Desmond Morse-Boycott reported that a contemporary described the activities of Park Village Sisterhood sometime between 1845 and 1850 in the following manner:

> "The Sisters were employed in visiting the poor and
> sick at their own homes, receiving and training
> orphans, giving shelter to women of good character
> while seeking occupation, also in the care of a day
> school for very poor children."

"The first Sisterhood had influential support," Morse-Boycott continued, "and was closely directed by Pusey and Dodsworth, but from the start, and as it grew in numbers, was an object of suspicion":

> From this community, Florence Nightingale chose her
> best nurses in the Crimean War, amongst them the

> Superior, Miss Langston. The Sisterhood moved in 1852
> into St. Saviour's Home, Osnaburgh Street, which was
> later given over to the All Saints' Sisters.[50]

When Gabriele died in 1854, Rossetti initially began doing parish district visiting on Robert Street. But she surprisingly culminated the year by applying for Florence Nightingale's campaign through the sisterhood at St. Saviour's Home. Nightingale herself was just thirty, resolved against facing a trivial existence as a middle-class wife, and fully ready to face the world.[51] Although Rossetti was rejected, ostensibly for being too young at twenty-four, her application signified her desire to identify with "unnatural," single women like Nightingale. Since the economic and social pressures on her at this time were severe, and she had valid reasons for expecting to be selected for Nightingale's competitive Scutari campaign, it is understandable that the rejection caused her to become depressed.

Although marriage was originally an option for Rossetti, she had been trained by her mother to be a governess, and her mother, maiden aunts, and older sister were all models in this field. Moreover, she had her own experience working as a governess both at home and in the homes of various family acquaintances where she occasionally stayed for a few weeks or a month at a time. Actually, though, Rossetti considered herself an "'escaped governess,'" probably because she was compelled to nurse her father for so long.[52] Even when the Rossetti family fortune was still not improved by 1851, Rossetti did not primarily do governessing. Instead, she helped her mother Frances by working as an assistant in two different day-schools that her mother managed. Rossetti's work experience therefore qualified her for joining Nightingale's ranks, especially since her mother's day-schools kept her in touch with the most recent educational ideas.

Her mother's first day-school was opened in 1851 in the family residence at 38 Arlington Street, Mornington Crescent in Camden Town. Encouraged by the sisterhoods, private day-schools mainly served young girls of tradespeople–the butcher, the baker, and the hairdresser–by providing their mothers with help in discipline and guidance. New methods were introduced including persuasion, playing on feelings, appeals to morality and social caste.[53]

Throughout the continuous financial stress and the daily stiff demands, Christina maintained self-respect in the face of disappointments and failure. She was writing steadily at this time, although not prolifically, and her ascendant themes explored the consequences of self-reliance, selflessness, and selfishness for women. She began *Maude* during this period. While she assisted her mother on Arlington Street, she composed "Behold, I Stand at the Door and Knock."

The day-school at Mornington Crescent drew only a few students, however, and was financially unsuccessful. The combined efforts of Maria, William, Frances, and Christina supported the family, but William had become the real mainstay. Gabriele was still sick, blind, clearly lacking the old exuberance, although he continued editing his poetry. He published a collection of evangelical hymns, *L'Arpa Evangelica*, in 1852.[54] Maria was a teacher of French and Italian; Dante Gabriel was still leading the life of a Bohemian artist and painting pictures that did not sell. William was steadily advancing as a clerk in the Inland Revenue Office. By 1851, he earned £110, plus £50 more as art critic for *The Spectator*. However, he could recall with horror a day when he was fourteen, unemployed, and without proper clothes. Spending the day with a wealthy friend, he had to paint the worn elbows of his jacket with blue watercolors.[55] Even on his present salary, he was unable both to support his immediate family and marry Henrietta Rintoul, daughter of *The Spectator*'s editor, with whom he was in love.

Frances was encouraged by her sister Charlotte's employer Lady Bath to set up a new day-school in Frome-Selwood, Somerset, where the vicar was Lady Bath's appointee. With the vicar's support, in a sympathetic, High Church parish, Frances' venture might have the help it needed. Gabriele would also benefit from the move to the country. In March 1853, Frances moved to Frome with Christina again as her assistant. Gabriele followed them shortly thereafter. Maria continued teaching and keeping house for William. By this time, Maria was also working as a volunteer for Mrs. Chambers' Young Women's Friendly Society on nearby Camden Street. This was a refuge for "fallen women" and a school for servant girls on their Sunday afternoons off. There they found recreation and religious instruction. The Church Penitentiary Association had contributed £100 to the establishment of the Friendly Society in an effort to make the parish more responsive to the needs of the poor who were critical of the elitism of the Romanish sisterhoods. Meanwhile, Dante Gabriele was set up at Chatham Place near Blackfriars where his mistress Elizabeth Siddall could spend as much time with him as they desired.[56]

Christina knew she could not totally depend on Dante Gabriel's assistance in promoting her writing. He was involved from 1850 on in the Pygmalion relationship with Elizabeth Siddall. Dante Gabriel was dazzled by Siddall's beauty. He wrote to Christina when she was doing some tutoring in Staffordshire: "Since you went away, I have had sent me, among my things from Highgate, a lock of hair shorn from the beloved head of that dear, and radiant as the tresses of Aurora, a sight of which perhaps may dazzle you on your return."[57] Dante Gabriel wanted Christina to develop stronger bonds with Siddall, but he was insensitive to the areas in which they were competitive, such as drawing, modeling, and writing poetry. In the same letter to Christina, he also wrote:

> Maria has just shown me a letter of yours by which I
> find that you have been perpetrating portraits of some
> kind. If you answer this note, will you enclose a
> specimen, as I should like to see some of your
> handiwork. You must take care however not to rival the
> Sid, but keep within respectful limits.

"The Sid" was Elizabeth Siddall. Dante Gabriel undertook promoting Siddall as a poet, model, and pencil sketcher. After 1850, within the Pre-Raphaelite circle, it seems Siddall elicited more fanfare than Christina. Packer pointed out that not only was "Guggums," as Dante Gabriel called Elizabeth, "beloved by Gabriel and admired by his circle, but she was also absurdly exalted as a great artist by Brown and Ruskin. The latter . . . settled £150 on her so that she could develop her talent without financial harassment."[58] As yet, Christina Rossetti had received slight recognition as a poet and had met with total frustration in her relationship with James Collinson.

Barbara Gelpi argues that as an artist of the mid-nineteenth century, Dante Gabriel Rossetti identified with the feminine, particularly as he was raised in a female-dominated household; Gelpi is thus sympathetic to Dante Gabriel's relationship with Elizabeth Siddall. But it is also clear from Dante Gabriel's letters that he conceived of Siddall more as a projection of his fantasies than as an individual in her own right. Moreover, he took risks with her health–despite his overscrupulous concern for her once she became intensely ill–which opened him to overwhelming guilt after her death, probably by suicide, in 1862.[59]

Meanwhile, in Frome, Christina's self-reliance was tested almost immediately. Just a month after Frances, Gabriele, and Christina had settled in Frome, Frances was called back to London to attend her mother's death. Christina's letter to Frances of April 28, 1853, assures her that she is able to handle the school alone:

> If you are only requiring my presence in London to save
> me trouble, pray do not let this weigh with you: I am

managing very well, and doubt not I shall continue
doing so. . . . Do not let Maria or any one at home
labor under the delusion that I do not care to see
them; but rather let them attribute my plan to that
strength of mind which characterizes me.[60]

That "strength of mind" carried Christina through the rather lonely
and unhappy eleven month stay at Frome by making it a productive period for
her writing. However, writing and publishing could still not receive her
full attention, and Dante Gabriel did not promote the pieces he promised.
She was writing short stories, critical articles, and creative essays as
well as poetry and had asked Dante Gabriel to push the story "Nick" with
the novelist James Hannay. But Dante Gabriel was more than busy promoting
his own career and Elizabeth's. He wrote to his mother at Frome that he
was "quite ashamed of not being able yet to tell" Christina "anything
positive about *Nick*": "I am constantly remembering it when Hannay is not
in the way, and always forgetting it when he is. I have now resolved to
remember it the next time I see him, and, if I am baulked again, to write
to him the next time I think of it."[61]   At the opening of 1853, Dante
Gabriel had sold only one painting– *The Girlhood of Mary Virgin*. He had no
private means, and *The Annunciation*, which he called "the blessed white
eyesore," failed to be sold. At one point, he even considered abandoning
both poetry and painting to become a telegraph clerk on the Great Northern
Railway and operate a telegraph machine. But through the help of Holman
Hunt and Ford Madox Brown, a Belfast merchant named Francis McCracken
decided to purchase *The Annunciation*.[62]

Dante Gabriel's father was continuing to decline physically. The
father begged his financially dependent son to regard his material
prospects more seriously. Dante Gabriel solemnly promised his father he
would be more conscientious about promoting his career as a painter.[63]
This involved maintaining an active social life which brought him, and
indirectly Christina, in touch with the most avant-garde literary and
artistic people in London.

Ruskin, of course, had come to the defense of the Pre-Raphaelite
Brotherhood in his famous articles in the *Times*, May 13 and 30, 1851.
Ruskin supported Pre-Raphaelitism in part because it followed his aesthetic
tenet of truth to nature, as put forward in *Modern Painters*.[64]   Dante
Gabriel met Ruskin personally through Coventry Patmore who, along with his
wife, were great admirers of Christina's poetry, even if Ruskin was not.
Other Pre-Raphaelite supporters in the early 1850s whom Christina knew
included Ford Madox Brown, William Bell Scott and his wife, Edward

Burne-Jones and his wife, and Arthur Hughes. As we have seen, Anna Howitt was struck by Christina's poem "The Ruined Cross" and illustrated it; Christina became close enough friends with the hostess Mrs. Orme's daughter to attend an art class with her at the Camden Town School run by Ford Madox Brown.[65]

Although Dante Gabriel knew and corresponded with the Brownings, whom he met through Patmore, Christina never actually met her literary foremother Elizabeth Barrett Browning. However, in the late 1850s and 1860s, she did meet other popular women poets like Dora Greenwell and Jean Ingelow.[66] In addition, she met a new wave of Pre-Raphaelites and their circle, including William and Janey Morris, Algernon Charles Swinburne, and Charles Lewis Dodgson.

However, the women whom Dante Gabriel was most anxious for Christina to meet were the radicals who would eventually form the Langham Place Group: Barbara Leigh Smith, a cousin of Florence Nightingale, and Bessie Rayner Parkes. Smith would bring the Married Woman's Property Bill before Parliament in 1857, and Parkes would found the *English Woman's Journal* the following year. It was when Christina was still in Frome that Dante Gabriel met Smith for the first time. He was obviously impressed. In his letter to Christina, he wailed,

> Ah if you were only like Miss Barbara Smith: a young
> lady I met at the Howitts' blessed with large rations
> of tin, fat, enthusiasm, and golden hair, who thinks
> nothing of climbing up a mountain in breeches, or
> wading through a stream in none, in the sacred name of
> pigment. Last night she invited us all to lunch with
> her on Sunday; and perhaps I shall go as she is quite a
> jolly fellow—which was Thackeray's definition of Mrs.
> Orme.[67]

To understand Rossetti's position on the Woman Question, it is important to speculate why she did not take up a stronger bond with members of the Langham Place Group. After all, many of its members were or became noted poets in their day. Bessie Rayner Parkes published several volumes of merit. Adelaide Procter, another member of the group, was Queen Victoria's favorite poet, and Isa Craig, who would become assistant secretary to the Association for the Promotion of Social Science—one of the first professional associations to admit women—was also a poet. Rossetti was enough on the periphery of this group to be asked by John Ingram to write a biography of Adelaide Procter in 1882 for his *Eminent Women* series.

However, Christina deferred to Anna Mary Watts (née Howitt) on this project. In her letter to William, she wrote: "Meanwhile it strikes me that the very person to write *A. A. Procter* would be not myself but Anna Mary Watts, who was in the heart of that social set instead of (as I was) on it merest outskirt."[68]   The Langham Place Group took a different approach to reform than the all-female day-schools, friendly societies, and ,sisterhoods with which the Rossetti women associated. When the group formed in the late 1850s, it became a hub of feminist activity including the first Women's Employment Bureau, the Victoria Press led by Emily Faithfull, and the Ladies Institute with reading room. Although Smith would later help to found Girton College for women, at this time her major focus was parliamentary reform, which culminated in her helping to organize the women's suffrage petition Mill presented to parliament in 1866.

The feminism of the Langham Place Group drew on the theoretical heritage of eighteenth-century rationalist philosophers and on Mary Wollstonecraft's *Rights of Woman* (1792). Smith had been educated by an Owenite teacher and exposed to theories of utopian communities in which equality of the sexes extended to the idea of free love. Smith and her co-workers claimed that the inalienable, God-given rights of men applied equally to women and that liberalism needed to include women as well as men in its reforms. Although these radicals drew inspiration and support from the evangelical reformers associated with the sisterhoods, and, in fact, published feature articles on the Sisters of Charity in the *English Woman's Journal*, they objected to the doctrine of separate spheres which the reformers accepted, and subverted, to their own ends.[69]

The basic theoretical difference between the Langham radicals and the evangelical reformers was in the latter's reliance on the church's doctrine of self-denial as the major source of power for women. The ability to be self-denying made women superior, spiritual beings compared to men. The Langham feminists had, on the other hand, a rational and liberal belief in the essential equality of the sexes. For them, women under oppressive social and economic conditions needed to make their demands known in the public, political sphere without being restricted to evangelical codes of modesty and decorum.

Like many women who began as reformers, such as the well-known Josephine Butler and the lesser known Emma Martin and Catherine Barmby, Christina Rossetti became more and more radicalized by her experience.[70] She went from governessing, to nursing and visiting through the sisters of charity, to petitioning as a more direct form of political action for certain causes. Her poetry from this critical decade for women's activity

(1856-1866) shows the influence of both radical and reform women's movements in such poems as "The Royal Princess" and "'The Iniquity of the Fathers Upon the Children.'" These and others will be fully discussed in Part III, "The Victorian World."

When the second day-school at Frome had clearly failed, and Frances Rossetti inherited in December 1853 a small sum from the death of her father, Frances moved back to London with Christina and Gabriele. There they joined Maria and William in a new residence on Albany Street which William's promotion and raise allowed him to rent. One month later, however, the sickly Gabriele died, at seventy-one. The loss undoubtedly brought Christina a mixture of sorrow and relief, as well as a growing fear about her own redundant future. After being her father's almost-constant companion, she had now to shape the course of her own life, and there were not many options. She disliked the governessing she was trained to do, but she was making no money from her poetry. One solution was to follow the lead of Maria who was volunteering at the Friendly Society.

As we have seen, Rossetti began visiting on Robert Street for the church. Then, she followed her Aunt Eliza who was, ironically, in a similarly redundant position. Eliza, who was the youngest Polidori daughter, had been the nurse for Christina's grandmother for many years, just as Christina, the youngest Rossetti, had nursed her father. When Christina's grandparents both died in 1853, Eliza decided to escape redundancy and extend her role beyond the family sphere by applying for Nightingale's Scutari campaign. To her honor, she was accepted; however, she served as a storekeeper instead of nurse as she had expected.[71] For nearly half a year following Christina's rejection, Christina suffered from writer's block.

Between 1860 and 1870, however, Rossetti renewed her involvement in the sisterhoods. She did visiting under the auspices of All Saints' Sisterhood in her parish district and in the Diocesan Penitentiary at St. Mary's Highgate. Thus, she achieved the status of "outer Sister." William Michael wrote to Christina's biographer:

> "She was . . . an outer Sister–but in no sort of way
> professed–of the Convent which Maria afterwards joined–
> Also at one time (1860 to '70) she used pretty often to
> go to an Institution at Highgate for redeeming 'Fallen
> Women'–It seems to me that at one time they wanted to
> make her a sort of superintendent there, but she
> declined–In her own neighborhood, Albany Street, she
> did a deal of district visiting and the like."[72]

These were the years, roughly from 1850 through 1870, when women's organizations of all sorts were coalescing: professional groups, like nurses; women's schools, like Queens College (1848), then later Girton (1873); and sisterhoods. At the same time, according to historian Barbara Taylor, attitudes toward feminism began to shift, since fears over more radical movements had subsided. The demise of the Owenite movement made it possible for middle-class women to organize without constantly being accused of socialism or sexual immorality. The connection between feminism and working-class radicalism was broken after the Chartist scare of 1848. In addition to antislavery and anti-Corn Law activists, many women like the Rossettis were involved in philanthropic schemes directed mainly at women, like rescuing prostitutes and providing for unwed mothers. Educational advances promised women a future of equality with men of their class. Harriet Taylor's ideas for women to become free agents like men in the laissez-faire business world and in the domain of sexual and marital relationships were in the air as possibilities. The feminist organizations of the 1850s and 1860s attempted, in the main, to allow women the free exercise of their individualities.[73] As one article from the *English Woman's Journal* illustrates, this could be accomplished with the help of God: "The first duty of women is to themselves, and that duty is to fulfill the will of God; by developing their nature to the highest, and thus progressing in the scale of spiritual intelligences."[74] Barbara Taylor commented that "by the late 1860s, feminism had become . . . an autonomous movement led almost entirely by women themselves."[75] This observation held true for both reform and radical women's movements.

Rossetti's poetic heroines in these years document the evangelical cause. Her heroines define themselves as social critics. They are resistant to oppressive moral and economic codes which thwart the development of individuals, especially women and the lower classes. The royal princess, in the dramatic monologue of the same name (1861), criticizes her aristocratic privilege not only because it divided her from the poor, but also because it fostered a stultifying and narcissistic self-interest:

> I, a princess, King-descended, decked with jewels,
>   gilded, drest,
> Would rather be a peasant with her baby at her breast,
> For all I shine so like the sun, and am purple like the
>   west.

. . . .

> All my fountains cast up perfumes, all my gardens grow
> Scented woods and foreign spices, with all flowers in
>   blow
> That are costly, out of season as the seasons go.
>
> . . . .
>
> All my walls are lost in mirrors, whereupon I trace
> Self to right hand, self to left hand, self in every
>   place,
> Self-same solitary figure, self-same seeking face.[76]

In chapter five, we show how the princess's identification with her father's subjects helps her to break through the limitations of material self-interest.

The illegitimate adolescent in the dramatic monologue "'The Iniquity of the Fathers Upon the Children'" (1865) prefers to trade her genteel status for membership in a working-class family. She is incensed that her mother—the Lady of the Hall—is compelled by moral and sexual double standards to hide her daughter's identity just because of her illegitimacy:

> I'd give my gentle blood
> To wash my special shame
> And drown my private grudge;
> I'd toil and moil much rather
> The dingiest cottage drudge
> Whose mother need not blush,
> Than live here like a lady
> And see my mother flush
> And hear her voice unsteady
> Sometimes, yet never dare
> Ask to share her care.[77]

In chapter six, we show how this monologue explored the patriarchal roots of women's subordination. Rossetti's earlier poetic heroines shared this general tone of resistance, but they aimed their criticism more ambiguously, ambivalently, and vaguely. The outsiders and wanderers of her early picaresque narratives are amazed at the evil in the world, but they do not probe for the sources of the problem. The precocious daughters and sisters of early dialogues are polite and contained at the same time they are headstrong. In the early poetry, the point that change is possible is only made indirectly, and on a personal scale, in psychological portraits that are linked by contrasting the perspectives of women with different levels of awareness.[78]

But the middle-period heroines identify the principles on which their resistance is based, and they actively push for change. They take off, in a sense, from where *Maude* left off in that they are not merely satisfied to blame themselves. The royal princess exists in an environment as claustrophobic as Maude's, but the princess acts to change her conditions.

Further, Rossetti's heroines play a wide variety of roles in this period—country maidens of fairy-tale and romance as well as country bawds; bluestockings; nuns; social outcasts and other renegades conceived with psychological realism; Tennysonian princesses who are parodied; rejected lovers like those she found in Gothic novels and poems of her female contemporaries. Her poetic forms are just as various—monodramas, dialogues, narratives, and dramatic monologues as well as lyrics.

But in Rossetti's later work, characterization fades. After 1865, Rossetti wrote no monologues in the developed sense that "The Royal Princess" or "'The Iniquity of the Fathers Upon the Children'" is a monologue, poems which belong to Rossetti's second major poetry volume, *The Prince's Progress and Other Poems* (1866). After 1866, it took Rossetti fifteen years before she published another totally new volume of poetry, not counting *Sing-Song* (1872), a collection of children's verse. The new poetry contained in her last two poetry volumes features a lyric voice which expresses faith in the power of love to create harmony in an otherwise bleak existence. In the intervening years, Rossetti published two volumes of short stories and six volumes of devotional prose (1874-1892).[79]

Why did Rossetti's social poetic vision shift markedly in the 1870s and 1880s? What happened to the poet who exposed the sad plight of unwed mothers and illegitimate children in her monologues and marital infidelities in her narratives? Why did she stop dating her poems and recording them systematically in notebooks, around the same time, ironically, that Emily Dickinson stopped organizing fascicles?[80] Excessive emphases placed by biographers and critics either on their general ill health, their romantic and religious preoccupations, or their eccentricities, overshadow other events that may be more significant to their development as poets. Without the support of a visible women's movement, it was more difficult for both poets to feel confident about expressing their public concerns. Especially for Rossetti, the question of whether she had violated her womanly nature by being an unmarried woman poet plagued her in the later years.

According to past biographers, 1866 marks the year Rossetti refused a second marriage offer, this one from Charles Bagot Cayley, a Dante scholar who had known Christina since adolescence when her father tutored him in Italian.   It is strange that we actually learn more about certain intimacies of Rossetti's relationship with Cayley after the marriage refusal.   It is obvious Rossetti was extremely fond of Cayley and valued his intellectual companionship, but she entered the relationship as one of equals and did not desire marriage as an endpoint.[81]

In the 1870s, Rossetti's siblings' lives changed drastically, and as a dependent sister, so did hers.   Partial blindness was setting in on Dante Gabriel who became quite sick after 1867.   He used chloral, later laudanum, and suffered from delusions.   Following Robert Buchanan's harsh critiques of the sensuality and phallic exhibitionism in Dante Gabriel's writing (1871-1872), he went into a deep depression which did not lift.   Christina and her mother clearly supported Dante Gabriel in his declining years and remained loyal and committed.[82]   Perhaps Buchanan's criticisms even influenced the direction of Christina's poetry insofar as they expressed a more generally   conservative aesthetic.   In a period described by its critics as increasingly decadent morally and aesthetically, Christina Rossetti clung more firmly to her principles and to the need for faith.

From 1870 to 1883, Rossetti visited as a nurse at the Convalescent Hospital at Meads, Eastborne,   which was affiliated with All Saints' Sisterhood, Margaret Street, the convent community which Maria joined as a novice in 1873.   Ellen A. Proctor, a good friend of Rossetti's in the later part of her life and her biographer, was "engaged in parish work in Ratcliff":

> My mission was to go on Monday nights to the Factory
> Girls' Club, London Street, under the special care of
> the vicar, Rev. R. K. Arbuthnot. Here congregated many
> of Bryant and May's workers, but ropemakers,
> satchelmakers, jam-makers, and all the industries of
> the East End were represented. Many were of Irish
> parentage and Roman Catholics. The object was to try
> and interest them in something, and get them into the
> club after work was over. Miss Rossetti took a deep
> interest in the welfare of these young people, and
> would herself have liked to become a working member of
> the club, had her nursing duties allowed it; but at

that time she had two aunts, invalids, to tend.[83]

Rossetti's political activism always had a religious basis, and the poetry she was writing stressed the need for faith. When William Michael married Lucy Madox Brown in 1874, Christina and her mother initially shared living quarters with them. Lucy, like William Michael, was an agnostic. The bickering that resulted from religious differences between Christina and Lucy eventually led Christina to move to her own residence at Torrington Square with her mother. After Maria Francesca had joined All Saints' Sisterhood, Christina and her mother were joined by Margaret and Eliza Polidori. Christina became the sick nurse for all of them in turn. Over the years, Christina nursed and witnessed the deaths of Maria Francesca, Dante Gabriel, Frances Lavinia, and Margaret and Eliza Polidori. She had been sick herself from 1871 to 1873 with exophthalmic goiter, but she lived until 1894 when she died from cancer.

The religious basis of Rossetti's activism caused her to doubt in the end whether or not she would be saved. Although many of her democratic ideas were consistent with her faith, the Woman Question raised profound contradictions in Anglicanism for her. Her antimaterialistic, nonhierarchical, and leveling ideas about the injustice of class divisions were harmonious with her belief. In *The Face of the Deep* (1893), one of her devotional prose commentaries, for example, she critically observed that the same two nations Disraeli had perceived were growing further and further apart over time:

> Alas England full of luxuries and thronged by stinted
> poor, whose merchants are princes and whose dealings
> are crooked, whose packed storehouses stand amid bare
> homes, whose gorgeous array has rags for neighbors!
> From a canker in our gold and silver, from a moth in
> our garments, from blasted crops, from dwindling
> substance, from righteous retribution abasing us among
> the nations, good Lord, deliver us. Amen.[84]

While she believed in the separation of church and state, she also supported the application of Christian principles to law. She was a known abolitionist and an active, petitioning antivivisectionist. She persuaded Dante Gabriel to sign a Parliamentary petition against vivisection in 1875 and convinced Mr. Frederic Shields to sign one eight years later. She also petitioned for a minors' protection bill concerning the age of consent and for a memorial against an Institute for Preventative Medicine which would have established "Pasteur's treatment and other horrors."[85]

But her belief in the moral superiority of women, and her own status as a heroic, unmarried saint, to recall Nina Auerbach's concept, conflicted with church doctrine.   Rossetti's dilemma is documented in her correspondence with the suffragist Augusta Webster which Mackenzie Bell reproduced. Rossetti wrote to Webster that she *could* support the vote for women, if that were the only means by which political equality could be gained. However, Rossetti also queried:

> "Does it not appear as if the Bible was based upon an
> understood unalterable distinction between men and
> women, their position, duties, privileges? . . . The
> fact of the Priesthood being exclusively man's leaves
> me in no doubt that the highest functions are not in
> this world open to both sexes."[86]

If the highest functions are not open to both sexes according to the Anglican Church, what punishments would she therefore have to suffer having violated women's subordinate role by pursuing a poetic vocation and never marrying? Her doubts, fears, and guilt surfaced in her closing years. Sonnet 27 from her series "Later Life: A Double Sonnet of Sonnets," published in the 1881 volume *A Pageant and Other Poems*, is especially graphic on this matter:

> I have dreamed of Death:—what will it be to die
>   Not in a dream, but in the literal truth
>   With all Death's adjuncts ghastly and uncouth,
> The pang that is the last and the last sigh?
>
> . . . .
>
> So long to those who hopeless in their fear
>   Watch the slow breath and look for what they dread:
> While I supine with ears that cease to hear,
>   With eyes that glaze, with heart pulse running down
>   (Alas! no saint rejoicing on her bed),
>   May miss the goal at last, may miss a crown.[87]

William Michael wrote that his sister's "forecast of death came singularly true; for, if one had been writing a condensed account of Christina Rossetti's last days and hours in December 1894, one might have described them very nearly in these terms."[88]   On her deathbed, William Michael had to console her and ease her fears.[89]

We have seen in the last two biographical chapters that two poets normally considered to be exclusively subjective were very much involved in their times and were writing poems about public issues. In spite of some important differences in their class, cultural, and religious backgrounds, they shared common experiences and problems as single women who were poets. Coming from educated families, they shared a similar advantage in being able to pursue poetic careers. However, Dickinson came from a position of greater wealth. Neither of them wanted to be limited by domestic roles. Their sisters were constant sources of support, while the intensified competition between them and their brothers seems also to have motivated their writing.

They both reached their writing peaks in the early 1860s, and their writing declines for some of the same and different reasons in the 1870s and following. They expressed a conflict that was common in women who wrote about public events, that is, they questioned the consequences of having pursued morally unsuitable paths for women. Since Rossetti was more religious in a traditional sense than Dickinson, her fears were greater than Dickinson's at the close of her life. Dickinson maintained her unique faith till the very end.

As a published poet, Rossetti received more recognition than Dickinson, although it is fair to say that both were misunderstood by their audiences. In Rossetti's case, she was often appreciated for the wrong reasons. By remaining unpublished, Dickinson was able to develop a more innovative and original poetic style. Dickinson's poetry expresses the transcendentalism and rugged individualism of romantic, ninteteenth-century America, while Rossetti's poetry expresses a blending of English and Italian romanticism with the evangelical optimism and faith of mid-century England.

We are now ready to examine the poetry that expresses the consciousness of their times. We begin with poems on one of the most crucial mid-century issues, namely the crisis of war.

PART III

THE VICTORIAN WORLD

Chapter 5

War Poems

War was an issue, like abolition and suffrage, which drew thousands of women in the mid-nineteenth century to take political positions when they felt otherwise marginal to the political process. Women's war poetry flourished from 1850 to 1865, but it has, for the most part, remained invisible. This is due to a larger problem: the invisibility of political poetry by women. Since most biographers and critics have treated the work of Dickinson and Rossetti in ahistorical ways, their responses to the major wars that touched their lives have been obscured and the ways the theme of war released their poetic power.

In this chapter, we look at Dickinson's and Rossetti's exclusion as women from the Crimean and Civil Wars as major turning points in their lives. A previously invisible thread of antiwar social commentary links several of Rossetti's strongest, most significant poems–"Repining" (1847), "The Lowest Room" (1856), "A Royal Princess" (1861), and "The Prince's Progress" (1865), while the extremely troubled Dickinson of the early 1860s is connected, through several of her most original and effective poems, to the Civil War and to her fears over the dissolution of her nation.

Middle-class women, like Dickinson and Rossetti, were in a contradictory situation in relation to war. Cast as spiritual vessels, they were supposed to protect peace and harmony. But since they were excluded from the political process, they could only apply their moral watchdog role within limited spheres. One sphere was literary, where their moral positions on war could be presented in fiction and poetry aimed at influencing public opinion. Ironically, the war poetry that flourished best *supported* wars rather than warned against them. During the Crimean War between England and Russia (1854-1856) and the American Civil War, two common themes in published women's war poetry were the elevation of select military officers to the status of Christian heroes, and the establishment of national wars as Christian and morally righteous.[1]   One of the most successful novels of the century, Harriet Beecher Stowe's *Uncle Tom's Cabin* (1852) generated massive antislavery sentiment which came to fruition almost a decade later in the outbreak of the American Civil War. Britain was coaxed out of its isolation from the rest of Europe in part by Elizabeth Barrett Browning's long poem "Casa Guidi Windows" (1851) in which she calls on her native country to abandon its "counterfeit" peace and to aid the Italian nationals in their struggle for independence against Austria.

There was, on the other hand, a culture of women writers, to which Christina Rossetti and Emily Dickinson belonged, whose poetry stressed the devastating spiritual costs of war, especially on women as powerless outsiders and pawns.

No situation illustrates the sexual divisions in society more graphically than war. As poets who followed a neoromantic code of truth to nature, with nature conceived as an harmonious, unifying spiritual force defying human control, Dickinson and Rossetti were morally committed to peace. The poet-sister in Rossetti's poem "The Lowest Room" objected to advanced weaponry, like gunpowder, for much the same reason Dickinson's "supposed person" objected to scientific classifications of nature in poem #70. Both developments signified a male-dominated hegemony bent on aggressively controlling nature which, after Darwin, was generally perceived as Tennyson described: "red in tooth and claw."

CHRISTINA ROSSETTI'S WAR POEMS

Rossetti expressed her pacifism most explicitly in correspondence with the suffragist, Augusta Webster. Rossetti wrote to Webster after having read her leaflets on suffrage printed by the Women's Suffrage Society. Mackenzie Bell reproduced their exchange in his biography: "'I think . . . that men should continue the exclusive national legislators, so long as they do continue the exclusive soldier-representatives of the nation, and engross the whole payment in life and limb for national quarrels.'" To the victor belongs the spoils. If the militarization of women was necessary to gain political power, Rossetti was against such pyrrhic victory: "'I do not know whether any lady is prepared to adopt the Platonic theory of female regiments; if so, she sets aside this objection: but I am not, so to me it stands.'"[2]

Christina Rossetti's war poems address the theme of the just and unjust war. Most wars are unjust to Rossetti, and her heroines either scoff at them or are passive witnesses. But she viewed the American Civil War, with its hope for ending slavery, as just, and her heroines of this period act to support war. Despite Rossetti's coherent attitudes on just and unjust wars, her biographers and critics have maintained the convention she herself felt compelled to invoke–that her poetry was personal, not political.

As Rossetti grew more involved with political and social reform, her poems address contemporary problems in innovative and dramatic ways. However, by emphasizing the personal and imaginative content of her poems, her critics have caused their historical and political meanings to disappear from the record. Rossetti's brother and editor William Michael considered her most democratic poem, "A Royal Princess" (1861), to be imaginative and fanciful, for example, rather than political.[3] Yet it belongs to an entire genre of abolitionist literature spawned by the wide success of Stowe's *Uncle Tom's Cabin*.

Rossetti's earliest attitudes about war were influenced by her father, Gabriele Rossetti. He had chosen exile over death in 1827 at the hands of Austrian King Ferdinand for his role in the constitutional movement in Naples. He never lost touch with his compatriots or interest in the destiny of his country. He hosted scores of Italian and other foreign visitors in his home where politics and ideas were discussed at length. The discussions often turned to the kind of service exiles could render from abroad to their native land and to the cause of Italian liberation. It has been said that Louis Napoleon conceived the idea for Latin unity while present during some of the conversations on Charlotte Street.[4]

That Rossetti developed an early grasp of England's powerful role internationally is clear from one poem in her juvenilia, "The Chinaman" (1842). She wrote the poem when she was twelve in response to an assignment William Michael was given in day-school to write "an original composition" in verse "on the subject of China" during the Anglo-Chinese Opium War. She wanted to try her hand at the task and focused on the issue of international spheres of influence by employing a poetic objective correlative: the Chinaman's queue or pigtail.

The pigtail is a synecdoche on two levels of cultural significance. On the level of myth, the pigtail signified the Chinaman's manhood–his self-respect among his peers. On the level of mythology, the pigtail signified China's attempt to gain greater international power. With an

early display of ironic reversal, Rossetti demonstrated England's greater
strength to diminish China's influence by clipping the Chinaman's tail:

> "Centre of Earth!" a Chinaman
>   he said,
> And bent over a map his pig-tailed
>   head,–
> That map in which, portrayed in
>   colours bright,
> China, all dazzling, burst upon the
>   sight;
> "Centre of Earth!" repeatedly he
>   cries,
> "Land of the brave, the beautiful,
>   the wise!"
> Thus he exclaimed; when lo his
>   words arrested
> Showed what sharp agony his head
>   had tested.
> He feels a tug–another, and
>   another–
> And quick exclaims, "Hallo! what's
>   now the bother?"
> But soon, alas, perceives. And, "Why,
>   false night,
> Why not from men shut out the
>   hateful sight?
> The faithless English have cut off
>   my tail,
> And left me my sad fortunes to
>   bewail.
> Now in the streets I can no more
>   appear,
> For all the other men a pig-tail wear."[5]

Just months before the outbreak of national revolutions in Italy,
France, and Germany, Christina Rossetti wrote "Repining" (1847) which
focuses on the theme of exclusion. As a woman and the daughter of an
exile, Rossetti felt doubly excluded. In the poem, Rossetti turned
exclusion around to express a woman's preference for being isolated from
war's insanity. Though she had developed a deep respect from her father

for the cause of liberty, she also learned the consequences of heroic acts in liberty's defense and that the stakes of any war were extremely high. "Repining" expresses a woman's rejection of war instead of a hero's praises.

"Repining" cleverly embeds two poetic structures–monodrama and narrative–in a contemporary version of the dream vision genre. Rossetti had found the dream vision in her reading of the Bible. Dante. Spenser, Coleridge, Byron, Keats, Tennyson, and the *Arabian Nights*. The genre includes an opening and closing prophetic scene that is usually set outside the bounds of temporality. These frame a long, sequential narrative which represents the limited, temporal realm.

The monodramatic aspects of Rossetti's structure derive especially from Gothic versions of the form she found in fiction by such authors as Maria Edgeworth, Robert Maturin, and Monk Lewis. A. Dwight Culler's research on Gothic fiction and monodramatic form indicates that "before and after the turn of the century several related art forms . . . focused on a solitary figure, most frequently a woman. who expressed through speech, music, costume, and gesture the shifting movements of her soul." That the figure was usually a solitary woman enforced the ideas of subjectivity and progressive and conflicting states of intense feeling. However, Rossetti creatively used these poetic sources only to reverse them. In her versions of the monodramatic form, the subjectivity of her heroines frees them from the constraints of linear history. Rossetti's heroines are not, as Culler described, "distracted, divided in will" or "torn between conflicting emotions."[6] Instead, they are strong and purposeful.

When the narrative opens, a Tennysonian maiden is alone, spinning and weaving. Although she experiences the loneliness of a typical Gothic heroine of monodrama. she also perceives the natural world, in her isolation, as the heroine of a biblical or medieval dream vision would–as holistic and harmonious:

> She heard the gentle turtle-dove
> Tell to its mate a tale of love;
>
> . . . .
>
> She knew each bird upon its nest
> Had cheering songs to bring it rest.[7]

She is initiated into "social company" and "human life" by a male savior, a counterpart of Tennyson's Sir Lancelot. He guides her through a series of worldly experiences—an avalanche, a tempest, and an uncontrollable fire—all of which cause huge numbers of deaths. These catastrophes temper the maiden's innocence and bring her to a new awareness of the unavoidable suffering which, in one sense, constitutes the human condition.

Rossetti took her basic theme, the idea of life passing like a shadow, from Ecclesiastes. But she extended the point in order to critique her society. While natural disasters cause all social enterprises to be vulnerable to decay, manmade disasters, like wars, can be prevented and are not. War, the last of the calamities to which the maiden is initiated, is the one she is least able to assimilate. After encountering it, she concludes that, "As a man soweth so he reaps": war is merely a reflection of the failure of social enterprise as presently constituted:

> As a man soweth so he reaps.
> The field was full of bleeding heaps;
> Ghastly corpses of men and horses
> That met death at a thousand sources;
> Cold limbs and putrefying flesh;
> Long love-locks clotted to a mesh
> That stifled: stiffened mouths beneath
> Staring eyes that had looked on death.

The poem closes appropriately for a dream vision. The humble heroine asks God for forgiveness. Moreover, she asks to be transported from the temporal and linear realm of human history to the spiritual realm governed by love. This progression corresponds structurally to the movement from monodramatic narrative to dream vision prophecy:

> She knelt down in her agony.
> "O Lord, it is enough," said she:
> "My heart's prayer putteth me to shame;
> Let me return to whence I came.
> Thou who for love's sake didst reprove,
> Forgive me for the sake of love."[8]

It is important to acknowledge that by this ending, Rossetti was reversing Tennyson's model. Tennyson's maidens, such as "The Lady of Shalott," "Mariana," and "Mariana in the South," all threaten the social fabric with their self-involvement. They either become mad, remain alienated, or die. But in Rossetti, the maiden's isolation is necessary for maintaining a sane subjectivity in the face of a human community fraught with disaster and contradiction. Rossetti's maiden winds up wiser as a result of her contact with war, greed, hypocrisy, and pride, but she also learns that she is powerless to change the course of linear history.

Six years later, when the Crimean War broke out between England, France, Turkey, and Sardinia against Russia, the typical war poem expressed a romantic British nationalism and righteousness of purpose. Tennyson's "Maud" (1855) captured public sentiment, with the young male hero's arousal to the nationalist cause presented as a productive way of personally transcending romantic disappointment.

Like Tennyson's hero, Rossetti looked to the Crimean War campaign for help in resolving a personal dilemma. At twenty-four, still unmarried and economically dependent on her family, she reached a low emotional ebb. Shortly before the war began, her father and maternal grandparents had all died, and she applied to join Nightingale's nurses as an outlet for her despair. The strategy backfired, however, and as we mentioned earlier, Rossetti took the rejection to heart. For six months, her writing process was blocked.[9]

The typical poems on the Crimean War that were written by women were expressions of nationalism that did not raise questions about women's role. Adelaide Procter, a popular poet of the day who was frequently compared to Rossetti, wrote two nationalist poems in response to the Crimean War. Although Procter was a leader among the strongminded radicals who organized for women's political reforms in the 1850s, her poems on the war uncritically supported Britain's military presence in the Crimea.

In "The Lesson of the War" (1855), Procter described the Crimean War as a way for the rich and the growing numbers of poor in Britain to transcend class divisions.[10] In fighting for a common, national goal, rich and poor alike had sacrificed their sons. She called on the national rulers to remember, when peace returned, the large part played by the poor in the Crimean War. However, she presented no particular political program, nor did she raise any question about women's role.

In "The Two Spirits" (1855), Procter had the spirit of the classical past debate the spirit of the Christian present regarding the ethics and morality of war.[11] The Christian spirit wins the debate for valuing peace, a higher moral good, over fame and revenge, the classical motives. However, the contradiction in using war as the method for achieving peace was not confronted, nor was pacifism offered as an option for Christians.

Such a debate was a common poetic way of writing about the Crimean War. Rossetti's poem "A Fight Over the Body of Homer," written a year later, used the same device, only Rossetti deepened the realism by creating two chatting sisters to discuss the issues within the format of a parlor debate. The highly original and complex poem was published eight years later in *Macmillan's Magazine* with a different title: "Sit Down in the Lowest Room." This was later abbreviated to "The Lowest Room." We have already examined the poem for its theme of marriage versus economic independence for women. Here we will trace its exploration of the war theme.

The poet-sister in the debate argues against Christian wars as she knows them. She sees little reason for British women to support modern wars, since they are unheroic by comparison to Homer's and provide women, as spectators, with little good "sport." While the more feminine, conventional sister is embroidering, the poet-sister defends the heroism of Homer's day:

> "Oh better then be slave or wife
>   Than fritter now blank life away:
> Then night had holiness of night,
>   And day was sacred day.
>
> "The Princess laboured at her loom,
>   Mistress and handmaiden alike;
> Beneath their needles grew the field
>   With warriors armed to strike.
>
> "Or, look again, dim Dian's face
>   Gleamed perfect thro' the attendant night;
> Were such not better than those holes
>   Amid that waste of white?
>
> "A shame it is, our aimless life:
>   I rather from my heart would feed
> From silver dish in gilded stall
>   With wheat and wine the steed—
>
> "The faithful steed that bore my lord
>   In safety thro' the hostile land,
> The faithful steed that arched his neck
>   To fondle with my hand."[12]

Startled by these comments, her sister stops embroidering and points out the precarious dependency embedded in her sister's attitude:

Her needle erred: a moment's pause,
    A moment's patience, all was well.
Then she: "But just suppose the horse,
        Suppose the rider fell?"

She reminds the poet that vengeance like Achilles', no matter how heroic, is essentially bestial, from a Christian perspective. This reasoning pushes the poet to a higher truth, which she attributes to the biblical Solomon, about the vanity of war. She remembers the historical and temporal place of war "beneath the sun" where "there's nothing new," where "men flow, men ebb, mankind flows on." Remembering Solomon also helps her expose the false ideology of causality invoked by war and the false dichotomy of win-or-lose:

"Vanity of vanities he preached
    Of all he found, of all he sought:
Vanity of vanities, the gist
    Of all the words he taught.

"This in the wisdom of the world,
    In Homer's page, in all, we find:
As the sea is not filled, so yearns
    Man's universal mind.

"This Homer felt, who gave his men
    With glory but a transient state
His very Jove could not reverse
    Irrevocable fate.

"Uncertain all their lot save this—
    Who wins must lose, who lives must die:
All trodden out into the dark
    Alike, all vanity."

Dante Gabriel criticized this poem for its "modern vicious style" and condemned its likeness to the masculine style of Elizabeth Barrett Browning and Jean Ingelow.[13] The poem was relevant to the American Civil War when it was published because British opinion about the Civil War was quite strong, and the poem raised connections between the position of women in society and that of slaves. Moreover, it queried whether wars were ever sufficiently moral to justify women's support and if morality was the proper standard of judgment.

In the 1860s, the social environment was more conducive to the participation of women in community and political work than it had been a decade ago. Lona Mosk Packer considered the span between 1860 and 1870 Rossetti's Highgate period, since Rossetti counseled and tutored unwed mothers, domestic servants, and prostitutes at the Highgate House of Charity.[14] Rossetti's commitment to enlarging women's sphere through social work and nursing became a deeper, more integral part of her life at this time, and poetically, she was highly productive. Her poetic heroines speak like assertive romantic heroes who are critical of the political, social, and psychological structures limiting their experiences as women. They are often willing to risk their lives for the important principle.

During the American Civil War, Rossetti's family belonged to a small but substantial segment of the London professional classes who supported the Yankees in their desire to end slavery. In his "Memoir" of Christina Rossetti, William Michael stated that his sister shared his abolitionist views.[15] He put these views forward in his article on the Civil War in *The Atlantic Monthly* (1866). There he named war a regrettable but necessary step towards ending the institution of slavery.[16]

The majority of British sentiment, however, sided with the Confederacy. The North threatened the survival of British cotton manufacturers. Many British abolitionists wished to convince their irate Lancashire neighbors that genuine struggles for liberty, like the American Civil War, were worth fighting, even if they sometimes meant sacrifice and loss. The first woman's press, run by Emily Faithfull, published a volume of poetry in 1863 to "relieve" the Lancashire cotton districts, that is, to help them financially and to elicit abolitionist support from them.[17] Rossetti's fascinating monologue, "A Royal Princess" (1861), was selected for inclusion in this volume, along with poems by Isa Craig, Mary Howitt, Dante Gabriel Rossetti, William Allingham, and others.

This poem represents Rossetti's most developed and cohesive use of the dramatic monologue form, a form she found in the work of Tennyson and Robert Browning but which she recreated in her own way. The dramatic monologue is distinguished from first-person narrative and monodrama, according to Robert Langbaum, by the nature of the response elicited from the reader.[18] The dramatic monologue calls on the reader to enter the the subjectivity of the speaker and to suspend moral judgment about the him as he confronts a critical moment, situation, or turning point in his development. By focusing on personalities who lack self-awareness, Robert Browning used the form to illustrate the limits of human subjectivity. In his dramatic monologues, like "Andrea del Sarto" or "My Last Duchess," the reader is exposed, as a horrified onlooker, to the levels of self-deception which blind Browning's speakers to their violations of moral and ethical codes. Rossetti's dramatic monologues, on the other hand, focus on speakers who are on the brink of self-discovery, whose subjectivities are presented in the process of expansion. The reader is engaged, as an inspired witness, to therapeutic self-disclosures, elaborate forms of confession, by speakers who develop realistically through carefully constructed attention to psychological detail.

"A Royal Princess" shows how a relatively privileged woman, like the princess, comes to support a peasant uprising against her father, the king, once she has acknowledged that the feudal hierarchy exploiting the peasants also oppresses her as a woman and daughter:

> Two and two my guards behind, two and two before,
> Two and two on either hand, they guard me evermore;
> Me, poor dove that must not coo—eagle that must not soar.
>
> . . . .
>
> As I am a lofty princess, so my father is
> A lofty king, accomplished in all kingly subtilties,
> Holding in his strong right hand world-kingdoms' balances.
>
> He has quarrelled with his neighbours, he has scourged his
>   foes;
> Vassal counts and princes follow where his pennon goes,
> Long-descended valiant lords whom the vulture knows,
>
> On whose track the vulture swoops, when they ride in state
> To break the strength of armies and topple down the great:
> Each of these my courteous servant, none of these my mate.
>
> My father counting up his strength sets down with equal pen
> So many head of cattle, head of horses, head of men;
> These for slaughter, these for labour, with the how and when.
>
> Some to work on roads, canals; some to man his ships;
> Some to smart in mines beneath sharp overseers' whips;
> Some to trap fur-beasts in lands where utmost winter nips.
>
> Once it came into my heart and whelmed me like a flood,

> That these too are men and women, human flesh and blood;
> Men with hearts and men with souls, tho' trodden down like
>   mud.
>
> Our feasting was not glad that night, our music was not gay;
> On my mother's graceful head I marked a thread of grey,
> My father frowning at the fare seemed every dish to weigh.
>
> . . . .
>
> Amid the toss of torches to my chamber back we swept;
> My ladies loosed my golden chain; meantime I could have
>   wept
> To think of some in galling chains whether they waked or
>   slept.[19]

When the rebellion breaks, the princess courageously abandons her position of privilege:

> With a ransom in my lap, a king's ransom in my hand,
> I will go down to this people, will stand face to face, will stand
> Where they curse king, queen, and princess of this cursed
>   land.
>
> They shall take all to buy them bread, take all I have to give;
> I, if I perish, perish; they today shall eat and live;
> I, if I perish, perish; that's the goal I half conceive:
>
> Once to speak before the world, rend bare my heart and show
> The lesson I have learned, which is death, is life, to know.
> I, if I perish, perish; in the name of God I go.

Although the déclassé princess's personal generosity can do nothing to change the injustice of the system, she is presented as heroic because of her willingness to risk her own status and life for Christian democratic principles.

Compared to the heroic princess, the prince in "The Prince's Progress" (1866) appears aimless and naive.[20] The structure of the poem is based on the kind of narrative journey the author employed fourteen years earlier in "Repining" and another long narrative, "The Dead City." "The Prince's Progress" is the poem with which Rossetti originally intended to "trip"

Tennyson up, although she later had doubts about her ability. She kept Tennyson in mind when she was unwilling to follow Dante Gabriel's suggestion to include a tournament in the poem: "How shall I express my sentiments about the terrible tournament? Not a phrase to be relied on, not a correct knowledge on the subject, not the faintest impulse of inspiration, incites me to the tilt: and looming before me in horrible bugbeardom stand TWO tournaments in Tennyson's *Idylls*."[21]

Her most obvious departure from Tennyson in the poem is her switch from Tennyson's usual focus on the maiden's world view as neurotic escapism to her own focus on the world view of an inept prince. The prince's mission fails to redeem the princess and the moral social order she represents because he is weak of purpose and will, an anti-Lancelot, who through sloth and infidelity sacrifices the princess to death and the social order to destruction:

> In his world-end palace the strong Prince sat,
> Taking his ease on cushion and mat.
> Close at hand lay his staff and his hat.

A chorus of female voices asks: "'When wilt thou start? the bride waits, O youth.'–" The prince responds, "'Now the moon's at full; I tarried for that, / Now I start in truth,'" but he does not begin his journey until the chorus answers a slew of questions he raises about his waiting bride. The chorus implores him to leave:

> "Time is short, life is short," they took up the tale:
>   "Life is sweet, love is sweet, use today while you may;
> Love is sweet, and tomorrow may fail;
>   Love is sweet, use today."

> While the song swept by, beseeching and meek,
> Up rose the Prince with a flush on his cheek,
> Up he rose to stir and to seek,
>   Going forth in the joy of his strength;
> Strong of limb if of purpose weak,
>   Staring at length.

He is "as goodly a Prince as ever was born," but considering his mishaps, Rossetti is not claiming much for princes. He is tried and is detained by an alluring milkmaid, a vast, disorienting expanse of wasteland, an old man on the brink of death, rushing water, and near drowning. Through the misguided prince, Rossetti expressed her criticism of empty, vainglorious heroism for heroism's sake and exposed the sham of male heroism as a means of delivering or advancing the position of women. The chorus sings at the poem's close:

> "Too late for love, too late for joy,
>   Too late, too late!
> You loitered on the road too long,
>   You trifled at the gate:
> The enchanted dove upon her branch
>   Died without a mate;
> The enchanted princess in her tower
>   Slept, died, behind the grate:
> Her heart was starving all this while
>   You made it wait.
>
> "Ten years ago, five years ago,
>   One year ago,
> Even then you had arrived in time,
>   Tho' somewhat slow;
> Then you had known her living face
>   Which now you cannot know:
> The frozen fountain would have leaped,
>   The buds gone on to blow,
> The warm south wind would have awaked
>   To melt the snow.

By 1870, when the Franco-Prussian War broke out, Rossetti returned to spiritual appeal as a means of capturing antiwar sentiment in a pair of linked poems, "The German-French Campaign, 1870-1871."[22] In the first poem, "Thy Brother's Blood Crieth," the voice of the visionary reminds "ye unwise among the people" that only the Lord has the moral power to invoke vengeance; therefore the arrogant ravagement of France must end. In the second poem, "Today for Me," the metaphor of France as a mournful mother bereaving the sons lost in war is extended and amplified. Only the Lord can bind the spiritual wounds of the war; but "thou people of the lifted lance," the Germans, must "roll back, roll back" from France.

Rossetti's poems treat war as a lethal male enterprise. Women are excluded from action and are expected to wait supportively for unheroic heroes who do not return. Women are critical of their powerlessness and of the society that uses and limits them, but except for the royal princess, they have no avenues for effective resistance or action. The royal princess achieves solidarity with oppressed peasants, but fully expects her revolutionary passion to cost her life. Precisely because the human cost of war is unavoidable, it is never justified to Rossetti. However, war sometimes seems the only human way to check more destructive social forces. In the end, Rossetti believed the taking of lives is God's business alone. It is worth noting that the only war Rossetti justified in her lifetime–the American Civil War–was one fought on foreign soil.

The poems we have discussed have usually been read for their confessional and psychological content. They have not been read as poems in which a major theme is Rossetti's response to war. It seems a surprising oversight to us, especially since Rossett's antiwar convictions released her creative power. The theme stimulated her to think of ironic possibilities for character development and to explore her poetic heroines with an impressive psychological depth. By placing these poems more firmly in their historical contexts, we can appreciate the way Rossetti used her exclusion as a woman critically to examine the complex experience of war.

EMILY DICKINSON'S WAR POEMS

An American example of the invisibility of women's war poems is the critical response to Emily Dickinson's poems written during the Civil War era. The first premise of traditional Dickinson scholarship is that she had no interest in external events. This, of course, fits well with the legend of her hermetically sealed life and, indeed, is often offered as the highest proof of her reclusiveness, despite the fact that she grew up in a politician's house, read *The Springfield Republican* every day, and larded her poems and letters with quick references to contemporary characters and events. Also, coincidentally or not, the years 1860 to 1865, particularly 1862, comprise the bulk of her writing, her most tortured and violent poems.

Only Shira Wolosky's *Emily Dickinson: A Voice of War* has broken ground by moving beyond the recluse myth assumed by most biographers. Wolosky demonstrates, "startling as this may be," that Dickinson's initiative as a poet may lie in "the public realm." Historical pressures, especially the Civil War, "implicate and generate linguistic configuration" in Dickinson's poetry. The reader might be surprised at the almost one hundred poems by Dickinson Wolosky identifies on the theme of war. However, Wolosky's primary emphasis is Dickinson's metaphysical use of history. The war prompts poems that are model instances of "confrontation with evil and suffering."[23]

We differ from Wolosky in that we believe Dickinson responded to the Civil War with a particularly feminist and feminine perspective. By no means have we dealt with all the poems on war in Dickinson's canon. Instead, we treat seven especially striking poems that illustrate our thesis, namely that in relation to war, Dickinson expressed a woman's view of events in which she was allowed no voice. When she projected herself imaginatively into these events, she had no interest in writing patriotic war epics, any more than she chose to express her theological doubts through closely reasoned sermons.

Most women loyally supported the war through activities such as sending medicines to the wounded, folding bandages, and preserving fruits for the soldiers. Although Dickinson revered Elizabeth Fry and Florence Nightingale as heroic individuals, she did not attempt to prove her valor by joining any voluntary group efforts such as nursing or community organizing. Instead, she questioned the entire idea of sacrifice for others.

Indirectly, it is possible to discern Dickinson's response to the efficacy of women's traditional activities. In a letter to a friend, Jane Humphrey, concerning a charitable sewing circle which she has refused to join, she remarks sarcastically that she is sure all the "hungry" will be "fed" and the "ragged clothed." It is possible to infer that she had similar feelings about a "woman's place" in relation to the war effort.[24]

Dickinson's consciousness of the war permeated her poems in two ways. One was to furnish them with vocabulary and images from the political and physical conflicts–North/South, Blue/Gray, bullets, armies, victories and defeats crowd her writing. Two poems written in 1860, before the actual outbreak of war, are subtle and indirect commentaries on it which effectively presage impending doom and tragedy to come. The third, written in 1863, expresses the present crisis of the nation in tumultuous terms that are, nevertheless, couched in spiritual and nature imagery.

In addition to these indirect expressions of her consciousness of the Civil War, Dickinson wrote two of her most moving elegies in 1862 specifically concerned with the war dead. These two poems imaginatively amplified the meaning of her one comment on war to T. W. Higginson, "War feels to me an oblique place."[25] The word "oblique" had two senses, both in use in 1860. One was the more common meaning of "not at a straight or right angle." The other was "morally deviant." In addition, a poem written during 1862, which is, in a sense, a sequal to "Success is counted sweetest," explores a recurrent theme and clearly shows her consciousness of the physical price of war.

Her own sense of dislocation, of wrenching apart, of death, was very acute through these years. This has commonly been ascribed to personal causes, usually the traditional feminine one of rejection by a man. Only recently has Wolosky connected the conflict to a sense of tragedy about the dissolution of her nation. Perhaps the early fragmented publication of her work kept any sense of these themes relevant to a particular period from emerging.

In 1862 the Union forces were discovering the intransigence of their opponents. There was supposed to have been a Southern rout which gobbled Northern resources and men and touched Amherst directly. Dickinson was loyal to Amherst and to her family. She may have gathered some of her ambiguous attitudes towards the war from her family's involvement with it. Though a distant cousin of hers was the first man from Amherst killed in battle, her immediate family was not so directly involved.[26] Her father was one of the founding members of the Republican Party but not a personal supporter of Lincoln. He saw Lincoln and the abolitionists as dangerous radicals who would destroy the Union. While he opposed extending the range of slave-owning territory, he wanted no part of ending the institution by force. Her brother paid a substitute to fight for him and spent the war at home.

When Dickinson assimilated these ideas with her own thoughts on sacrifice and victory, the result was two elegies which are questioning and ambiguous, tones at odds with the usual confident pomp of war poetry. Both call into question the underlying assumption of the necessity for war—sacrifice for others. Both also raise the issue of women's role in relation to war, as the passive recipients of sacrifice, though, of course, they do not have access to the political process which determines whether wars are to be fought. Dickinson records the feelings aroused in her by such enforced passivity.

The first war elegy, #444, may be read as a meditation by the excluded on institutions in which she has no part:

> It feels a shame to be Alive—
> When Men so brave—are dead—
> One envies the Distinguished Dust—
> Permitted—Such a Head—
>
> The Stone—that tells defending Whom
> This Spartan put away
> What little of Him we—possessed
> In Pawn for Liberty—

The price is great–Sublimely paid–
Do we deserve–a Thing–
That lives–like Dollars–must be piled
Before we may obtain?

Are we that wait–sufficient worth–
That such Enormous Pearl
As life–dissolved be–for us–
In Battle's–horrid Bowl?

It may be–a Renown to live–
I think the Man who die–
Those unsustained–Saviors–
Present Divinity–

The poem begins with the emotion of shame. similar to the shame felt by the heroine of "Repining" at her first contact with war. In Dickinson's poem, the poet is ashamed at being the observer of so many deaths. She envies soldiers their active parts and identifies herself as one of "we that wait," questioning whether these are worth enough to justify others' deaths in "Battle's–horrid Bowl."

The question of worth is then more fully and originally explored. Stanzas two and three are concerned with valuing, in terms of dollars or of gems, the worth of one life for another. Particularly striking is the curious statement, a parody of the elegy, "That lives–like Dollars–must be piled," which sharpens and particularizes the first line of the stanza, the more conventional "The price is great–Sublimely paid." The notion is reinforced in the fourth stanza, "Are we that wait–sufficient worth– / That such Enormous Pearl," and expresses her awareness of the relationship between war and economic institutions. from which women are also excluded.

The last stanza restates this sense of exclusion in religious terms, equating the men who die with Christ, a figure women, by reason of gender, were not expected to emulate. This implicates and underscores the church's role in supporting "just wars" for liberation. while still leaving women among those who "wait," that is outside any real positions of religious power.

The pronouns in the poem interestingly move from the impersonal passive. "It feels," to the impersonal active. presumably editorial. "we" and "Us" of the next three stanzas. to the "I" of the last stanza, as if the author has worked through to a position of responsibility. Indeed, from the beginning, she allows herself more involvement with the subject than a traditional, third-person elegy.

In the second inventive elegy, #596, her relationship with the subject of the poem is stated early:

> When I was small, a Woman died–
> Today– her Only Boy
> Went up from the Potomac–
> His face all Victory
>
> To look at her– How slowly
> The Seasons must have turned
> Till Bullets clipt an Angle
> And He passed quickly round–
>
> If pride shall be in Paradise–
> Ourself cannot decide–
> Of their imperial Conduct–
> No person testified–
>
> But, proud in Apparition–
> That Woman and her Boy
> Pass back and forth, before my Brain
> As even in the sky–
>
> I'm confident that Bravoes–
> Perpetual break abroad
> For Braveries, remote as this
> In Scarlet Maryland–

The poem begins, "When I was small, a Woman died– " putting both herself and the woman at the center of attention and only then moving on to a consideration of the woman's son, killed "In Scarlet Maryland– " who would usually be the focus of most conventional war poems. The poem thus appears to be a working out of women's participation in male sacrifice in war, since the rest of the poem is careful to link his heroism with hers. Indeed, the whole point of the son's death is to be able to "look at her" (his mother), and *"their* imperial Conduct–" is praised. The image presented of them resembles a Madonna-Christ. "But, proud in Apparition– / That Woman and her Boy / Pass back and forth, before my brain / As even in the sky–." This is one of Dickinson's visualizations of the cult of motherhood.

The explicit meaning of the poem is a tribute to a brave soldier and his mother's pride which extends beyond the grave, but the poem actually focuses on the woman rather than the warrior. At the same time, the author, through her insistence on remaining an active participant in the poem, links herself with their courage. The use of first person is maintained except in the third stanza, the most tentative and questioning, where "Ourself" is used instead. Thus, the poet *and* the mother participate in war and Christlike sacrifice.

The third poem for consideration is #639, also written in 1862. When it is contrasted with the earlier "Success is counted sweetest," it attains new significance as a demonstration of the effect of war reports on Dickinson. The last two stanzas of "Success is counted sweetest" contain the essential theme:

> Not one of all the purple Host
> Who took the Flag today
> Can tell the definition
> So clear of Victory
>
> As he defeated–dying–
> On whose forbidden ear
> The distant strains of triumph
> Burst agonized and clear!

Dickinson often pursued one idea through many poems, elaborating and deepening her analysis, sometimes contradicting an earlier thought. This relationship of victory and defeat to death was one such idea which she used later in #639:

> My Portion is Defeat–today–
> A paler luck than Victory–
> Less Paeans–fewer Bells–
> The Drums don't follow Me–with tunes–
> Defeat–a somewhat slower–means–
> More Arduous than Balls–
>
> 'Tis populous with Bone and stain–
> And Men too straight to stoop again,
> And Piles of solid Moan–
> And Chips of Blank–in Boyish Eyes–

And scraps of Prayer–
And Death's surprise,
Stamped visible–in Stone–

There's somewhat prouder, over there–
The Trumpets tell it to the Air–
How different Victory
To Him who has it–and the One
Who to have had it, would have been
Contenteder–to die–

In the 1862 poem, she shifted the narrator from third person to first so the defeated soldier expresses his own emotions directly. Moreover, she intensified the dramatic quality of the narration by a realistic description of a battlefield strewn with dead and dying, a change from the rather abstract formulation of war in the 1859 poem.

The conclusion of the earlier poem, that victory is only clearly understood by the defeated, is broadened in the later poem into an elaborated description of the agony of defeat, an agony so great that death in victory is seen as preferable to life in defeat. Had the descriptive middle stanza not been included, the end of the poem would have been less ambiguous, but the vivid account of unidealized death undercuts any such ending, keenly turning desire for death from nobility to the macabre. The poem also keeps the desire for victory within the bounds of the "I," the speaker of the poem, who is given the masculine heroism of the soldier. Nowhere is there a hint of the Christlike suffering for others, only the desire for victory for the sake of victory, even at the expense of many lives.

Three poems written before the outbreak of war mysteriously predict the crisis to come. One poem, #152, possibly written in early 1860 (if one accepts Thomas Johnson's chronology) contains interesting martial references in an otherwise peaceful hymn to evening. This poem captures some of the suspense and excitement associated with the possibility of war:

The Sun kept stooping–stooping–low!
The Hills to meet him rose!
On his side, what Transaction!
On their side, what Repose!

Deeper and deeper grew the stain
Upon the window pane–

Thicker and thicker stood the feet
Until the Tyrian

Was crowded dense with Armies–
So gay, so Brigadier–
That *I* felt martial stirrings
Who once the Cockade wore–
Charged, from my chimney corner–
But Nobody was there!

There is a menacing quality to this highly metaphoric poem at odds with the subject matter. The stain upon the window and the armies' slow advance, especially when read in 1860, have dimensions it is hard to avoid. The gradual inching toward conflict would be something a politician's daughter would have difficulty ignoring and may be linked to her remark to her cousin in the spring of 1861, "When did the war really begin?"[27] The humorous ending to the poem, which has nothing to do with sunsets, may be taken either as a comment on the ridiculousness of martial attitudes or as Dickinson's comment on her exclusion from such activities as a woman, or both. Poems written later in the war certainly indicate that she held both these attitudes.

Another poem of 1860, #204, a poem to both evening and morning, uses interesting and suggestive color imagery, especially in the section devoted to evening:

A slash of Blue–
A sweep of Gray–
Some scarlet patches on the way,
Compose an Evening sky–
A little purple–slipped between–
Some Ruby Trousers hurried on–
A wave of Gold–
A bank of Day–
This just makes out the Morning Sky.

The color images in the "morning" section contain curious, if more tangential, references. Dickinson previously used purple to refer to armies in poem #67, "purple Host," and the color gold was linked to money in #23, "guinea golden." These, when placed in conjunction with "Bank of Day," make a significant combination and point the way to the elegy we have already discussed, #444, which links money and war. It is intriguing to think of the "Ruby Trousers," surely not a common sight in sober Amherst, in a military connection, since some Civil War regiments, for example the Zouaves, with their Oriental uniforms, were very flashily attired.

A third intriguing poem, #721, may be interpreted as an illustration of Dickinson's personal response to the crisis of her country. Conventionally interpreted as an illustration of madness or of religious ecstasy at immortality, it uses words which must have had other echoes in 1863:

> Behind Me–dips Eternity–
> Before Me–Immortality–
> Myself–the Term between–
> Death but the Drift of Eastern Gray,
> Dissolving into Dawn away,
> Before the West begin–
>
> 'Tis Kingdoms–afterward–they say–
> In perfect–pauseless Monarchy–
> Whose Prince–is Son of None–
> Himself–His Dateless Dynasty–
> Himself–Himself diversify–
> In Duplicate divine–
>
> 'Tis Miracle before Me–then–
> 'Tis Miracle behind–between–
> A Crescent in the Sea–
> With Midnight to the North of Her–
> And Midnight to the South of Her–
> And Maelstrom–in the Sky–

Its references to a "Dateless Dynasty," a firm, indissoluble state which will begin sometime after "Death but the drift of Eastern Gray," must have been appealing in the height of the "Maelstrom" and Northern and Southern Midnights of 1863.

By the 1860s, Dickinson had chosen not to be a public person, let alone a public poet. She did not see her poetic role to write battle hymns for any republic, but to explore the implications of war from her own perspective–that of a woman. Her poems weave unique and subtle metaphors in structures that defy traditional genres.

CONCLUSION

The poetry of Christina Rossetti and Emily Dickinson offers complex insights into women's relationships with the public institutions which shaped their lives. However, they chose to develop their insights by linking images creatively rather than by means of logical argument, by such devices as framing a poem overtly about war in a parlor debate about women's rights throughout the ages, or using a Madonna-Christ image in a soldier's elegy. In the case of both poets, the subject of war called forth their most characteristic poetic strengths. For Dickinson, these strengths include mastery of metaphor, highly suggestive syntactic compression, and an unusual, striking, and original perspective. For Rossetti, the war theme elicited complex narratives embedded within narratives, heroic romantic speakers, and ironic toning. These strategies of poetic expression, as well as the emphasis by biographers on their isolated lives, make it easy to miss the political implications in their work. In addition, it is difficult to pierce the habit of seeing political issues under the boldface subheadings of the textbooks–pacificism, abolition, and others, and easy to forget that in most women's lives, the more immediate sensation was that of exclusion from war as an extension of other rejections. As single women lacking even the influence wives and mothers were assumed to exert and living the proscribed lives of Victorian spinsters, these poets were at an advantageous position to describe exclusion and to offer an alternative to the male fantasy of women as passive supporters and idolizers of male heroism.

Chapter 6

The Market Is for Bankers, Burglars and Goblins

As urbanization altered the agrarian landscape and the countryside diminished, women gradually lost their once essential roles within domestic economies. Their decreased value to the economy made them less equal as wives, although they became more valorized as mothers. Throughout industrialization, women were part of the working population, but they were treated as more expendable to the economy and they earned less in factories than their male counterparts. Women became visible among those growing poor, as urbanization advanced, and the number of prostitutes grew as cities did. Many women concluded it was more profitable to sell their bodies than to be exploited by factory bosses. In the meantime, myths of women as fragile and innately sick were used to keep middle-class women at home and to prevent them from challenging men for jobs and for control of the public sphere.[1]

The poetry of Emily Dickinson and Christina Rossetti incorporated the skepticism towards industrialism of several progressive movements, but they also tied their view of the problem to the situation of women as outsiders. We will show that Dickinson's and Rossetti's radical responses to industrialism resulted in poems of exceptional originality and power and that their poems examining the institution of marriage are integrally connected to their critiques of industrialism.

Though they were both rather privileged witnesses of the profound changes taking place in women's work lives, they responded deeply as redundant women, that is as unmarried, dependent daughters, to the divisions growing around them between rich and poor, public and private.

While their poems undoubtedly reflect differences in cultural and religious backgrounds, they also express similar criticisms of the industrial system and of all the ideologies concerning women as weak, passive, and domestic which it claimed to require–the cults of romance, marriage, and motherhood and the privatization of women's sphere. Moreover, Rossetti was particularly critical of the sexual objectification of women that accompanied urbanization.

As in the case of their treatment of war, Dickinson's and Rossetti's treatments of industrialism are often subtle and indirect. Since their critiques can be elusive, they have been either invisible or misconstrued. For example, previous critics of Emily Dickinson's financial and business imagery have theorized that she used these images in imitation of the conversation of her father and brother, both lawyers, like some sort of verbal resolution of penis envy or a mere parroting of words made familiar at the dinner table. This ignores her precise use of these terms and her contribution to a critique of an emerging industrial economy. Rossetti's critics have been blinded by her religious commitment, and they falsely divide her spiritual and symbolic goals as a poet from the social/political goals she also hoped to achieve. Critics who stress Rossetti's piety alone ignore her ties to the radical Langham Place Group through her brothers and to the insurgent and controversial Anglican Sisterhoods through her own work as a social worker and nurse. Both these movements challenged the materialism of industrial society from a woman's perspective and advocated alternative forms of social organization.

Rossetti's and Dickinson's responses can be gauged primarily through their use of poetic language, particularly their imagery and dramatic characterizations. They challenged market relations for commodifying and objectifying women and for using them as currency. They associated industrialism thematically with shallow, misdirected materialism, and they also represented the culture of the mart or marketplace through various, oppressive patriarchal images, ranging from "Fathers" to goblin-merchant men. In addition, from the late 1850s to the mid-1860s, they added to their repertoire an exploration of different forms of male-dependency. It is as if they hoped to learn from working through this theme, through revulsion, as it were, to avoid its debilitating emotional and economic consequences. Finally, Dickinson's and Rossetti's female speakers embody critiques of industrialism in their active agency. They find ways to survive as outsiders by not succumbing to victimization, but rather by demonstrating their equivalency with the world.

By the 1850s and 1860s, patriarchal control over industrialization was clear. Bourgeois men controlled the means of production while men in the professional and working classes cornered the employment market. Women of the middle and upper classes were encouraged to manage households and to mother, while women of the lower and working classes provided sex and cheap labor.

The popular American and British ladies' journals were advising respectable women to avoid all unnecessary contact with the male marketplace. Young ladies were not to loiter on village and city streets, take walks and railway journeys alone, own a dog, which required walking in public places, ride to hounds, speak to young men–indeed, think for themselves. These restrictions which men argued were necessary for ladies' safety and the smooth running of capitalism robbed women of the conditions necessary for growth and development. By the later half of the decade, women radicals and reformers alike were drawing connections between the rise of industrialism and the cult of separate spheres used to exclude women from the center of economic and political activity.

THE MARKET IS FOR GOBLINS

The Langham Place Group held the male-constructed cult of domesticity responsible for marginalizing working women and for labeling unmarried women "redundant." In their periodical the *English Woman's Journal*, the Langham radicals demanded to know the good of proposing the cult of domesticity to the 876,920 redundant women who inhabited England, not to speak of the other million and a half who were forced by poverty into the labor market.[2] As well-educated, unmarried, middle-class women, Dickinson and Rossetti both belonged to this new "class" who were considered essentially useless to society.

After doing parish district visiting on Robert Street, Rossetti soon realized unmarried women of all classes were society's largest group of outsiders. They were outsiders not only because they composed more than half of the British poor, but also because as prisoners, vagrants, prostitutes, mistresses, spinsters, or widows, they were legally and politically devalued, economically dependent on men and vulnerable to romantic oppression and physical abuse. Recent discussions of Rossetti's "alien" vision have focused on her sensitivity to women's invisibility in the urban marketplace and their sexual and social vulnerabilities.[3] We wish to show that her alien vision is also tied to the active social and political movements against industrialism.

During the 1850s and 1860s, women reformers and radicals Rossetti knew personally were beginning to organize around women's exclusion from the workforce and their lack of educational, professional, and political opportunity. Initially, however, they approached the struggle for women's economic independence by focusing on legal rights in marriage and divorce.

Instead of changing the structure and organization of work to accommodate more women, the initial approach taken was to change the legal situation of married women so that they could individually benefit from paid employment. It was assumed that married women did not compose a signfificant portion of the workforce, as they do now, in part because they did not have the right to keep their own earnings. The Langham Place leaders introduced the Married Woman's Property Act as early as 1856. This radical proposal gave married women who worked the right to keep their own earnings. Severely threatening the sexual division of the spheres, this proposal prompted such a public controversy over sex roles, that the Langham leaders were forced to change their entire political direction.[4]

Women trapped in bad marriages needed to secure the right to divorce so that they could attempt to become economically independent. The Divorce Reform Bill, encouraged by Mrs. Caroline Norton's efforts, was passed by Parliament in 1858.

Several of Rossetti's poems compose an antimarriage and antiromance cluster which reflects the marriage reform focus of the British women's movement at the time. From one perspective, marriage and romance were viewed as limitations on women's economic independence, free choice, and self-reliance. The antimarriage group includes such narratives and dialogues as "The Hour and the Ghost," "A Triad," and "Love From the North" (all 1856); "Maude Clare" (1858), "Cousin Kate," "Goblin Market" (both 1859), and "'The Iniquity of the Fathers Upon the Children'" (1865). The narrative, "An Apple Gathering" (1857), and the monologue, "From Sunset to Rise Star" (1865), also belong in this group, although they focus more on romantic oppression and sexual double standards.

"The Hour and the Ghost" is one of the earliest antimarriage poems. In it, the wife's consciousness is controlled by her dead husband's ghost who demands loyalty from her beyond the grave: "For better and worse, for life and death, / Goal won with shortened breath!"[5]

The focus is on the controlled consciousness of wives again in "A Triad" where the usually exalted wife is paralleled with the spinster and whore. All three are equally judged as being "short of life," since they all exist in dependency relation to men. The critic McGann stressed that the spinster and whore (then known as "fallen woman") are lacking because "they are not self-conscious about the meaning of their choices and . . . none of them is truly 'single' since each one's personality exists in a dependency relation to something or someone else."[6]   It is therefore not surprising that the honesty of this poem, which has the "sluggish wife" grow "gross in soulless love," grated on its Victorian audience.   *The Spectator*, according to Packer, accused the poem of having a manly "'voluptuous passion.'"[7]

A day after writing "A Triad," Rossetti turned to the subject of brides in "Love From the North." In this deceptively romantic narrative, a bride is seized on her wedding day by a strange, "strong man from the north" who, as Packer explained, "carries her off without asking her consent."[8]   Left without an alternative, "made . . . fast with book and bell," she comes to have "neither heart nor power / Nor will nor wish to say him nay."[9]   The speaker in "An Apple Gathering" has been sexually dishonored, although we know this only through the metaphor of apple plucking. The speaker's early plucking of apple blossoms, which leaves her apple orchard fruitless, becomes a metaphor for her premature sexual looseness with Willie, who fails to meet her at harvest time when other maids, like "plump Gertrude," have "stronger hands" to "help" them "along." The speaker's loitering at the poem's close, after "the night grew chill," marks her as a tainted outsider:

> I let my neighbors pass me, ones and twos
>> And groups; the latest said the night grew chill,
> And hastened: but I loitered, while the dews
>> Fell fast I loitered still.[10]

Rossetti's heroines began to identify more direcly the male agents responsible for these abuses in the same years that the Langham Place Group was meeting in its London headquarters and beginning to publish the *English Woman's Journal*.   In "Maude Clare," for example, the speaker is an outspoken "other" woman who has been abandoned by her promiscuous lover, Thomas. Risking social censure as a fallen woman, the speaker appears on Thomas's wedding day to inform his new bride of Thomas's disloyalty:

> "Take my share of a fickle heart,
>> Mine of a paltry love:
> Take it or leave it as you will,
>> I wash my hands thereof."[11]

While Maude Clare's exposé of the sexual double standard is significant, it is interesting to note also that the manuscript version of the poem was more critical of the marriage system than the published version. In manuscript, the poem is longer and, with Thomas marrying Nell for her gold, it critiques the commercialization of the marriage market. Evidently, it was safer to be critical of the sexual double standard than of the connection of women with property. This makes sense, given the controversy generated by the proposed Married Woman's Property Act.

"Cousin Kate," written just two weeks after the publication of "Maude Clare" in *Once a Week*, used an agrarian, romantic pattern to show the sexual objectification of women that accompanied urbanization. Sometimes Rossetti drew characters and images from Gothic and pastoral romance to depict conflicts and contradictions in industrial capitalism.

A fair, flaxen-haired "cottage maiden" is abducted by a "great" feudal "lord." In the old, conventional pattern, the lord would rescue the maiden, marry her, and live happily ever after. In some working-class poetry, this pattern became the tale of the factory girl marrying the rich stranger.[12]

In "Cousin Kate," Rossetti employed the old pattern, but she altered the significance of the lord. Instead of signifying positive, upward mobility, he signifies hypocrisy and moral corruption. As a figure, he is a synthetic construct of a transitional ideology. On the one hand, the lord is a stock figure of romance who offers an escape to women of the worker class. On the other hand, the lord is the new bourgeois of realism who divides women morally into two groups–whores and ladies.

The lord leads the speaker to "a shameless shameful life" as his "plaything" and "love." After he wears her "like a silken knot," he exchanges her as easily as "a glove" and chooses to marry her cousin Kate instead. The speaker recounts:

> O Lady Kate, my cousin Kate
>   You grew more fair than I:
> He saw you at your father's gate,
>   Chose you, and cast me by.
> He watched your steps along the lane,
>   Your work among the rye;
> He lifted you from mean estate
>   To sit with him on high.[13]

Intent on exposing the lord's fraudulence, the speaker rebukes him for abusing her sexually, for abandoning her after the birth of their son out of wedlock, and for oppressing her with rigid, bourgeois sexual double standards. She criticizes Kate for not rejecting the lord as a husband because of his dishonest and abusive treatment of her. The speaker says to

Kate:

> Because you were so good and pure
> He bound you with his ring:
> The neighbors call you good and pure,
> Call me an outcast thing.
>
> . . . .
>
> O Cousin Kate, my love was true,
> Your love was writ in sand:
> If he had fooled not me but you,
> If you stood where I stand,
> He'd not have won me with his love
> Nor bought me with his land;
> I would have spit into his face
> And not have taken his hand.

It is significant that in these lines, Rossetti is speaking through the voice of the fallen woman. Equally important is that the fallen woman expects to find an ally in the other, "purer" woman. This bonding among women was common in the Houses of Charity where Rossetti counseled fallen women for over a decade. Rossetti's brothers tried to discourage her from identifying too closely with these fallen women, but Rossetti was too serious about issues of sex and class equality and too sensitive to her own vulnerabilities as a woman to abandon the subject.

In 1856, Rossetti wrote two monologues whose speakers were modeled on women she undoubtedly met through her experiences at St. Mary Magdalen's Home for Fallen Women on Highgate Hill. The monologue published as "From Sunset to Rise Star" (22 February 1865) is named "Friends" in Rossetti's manuscript notebook and has the words "House of Charity" penciled in against the title. While the monologue obviously gives voice to the perspective of a fallen woman at Highgate who identifies as an outsider—"I live alone, I look to die alone"—William Michael Rossetti insisted that the monologue was "deeply personal."[14] Dante Gabriel Rossetti had a similar response to the other monologue of that year, "'The Iniquity of the Fathers Upon the Children.'" The speaker of this monologue is a young girl in the process of discovering the circumstances of her illegitimacy. Packer called Rossetti's treatment of the illegitimate child in this monologue "frank, realistic, unsentimental, and psychologically convincing." With reference to Dickens' Little Emily and Mrs. Gaskell's Ruth, Packer appreciated the unconventionality of Rossetti's character who is "decades ahead of the mid-century Victorian novelists on the same subject."[15]

Rossetti had already introduced illegitimate children in her poems, though not as speaking characters, in "Light Love" (1856) and "Cousin Kate." In both of these early poems, illegitimate children are used as symbols for contradictions in dominant sexual, social, and moral codes. In these poems, unwed mothers have been abandoned by their children's fathers and must face their lives as social outcasts alone. The fathers are free from responsibility; but the children, while personally enriching the mothers' lives, remain as tangible marks of their mothers' shame.

"'The Iniquity of the Fathers Upon the Children'" is a moving dramatic monologue in which the illegitimate child, who has been abandoned by both father and mother, undergoes a process of heroic self-discovery and realization. This leads her to understand the patriarchal roots of her oppression and motivates her to try, in her own way, to change the system:

> 'All equal before God'—
> Our Rector has it so,
> And sundry sleepers nod.
> It may be so; I know
> All are not equal here,
> And when the sleepers wake
> They make a difference.
> 'All equal in the grave'—
> That shows an obvious sense:
> Yet something which I crave
> Not death itself brings near;
> How should death half atone
> For all my past, or make
> The name I bear my own?[16]

Writing in a poetic form which Louise Bernikow identified as the "I am not yours" pattern, and which Cheryl Walker described as a rejection-of-marriage genre, Rossetti gave her child-speaker the resolve to reject marriage as an alternative to redundancy. The young girl vows to lead the life of a single woman and refuses to define herself in conventional terms as the property of a man. Her life serves as an example of resistance to patriarchal law which unjustly allows fathers to abandon children out of wedlock:

> I think my mind is fixed

On one point and made up:
To accept my lot unmixed;
Never to drug the cup
But to drink it by myself;
I'll not blot out my shame
With any good man's name;
But nameless as I stand,
My hand is my own hand,
And nameless as I came
I go to the dark land.

Dante Gabriel advised his sister not to include this monologue (originally titled "Under the Rose") in her 1866 volume because of its unladylike subject and style. But Rossetti defended herself, arguing strongly that the subject was within the female range and that her "Poet mind" had the ability to create such a character even if it was *not* indeed based in her own personal experience:

> I yet incline to include within the female range
> such an attempt as this. . . . Moreover, the sketch
> only gives the girl's own deductions, feelings and
> semi-resolutions; granted such premises as hers, and
> right or wrong it seems to me she might easily arrive
> at such conclusions: and whilst it may truly be urged
> that unless white could be black and Heaven Hell my
> experience (thank God) precludes me from hers, I yet
> don't see why "the Poet mind" should be less able to
> construct her from its own inner consciousness than a
> hundred other unknown quantities.[17]

Given these dominant views about appropriate subjects for women's poetry, it is understandable that Rossetti embedded her most radical critique of marriage, romance, and capitalist society within a seemingly conventional moral tale. "Goblin Market" should be read in the context of Rossetti's poems of social protest. Written in the same period as the antimarriage poems, the same year as "Cousin Kate," it expresses one of the nineteenth century's most vivid nightmares of female violation in the marketplace and one of the most brazen fantasies of the redemptive powers and pleasures of sisterly love. Moreover, the poem reveals Rossetti's sharp and modern insight into women's dual role in the marketplace as both objects and perpetually unfulfilled consumers.

This masterpiece appears on the surface to be a simple narrative advising young women about the value of sisterhood, especially from Laura's chanting words which close the poem:

> "For there is no friend like a sister
> In calm or stormy weather;
> To cheer one on the tedious way,
> To fetch one if one goes astray,
> To lift one if one totters down,
> To strengthen whilst one stands."[18]

But the deeper significance of Laura's bonding with her sister Lizzie is revealed only by examining their alienation from one another and from themselves.

On a social/historical level, "Goblin Market" is about women's encounter with the male-dominated marketplace and their different accommodations to it. Lizzie, Laura, and Jeanie represent scores of young country and village women whose lives were displaced by capitalism, signified in the poem by the goblin-merchant men. Whereas McGann already offered this interpretation of the goblins, he did not use it to develop a fuller interpretation of the poem as a whole or of Lizzie's and Laura's alienation. For example, ultimately McGann does not decide whether "Goblin Market" is a religious poem with the goblins representing the evil merchants in Revelations or a social protest poem in which the goblins "appropriately" represent the "men of the world" who "have become these merchants."[19]

In "Goblin Market," Rossetti represents the market relation from a woman's point of view—as a sexual violation and as an emotional/psychic manipulation. Fallen women like Jeanie get caught in the marketplace as sexual victims. "Soiled" outcasts from respectable middle-class society, they become dependent on the very networks which abuse them. In "Goblin Market," Jeanie, "who for joys brides hope to have," met goblin merchant men "in the moonlight,"

> Took their gifts both choice and many,
> Ate their fruits and wore their flowers
> Plucked from bowers
>
> . . . .
>
> But ever in the moonlight

She pined and pined away;
Sought them by night and day,
Found them no more but dwindled and grew gray;
Then fell with the first snow.

Lizzie and Laura represent very different accommodations to the marketplace. Initially, they are introduced as golden innocents, heroines of idyllic, pastoral romance where domestic and farm work and cottage industry reign supreme untouched by commercial capitalism:

Golden head by golden head
Like two pigeons in one nest
Folded in each other's wings,
They lay down in their curtained bed:
Like two blossoms on one stem

. . . .

Cheek to cheek and breast to breast
Locked together in one nest.
Early in the morning
When the first cock crowed his warning,
Neat like bees, as sweet and busy,
Laura rose with Lizzie:
Fetched in honey, milked the cows,
Aired and set to rights the house,
Kneaded cakes of whitest wheat,
Cakes for dainty mouths to eat,
Next churned butter, whipped up cream,
Fed their poultry, sat and sewed;
Talked as modest maidens should:
Lizzie with an open heart,
Laura in an absent dream.

Since Laura entered into an exchange relation with the same goblin merchant men responsible for Jeanie's death, she has become alienated from her pastoral environment. The goblins, who hover in the "woodland glen," prey on women as sexual objects and as dependent followers. To foster dependency, they entice them with irresistible fruit. Through an exchange relation, the fruit is associated with an intense, passionate release which, it seems, only the goblins can offer. Laura—young, curious, naive, confined by the regimen of her domestic and farm economy—exchanges a lock of her hair, traditionally a literary symbol for loss of virginity, for the extraordinarily luscious fruit on which the goblins convince her to gorge. She "sucked their fruit globes fair or red":

> Sweeter than honey from the rock,
>
> . . . .
>
> She never tasted such before,
> How should it cloy with length of use?
> She sucked and sucked and sucked the more
> Fruits which that unknown orchard bore;
> She sucked until her lips were sore;
> Then flung the emptied rinds away
> But gathered up one kernel-stone,
> And knew not was it night or day
> As she turned home alone.

The fruit elicits a deadly dependency, but one which is strangely familiar. One longs for more, but once satiated, one can never hear the goblins or find the fruit again. This myth of the disappearing goblin fruit captures the elusive essence of the exchange relation Karl Marx developed in *Grundrisse* (1857):

> The process, then, is simply this: This product
> becomes a commodity, i.e. a mere moment of exchange.
> The commodity is transformed into exchange value. . . .
> Because the product becomes a commodity, and the
> commodity becomes an exchange value, it obtains, at
> first only in the head a double existence. This
> doubling in the idea proceeds (and must proceed) to the
> point where the commodity appears double in real
> exchange: as a natural product on one side, as
> exchange value on the other.[20]

Laura has falsely associated the goblins with the social meaning and erotic/emotional intensity lacking in her own circumscribed existence. The depth of Laura's need is not only measured in the primal fierceness of her sucking, but also the depth of her false consciousness is measured in the perpetual unfulfillment of her need. While the critic McGann does not employ a Marxist analysis, he comes to Marxist conclusions about Laura's "illness." She fell subject to a "spell of erotic illusions." Her development depends on her ability to release herself from an "erroneous belief" in her dependency on the goblins.[21]

Lizzie becomes the agent of change, but only once she frees herself from her own dependency on Victorian prudery and propriety. Left to her own devices, she adheres to regimen, avoids experience, and gladly ignores the goblin men. However, to save her sister from death, she confronts them with groundbreaking courage. Attempting to procure the fruit without drinking any of their juices herself or being used sexually, she bargains for the fruit with a coin—a silver penny—instead of the symbolic lock of hair. Offering money instead of sex immediately incites the goblins' wrath and abuse:

> They began to scratch their pates,
>
> . . . .
>
> Grunting and snarling.
> One called her proud,
> Cross-grained, uncivil;
> Their tones waxed loud,
> Their looks were evil.
> Lashing their tails
> They trod and hustled her,
> Elbowed and jostled her,
> Clawed with their nails,
> Barking, mewing, hissing, mocking,
> Tore her gown and soiled her stocking,
> Twitched her hair out by the roots,
> Stamped upon her tender feet,
> Held her hands and squeezed their fruits
> Against her mouth to make her eat.

She defeats them only through unflagging resistance. Without drinking a drop, she manipulates them into squeezing the juice over her face and neck:

> Tho' the goblins cuffed and caught her,
> Coaxed and fought her,
> Bullied and besought her,
> Scratched her, pinched her black as ink,

Kicked and knocked her,
Mauled and mocked her,
Lizzie uttered not a word;
Would not open lip from lip
Lest they should cram a mouthful in:
But laughed in heart to feel the drip
Of juice that syruped all her face,
And lodged in dimples of her chin,
And streaked her neck which quaked like curd.

In a scene unprecedented in Victorian literature for its bold, unconventional physicality, Laura is released from what McGann called "the pursuit of truth" in its illusive forms. Laura achieves release only after literally sucking the juices off Lizzie's body. Lizzie cried:

"Laura," up the garden
"Did you miss me?
Come and kiss me.
Never mind my bruises,
Hug me, kiss me, suck my juices
Squeezed from goblin fruits for you,
Goblin pulp and goblin dew.
Eat me, drink me, love me;
Laura, make much of me;
For your sake I have braved the glen
And had to do with goblin merchant men."

. . . .

"Lizzie, Lizzie, have you tasted
For my sake the fruit forbidden?"

. . . .

She clung about her sister,
Kissed and kissed and kissed her:
Tears once again
Refreshed her shrunken eyes,
Dropping like rain
After long sultry drouth;
Shaking with aguish fear, and pain,

She kissed and kissed her with a hungry mouth.

The juice—received through Lizzie this time, not the goblins—triggers a positive catharsis. "Laura awoke as from a dream, / Laughed in the innocent old way." Her false dependency on the goblins is broken.

This points to a distinction between the fruit itself—representing physical gratification, joy, exuberance—and the goblins' malign, sadistic purposes. This poem is partly about women's exploring and taking control over their own sensual natures, identifying pleasure, and experiencing joy. At this climactic point in the poem, Lizzie and Laura find emotional/erotic release within their own relationship.

Yet, to express their newfound sisterhood openly required another concession to convention on Rossetti's part. When Laura's crisis is over, she hugged Lizzie, "but not twice or thrice":

> Days, weeks, months, years
> Afterwards, when both were wives
> With children of their own;
> Their mother-hearts beset with fears,
> Their lives bound up in tender lives;
> Laura would call the little ones
> And tell them of her early prime,
> Those pleasant days long gone
> Of not-returning time:
> Would talk about the haunted glen,
> The wicked, quaint fruit-merchant men,
> Their fruits like honey to the throat
> But poison in the blood.

Clearly the "pleasant days long gone" refer to more exciting roads not taken. This surface support of marriage and motherhood rings hollow. It is anticlimactic given the focus on sisterhood and the absence of any men except for the goblins. The poem also reinforces the antimarriage themes in Rossetti's other work. Again, as McGann has pointed out:

> The spectacle of the Victorian marriage market appalled
> her. Wives, she says in "A Triad" (Crump, p. 29) are
> "fattened bees" who "grow gross in soulless love." . .
> . Her heroines characteristically choose to stand
> alone, as Agnes does in *Maude*. Those who do not—those
> who choose either love and marriage or love and

romance—almost invariably find either disaster or
unhappiness or a relationship marked by a sinister and
melancholy ambiguousness. . . . But the poem [Goblin
Market] is unusual in Christina Rossetti's canon in
that it has developed a convincing positive symbol for
an alternative, uncorrupted mode of social relations—
the love of sisters.[22]

How to portray the love of sisters in 1859 was Rossetti's challenge in
"Goblin Market." She had to consider the large segment of public opinion
enraged against the image of the independent woman put forth by the Langham
reformers. The dominant view expressed in *The Saturday Review* and in the
serious press was that women's "profession" should be married life, and her
training should consist of learning to be dependent. If women were
redundant, it was because they would *not* marry. Trying to make the single
life worthwhile and pleasant for women was nonsense which would destroy
marriage and the home.

Moreover, the model for sisterhood Rossetti found in the Anglican
Sisterhoods was regarded with distrust and skepticism, especially because
of the conventual vows. Requiring poverty, chastity, and obedience, the
vows challenged male access to female sexuality and property. Most critics
asked why Sisterhoods could not exist without vows. Was it not possible
for women to be kind to the sick and poor and to educate the young without
vowing to remain chaste for life and giving up their private property to
the convent?

In considering how to portray the genuine functions and values of
sisterhood, Rossetti chose to warn about the self-destructive aspects of
male-dependency which threatened women of all classes, from fallen women
like Jeanie, to self-sufficient wives and mothers like Lizzie and Laura.
In bonding and networking, married and single women alike could defend
themselves against the assaults of capitalism.

McGann commented that in "Goblin Market," Rossetti used "the
Christian material . . . to mediate for the audience the poem's primary
arguments about love, marriage, sisterhood and friendship."[23] However, the
poem does not actually seem to be about marriage or heterosexual love at
all. We suggest Rossetti used the marriage and motherhood material to
mediate for the audience the primary arguments about sisterhood, women's
autonomy, and the power of women to survive by accommodation in a hostile,
male-dominated marketplace.

THE MARKET IS FOR BANKERS AND BURGLARS

Emerging capitalism in America narrowed women's options and changed the traditional relation between man and his "helpmeet" for all classes. It profoundly altered the rural towns of New England, corrupted relations between neighbors, and changed even the landscape. Increasingly, marginal hill farms were supported by daughters' wages from the Lowell mills or from schoolteachers' meager pay. For middle- and upper-class women, housewifery skills were coming to mean supervision of servants, either Irish immigrants or surplus farm girls, and consumption of items formerly made at home. Men disappeared into the world of getting while women were stranded in the home of spending. In all cases, woman's status depended on her husband's. One could marry up, as Sue Gilbert did when she married Emily Dickinson's brother, and be rescued from mill work or the horrors of teaching for little pay or security; but one could also lose status through marriage. As the daughter of one of Amherst's leading citizens, Emily Dickinson was faced with a limited market if she wished to maintain her position.

In her poems, Emily Dickinson depicted a time in which the Amherst community had changed from a farming village directly linked to nature to a mercantile center in which more natural relationships had been replaced by artificial intermediaries. Dickinson questioned dominant assumptions about prosperity in a cluster of poems written from 1858 to 1862 by linking the village and the factory to images of poverty, horror, and personal struggle. Moreover, her poems on marriage show that love is no longer possible within an institution dominated by commercial and contractual concerns. The poems are feminist metaphors for changing economic relations between men and women from agrarian to industrial times.

Though Dickinson used many images to explore themes of isolation and alienation, when she chose the vocabulary of the marketplace to replace the more familiar nature images, she commented not only on the personal plight of the superfluous, but more specifically about the conditions which dictated her separation from the central action of her time. These conditions, according to feminist historian Ellen Dubois, consisted of women's total "dependence on marriage and the sexually segregated nature of the labor force."[24] Indeed, the relations of the market impinge on every relationship, especially the relations between men and women in marriage.

Of course, there was marriage for love, which justified whatever choice a young woman made. "Romance" was a potent and potentially unsettling force in the 1850s and 1860s. However, despite its allures, few if any of Emily Dickinson's friends appear to have made runaway matches with their grooms or with Irish laborers. In poem #580 (1862), Dickinson cleverly describes marriage to someone of the same class in metaphoric terms which lay bare the economic underpinnings of the institution:

> I gave myself to Him—
> And took Himself, for Pay,
> The solemn contract of a Life
> Was ratified, this way—
>
> The Wealth might disappoint—
> Myself a poorer prove
> Than this great Purchaser suspect,
> The Daily Own—of Love
>
> Depreciate the Vision—
> But till the Merchant buy—
> Still Fable—in the Isles of Spice—
> The subtle Cargoes—lie—
>
> At least—'tis Mutual—Risk—
> Some—found it—Mutual Gain—
> Sweet Debt of Life—Each Night to owe—
> Insolvent—every Noon

Most feminist thinkers of the 1840s and 1850s concentrated their efforts on reforming marriage rather than attacking the institution of marriage itself. They believed civil rights for women would restore them to their equal position within marriage before industrialization. Historian Susan Conrad records that leading intellectuals of the movement, such as Pauline Wright Davis, described contemporary postmarriage life as a living death in a "'series of dissolving views.'"[25]   Immediately after marriage, the woman became the "child bride," and from there, soon declined into different states of dependency, without ever having been a mature adult.

In a series of poems written from 1860 to 1863, supposedly the time in which she was most involved in an unconsummated, heterosexual passion, Emily Dickinson imagined herself a bride or a wife and, through this persona, explored the state of marriage. These poems are commonly interpreted as a longing for the image and exaltation of matrimony, an exaltation which extends to divine marriage with Christ.[26]   However, it is only possible to so read these poems by excluding troublesome and paradoxical lines and by ignoring Emily Dickinson's own advice, "Tell all the truth." *It is certainly possible to read these poems as, at least, ambivalent about marriage* and, possibly, as a gloss on feminist criticisms of marriage of the prewar era.

Several lines recall the notion of the "child bride." Poem #473, for example, ends with the line, "Baptized–this Day–A Bride–." In poem #1072, she begins to "rot" before maturation. She is "Born–Bridalled–Shrouded– / In a Day–." Comparisons between marriage and death appear throughout poem #649, "Her Sweet turn to leave the Homestead / Came the Darker Way–." In the third stanza, kinsmen kneel to salute a bride's "forehead," which suggests a comparison between the "Bride" and a corpse:

> Never Bride had such Assembling–
> Never kinsmen kneeled
> To salute so fair a Forehead–
> Garland be indeed–

However, in poem #470, "I am alive–I guess–" (a description of ecstasy so intense, it has caused her to be born again), Dickinson lists a number of signs that enable her to know she has *not* died:

> I am alive–because
> I do not own a House–
> Entitled to myself–precise–
> And fitting no one else–
>
> And marked my Girlhood's name–
> So Visitors may know
> Which Door is mine–and not mistake–
> And try another Key–

These two stanzas set forth the terms on which a woman in America before the Civil War could own a house, or her own "Girlhood" name, or even the "Key" to her own identity. She had the choice of a living death in which her legal, psychic, and economic identity was expected to be taken over by an all-controlling husband, or she could remain within her "Girlhood's name," even though nothing "Entitled to myself" would be hers until she was, in fact, dead.

Her other poems, far from extolling the conventional Victorian marriage, make it clear that love itself is not possible within marriage, given the narrow economic terms in which it is conceived. In poem #199, she is not wife, but "Wife," a state she also occupies in poem #1072, "Title Divine—is mine! / The Wife—without the Sign!" or in poem #1737, "Rearrange a 'Wife's' affection!" Of course, this qualification on her wifehood is usually considered to be evidence of her attachment to one or another married man, such as Wadsworth or Bowles, whom she considered her true husband. Far from constituting an attack on marriage, these poems seem to reinforce the idea that marriage is the best state, one to which she desperately, and vainly, aspired.

This view of Emily Dickinson as a tragic spinster overlooks these lines from poem #199: "I'm Czar—I'm 'Woman' now— / It's safer so—." This is an odd choice of lines which is not so easily explained away by references to "Czar" indicating how supremely royal marriage makes her feel. Surely, words such as "Empress," "Queen," or even the more neutral "Ruler," were equally available to her. At the very least, her diction indicates a recognition that to be truly in command requires a male brand of ruler. "I'm 'Woman' now—" with its careful use of quotes, when coupled with the quotes around "Wife," undercuts the simple explanation that she was a "wife" in her own mind, if not in the world's. If, by pledging herself to a man whom she considered her husband, she considered herself a woman, why the use of quotes? She then follows this already qualified definition with a line that, to say the least, lacks romantic sweep: "It's safer so—."

There is another explanation for these odd juxtapositions, one which is not at variance with other views Emily Dickinson was known to have. At one point, she chides other women for their "Dimity Convictions" (#401), and in a letter to Abiah Root which has usually been interpreted as referring to religious doubts, she contrasts the safety of life in a calm harbor with her desire to brave the sea, *alone.*[27]

The marriages with which she was most familiar, her parents' and her brother's, were hardly models for wedded bliss. Her mother was a weak, ineffectual woman, in awe and terror of her domineering husband. There is evidence that Emily Dickinson devalued her mother and adored, as well as feared, her autocratic father. Indeed, she only learned to love her mother after her mother was incapacitated by a stroke, and Emily cared for her as if she had been a child.

Although Sue Gilbert's marriage to Austin Dickinson improved Sue's social status, it ended her friendship with Emily who had envisioned a happy threesome. Emily Dickinson never had to endure the kind of poverty that many women like Sue married to escape. Dickinson's poems may well have been expressing her criticism of these women who married to gain the safety and security which only wifehood offered.

The rest of poem #199 can be read as ironic exaggeration of the importance wifehood bestowed on its possessor. The wife is immortalized, unlike the "Girls" she leaves behind. Becoming a wife would clearly make her "Czar," as Sue was rumored to be in her own house and, at least, would enable her to take precedence over her unmarried friends and kin. The last stanza, with its tortured logic, "This being comfort—then / That other kind—was pain—" loses some of its oddity if it is read as a questioning of the first premise, that marriage *is* comfort. It may account for the abruptness of the ending lines, "But why compare? / I'm 'Wife'! Stop there!" Wives may have safety, title, and comfort, but are they, like Princess Ida wished to be, "whole" in themselves and "owed to none"? Dickinson's answer seems to be "No."

Poem #493 relates a different relationship, less a comment on the state of marriage in general and more on a particular relationship. While commonly read as an exaltation of marriage, it, too, contains interesting discrepancies. In the first place, the poem slips from first person into third person immediately after the first two lines, "The World—stands—solemner—to me— / Since I was wed—to Him—." From that point on, the poem involves itself in complicated passive constructions. Even in the second line, the persona of the poem is "wed to him" rather than *weds* him, and this sense of physical joining is echoed in the "binding" and "clasping" which the man enforces on the woman in the seventh and eighth lines.

Lines three and four set up the power dynamics of this marriage, "A modesty befits the soul / That bears another's name—" with the word "bears" having its double connotation of being "designated by" and "holding up." Bearing this burden clearly worries the poem's speaker, who feels herself unworthy of the gift she is receiving, the "munificence, that chose— / So unadorned—a Queen—." The soul of a woman being married, then, is supposed to experience modesty, doubt, prayer, and gratitude. The burden of her prayer, "that it [her soul] more angel—prove— / A whiter Gift—within—" recalls Coventry Patmore's poem to the model Victorian wife, *The Angel in the House*. This poem perfectly delineates the Victorian marriage with the woman's soul burdened, clasped, and bound.

The world is indeed solemner in poem #732 as well:

> She rose to His Requirement—dropt
> The Playthings of Her Life
> To take the honorable Work
> Of Woman, and of Wife—

One expects to hear following this first stanza those things which will justify this honorable work, but what follows is no paean to the glories of marriage, but a discussion of deficiencies or disappointments:

> If ought She missed in Her new Day,
> Of Amplitude, or Awe—
> Or first Prospective—Or the Gold
> In using, wear away

God, the husband, does not appear as omnipotent, close up. However, the stanza break at this point clearly builds up suspense. Now, we feel we are going to learn what makes this all worthwhile. Now, the conventional Victorian pieties:

> It lay unmentioned—as the Sea
> Develop Pearl, and Weed,
> But only to Himself—be known
> The Fathoms they abide—

Whether this is God Himself or Husband Himself, the images of irritants— even "Pearl" building from an irritant and "Weed" as the fruition of this union—are not the answer we expect. The reality of this imagined, supernatural, or actual marriage is unmentioned and unmentionable.

Where, then, does love occur? For Emily Dickinson it is clear that it occurs outside marriage, in a relationship that will only be consummated after death. This world offers only the disappointment of conventional marriage. In poem #472, for example, instead of achieving bliss, amidst her hopes that she, despite her ignorance, will be worthy of this state, she is denied all her hopes:

> But just to hear the Grace depart—
> I never thought to see—
> Afflicts me with a Double loss—
> 'Tis lost—And lost to me—

In poem #473, there are echoes of poem #493 in that here, too, is an unworthy bride:

> I am ashamed—I hide—
> What right have I—to be a Bride—
> So late a Dowerless Girl—

A series of images are then added which stress not only her unworthiness for marriage, but also her lack of a mentor to instruct her how to behave or to array herself as she ought. Whatever her hopes for marriage, they involved something so different, she despaired of finding anyone to teach her "that new Grace–." She is the orphan child shut out of a world of riches, the foreigner, the refugee. But again, when she is exalted, she is exalted like a man. She hopes for "Skill–to hold my Brow like an Earl–."

In poem #322, again her bliss is snatched from her at the last minute. But in this poem, we get a glimpse of what might have happened and where the ideal union might take place:

> Each was to each the Sealed Church
> Permitted to commune this–time–
> Lest we too awkward show
> At Supper of the Lamb

These two are ultimately isolated from each other, with two different futures, "So faces on two Decks, look back / Bound to opposing lands–." However, they are allowed to commune once within time's boundaries as practice for what they will be allowed to do outside of time, "At Supper of the Lamb." This will be allowed after life because

> Each bound the Other's Crucifix–
> We gave no other Bond
> Sufficient troth, that we shall rise–
> Deposed–at length, the Grave–
> To that new Marriage
> Justified–through Calvaries of Love–

Within their lifetimes, they are bound only to each one's separate misery. "Communing" is not possible within this life. Poem #1072 which begins, "Title divine–is mine! / The Wife–without the Sign!" is a further elaboration on the images raised in poem #199, in which the married woman is "Czar," absolutely separated from the life of mere "Girls." In #1072, the speaker is also "Royal–all but the Crown!" and is, in fact, "Empress of Calvary!" Again, she contrasts her state with that of "women" in what seems like sarcastic tones:

> Born–Bridalled–Shrouded–
> In a Day–

> "My Husband"—women say—
> Stroking the Melody—
> Is *this*—the way?

This trilogy of victories recalls the advice to young women of the period, that the only times a lady had her name in print was when she was born, married, and died. The last three lines emphasize Emily Dickinson's difference from the truly married and can be read variously as envious imitation of married women's security, or as sarcastic imitation of the smug matron.

Poem #1737 does not have a date assigned to it in Johnson's edition of the collected poems. Its theme and many of the images make it a compendium of Emily Dickinson's concerns about marriage. It begins with the theme of the wife who is not a wife: "Rearrange a 'Wife's' affection!" However, this "wife" is truer than the merely married. Her affection will only be rearranged

> When they dislocate my Brain!
> Amputate my freckled Bosom!
> Make me bearded like a man!

These lines not only emphasize her constancy but also imply that if she were to be untrue, she would be a man. "Freckled Bosom" recalls the lines in poem #401 which satirized the "Gentlewomen" of her day:

> Such Dimity Convictions—
> A Horror so refined
> Of freckled Human Nature—

The next stanza of poem #1737 emphasizes her "unacknowledged" state and concludes with "Seven years of troth have taught thee / More than Wifehood ever may!"—an explicit statement about the superiority of love outside of marriage. Interestingly, the point is made by having the speaker take on the role of Jacob who labored seven years for Leah and seven years for Rachel.

The next four stanzas place the narrator in a Christlike role that recalls the Empress of Calvary motif of previous poems. "For I wear the 'Thorns' till *Sunset* / Then—my Diadem put on." In this poem, as in the others in this group, love in this life is only possible through Christlike or heroic suffering on the part of the woman.

The androgynous hero of poem #1737 takes on more ambiguous

characteristics in poem #631, "Ourselves were wed one summer–dear–" with its first pronoun which does not resolve whether these two were "wed" to each other or to other people at the same time. The rest of the poem recalls poem #322, "There came a Day at Summer's full," in that this wedding also occurs in June. But from that event on, the two people are destined to opposite fates:

> 'Tis true–Our Futures different lay–
> Your Cottage–faced the Sun–
> While Oceans–and the North must be
> On every side of mine

However, the participants in this drama are not male heroes or Christlike figures, but earthly royalty, "And yet, one Summer, we were Queens– / But You–were crowned in June–."

This is not the only time Emily Dickinson plays with changes in gender roles. In poem #494, Versions I and II, she wrote the same love poem from the perspective of different genders. She further experimented with gender changes for marriage partners in poem #518,

> Her sweet Weight on my Heart a Night
> Had scarcely deigned to lie–
> When, stirring, for Belief's delight
> My Bride had slipped away–

In none of the poems explicitly concerned with marriage as opposed to love does Emily Dickinson present a view of marriage as bliss for the dependent woman. Rather, there is a critique of life within marriage, of the contractual terms in which marriage is conceived, and a desire for true equality and balance, if only through suffering and experimentation with the boundaries that divide men from women. If so many of her poems express longing for true communion that cannot be fulfilled, this reflects a system of beliefs which held that men and women were as separate as the magnetic poles of the earth. While some of her critiques of marriage use the reformers' views of the death-in-life marriage brought to Victorian women, others go beyond criticism to an imaginative longing for an end to the sealed lives of men and women.

Sometime in 1858, Dickinson wrote poems #10, #22, #49, and #54 which are part of a sequence of poems concerning risk, loss, death–not uncommon themes. Many of the poems of this year use natural images such as the death and rebirth of the seasons. These were familiar to her contemporaries. However, with characteristic boldness, Emily Dickinson transformed these conventional images. With irony, she added not only exotic symbols for gain and loss such as gold, foreign coins, and jewels, but also images well understood by those of her time—looms, salaries, stocks, and dividends. She placed herself in relationship to these images exactly where all women of her class and time were—passively observing or being acted upon, never the agent manipulating these new, powerful symbols. The active and often denying agents in the poems are "gentlemen" or "Gentlemen," "brokers" or "Brokers," "Bankers," "Burglars," and—"Fathers."

For example, Dickinson's poem #10 (1858) employs imagery from the textile mills to reflect metaphorically on one's narrow choices in life. The speaker's life is as meaningless, routine, and painful as that of the textile worker who operates her "wheel" in the "dark":

> My wheel is in the dark!
> I cannot see a spoke
> Yet know it's dripping feet
> Go round and round.

The speaker then muses, "Some have resigned the Loom—" while others, without alternatives, still "find quaint employ" in the "busy tomb," a reference to the tomblike quality of the mills themselves. Others, who die, pass "royal thro' the gate—" and fling "the problem back / At you and I!" In historical context, the "problem" is meaningful work for women. The speaker, a poet, has her foot, not on a wheel, but on "the Tide! / An unfrequented road—." Though riding "the Tide" may be less tedious than working "a wheel," it is just another lonely "Road." She hopes "all roads" have a "clearing in the end."

The first Dickinson poem which introduces the cast of patriarchal characters held responsible for the robberies of capitalism is #22, "All these my banners be—" a poem concerned with the contrast between earthly spring and eternal life. In eternity, "The Burglar cannot rob—then / The Broker cannot cheat," an interesting contemporary comment on the folly of laying up treasure on earth, one in which the facilitator of capitalist development is equated with a thief.

These are not common thieves, but capitalized "Crooks," the significance of which is explained in the next poem in the sequence. Poem #49, "I never lost as much but twice," identifies the "Burglar" in such a way that intensifies the absurdity of storing up earthly treasure, even the treasure of earthly love. The poet evidently fears metaphysical crooks, but she continues by linking burglarhood to more respectable male roles. In a trinity which must have outraged her Congregationalist neighbors, she names the three aspects of God as "Burglar, Banker, Father." She approaches this trinity only as a humble supplicant, "Twice have I stood a beggar." As in the war poems, she is outside the action, outside the door.

This sense of exclusion is intensified in poem #54, probably her most satirical comment on the contrast between human and business concerns. In this poem she paints a frenetic pastoral in which bees, birds, commerce, and trade dance in staccato rhythm completely oblivious to her death.

> If I should die,
> And you should live—
> And time sh'd gurgle on—
> And morn sh'd beam—
> And noon should burn—
> As it has usual done—
> If Birds should build as early
> And Bees as bustling go—
> One might depart at option
> From enterprise below!
> Tis sweet to know that stocks will stand
> When we with Daisies lie—
> That Commerce will continue—
> And Trades as briskly fly—
> It makes the parting tranquil
> And keeps the soul serene—
> That gentlemen so sprightly
> Conduct the pleasing scene!

The poem consists of two parts, with the first ten lines providing a cynical look at the triviality of one life placed against the teeming life of nature. The choice of such phrases as "And time sh'd *gurgle* on— / And morn sh'd *beam*" certainly remove it from the category of a sentimental nature poem. The two lines which end this section culminate in an exclamation point and provide one possible ending for a restatement of this old cliché. However, the words "option" and "enterprise" acquire a different, more somber meaning, as these two lines function both as an end to the first, lighter section of the poem and an introduction to the second half.

In this eight-line section, nature imagery is replaced by the vocabulary of the world of business, an arena in which her father and brother moved freely and in which she, had she been a boy, would have been expected to move with the same ease. In this section, "Commerce" and "Trade" are capitalized in a mirror of the "Birds" and "Bees" of the first section. "Daisies" are where "we" lie, tranquil and serene, while "gentlemen so sprightly," like some kind of wind-up toys run amuck, "conduct the pleasing scene!"

Who are these "gentlemen" directing this manic, mechanized diorama, undiminished by the loss of human life? Unlike the "Burglars" and "Bankers" of the earlier poems, they are uncapitalized, uncelestial, earthy–and as indifferent to the narrator of the poem as the foreign world of nature. Again, the poet, who is too honest for sentimentality and too aware of her position as a woman to comfort herself with the recompense of the separate sphere, writes of having no place, neither raw nature, nor overcooked Victorian mercantile culture in which to live or die.

Again in poem #112 (1859), we meet "Gentlemen," not "sprightly" this time, but nimble, and though they are capitalized "Gentlemen," having left the earthly dross, they are no longer in charge. Indeed, they are forced to keep their rooms. Other items Emily Dickinson felt she had no power over are also kept in check in this vision of paradise. One, the bells, is repeated as a threat. In the first line, in this heaven, bells can no more "affright the morn–." In the last two lines, neither "Father's bells–nor Factories, / Could scare us any more!" Therefore, the first stanza includes both "bells" and "Gentlemen," while in the next to last line, the bells are clearly the "Father's." The "Factories"–an odd choice of word for a simple country girl–are also linked to these bells. Only in heaven will these images of mortality lose their power, when the poet is protected by the certainty of immortality and a protective father, the "Pater" of line eight, to whom the poet will appear again as a supplicant.

This poem appears in a cluster which are speculations on immortality. Emily Dickinson is commonly praised for her interesting and fresh wedding of uncommon images to renew poetic conventions. But why would she have chosen these particular images which seem, at first glance, to be hopelessly jumbled? The system described in this poem, a web of terror and longing, leaves the supplicant begging from the very person she is tormented by, a supreme paternalistic being who, as in the earlier poem, gives and takes away.

As Herbert Gutman has pointed out in his work on early American industrialization, one of the hardest tasks for factory owners and foremen was to accustom rural workers to measured time, time demarcated not by their own sense of what the job took but by bells, factory bells, Father's bells.[28] Although Emily Dickinson is an unlikely commentator on manufactured time, it is clear from other evidence, such as Samuel Bowles' comment on her agricultural knowledge, that she was interested in more than her male acquaintances supposed.[29] More to the point, she is clearly interested in portraying a changed landscape in which she has no control and in which the images of the new technology stand for death.

These poems are early works written during 1858-1859. They are also not among her more popular works. All of them link aspects of modern male power positions–brokers, bankers, factory owners–with God-like qualities, excluding the feminine narrator who then has refuge only in sarcasm (poems #22 and #54) or supplication (poems #10, #49 and #112) in order to present her concerns in these dramas of the masculine sphere. Now, consider a later and much more famous poem, #585, written in 1862.

The train described in this poem certainly had personal meaning for Emily Dickinson since it was her father who brought the railroad to Amherst. Dickinson associated the concept of power with fathers. Asserting herself in relation to this power, Dickinson expressed ambivalence, questioning, and fear in her letters. Dickinson's letter to her brother Austin, for example, about the completion of the Amherst and Belchertown Railroad in 1853 shows her recoiling before her father who was largely responsible for the enterprise. "Father" is as "usual, Chief Marshal of the day"; but Emily watched the event from "Prof. Tyler's woods and saw the train move off, and then ran home again for fear somebody would see" her "or ask how she did."[30]

Instead of going to the ceremonies, she wrote this commemorative poem to a monster:

> I like to see it lap the Miles–
> And lick the Valleys up–
> And stop to feed itself at Tanks–
> And then–prodigious step
>
> Around a Pile of Mountains–
> And supercilious peer
> In Shanties–by the sides of Roads–
> And then a Quarry pare
>
> To fit it's sides
> And crawl between
> Complaining all the while
> In horrid–hooting stanza–
> Then chase itself down Hill–

And neigh like Boanerges–
Then–prompter than a Star
Stop–docile and omnipotent
At its own stable door–

Emily Dickinson chose to describe the onslaught of the train's presence on her countryside by mixing mechanized and natural images in an attempt to accommodate this new phenomenon to her imagination. In a similar vein, in poem #54, she replaced "Birds" and "Bees" with "Commerce" and "Trades." Therefore, this new creature, reassuringly, crawls and hoots. If it neighs like tumult, at least it neighs, has a stable, and its unnatural exactitude can be compared to a "Star."

However, the overall impression is much more sinister. Surpassing her contemporary, Emerson's remark, "Things are in the saddle and ride mankind," she has constructed a scene in which people are superfluous and so, absent. This juggernaut doesn't need human aid as it devours the landscape, so that now both time and space are altered. It may peer supercilious in "Shanties," but no one is in them. No one needs to be, for the immigrant Irish who would have inhabited them are not needed to dig the railroad bed. It does this for itself. Well it might, for, in a teaming of opposites that perfectly describes machine servants, it is docile *and* omnipotent.

This is far from, say, Whitman's vision of the new industrial age. It is no celebration of possibility. Instead, a profound sense of unease, of powers about to run amuck, hovers about this poem. Certainly, the speaker feels little sense of control.

Is this another way of expressing the old saw about women's conservative position on innovation? In light of what we now understand about the consequences of industrialization, it would be naive to pose this as an either/or question. What emerges most powerfully from these poems is a sense of displacement and accommodation. Emily Dickinson never asks for a return to an imaginary golden age. She simply describes, not events, but her relationship to these events. In all these poems, intermediaries, mechanized or monied, have replaced more natural relationships and have placed the woman who writes of these changes in an increasingly irrelevant position. She is not without status; though, as with most women of her time, it is a borrowed vision, dependent on the status of her male relations. With this borrowed eye, an upper-middle-class one, she sees "Bankers" and "Brokers," but not Irish laborers. Since she is the recipient of advantages of this system, but permitted to have no share in deciding its shape, she permits herself the luxury of subjectivity. Through exploring the nature of the changes effected in her by external change, she has the ability to express a sense of the profound alterations in control and participation going on around her.

We have seen in this chapter that Dickinson's and Rossetti's poems on industrialization are integrally tied to the themes of women's displacement, their economic devaluation, and their relegation to superfluous roles in the home. Women's declining value in the workplace affected their position in the home, as marriage for women became a "series of dissolving views" or contractual arrangements whereby women are "insolvent every noon." Love and romance are overshadowed by sexual commerce and trade, and women are either "dimity" ladies or outcast whores. These themes not only inspired some of Dickinson's and Rossetti's best known masterpieces; they have pointed us to unfamiliar poems of marked strength.

We now move to Dickinson's and Rossetti's poems on women's nature which include their most spiritually probing pieces. Struggling with the question of women's essential nature, they confronted the dominant view that women writers, and especially women poets, were contradictions in terms.

Chapter 7

Women's Place/Women's Nature

As economic power increasingly solidified in male hands following the Industrial Revolution, and women were increasingly deprived of opportunities for independent living, feminist reformers claimed moral superiority for women to justify the separate spheres to which women were being relegated. These separate spheres offered women opportunities for intellectual and spiritual development and meaningful work not provided by the larger society.

The ideology of women's spheres came to the fore during the period we have been examining in England and America, the 1850s and 1860s. Acknowledging this fact, Tillie Olsen reclaimed the term "the feminine fifties" by stressing women's real advances.[1] Not only had feminists drawn attention to women's rights, but women writers, especially novelists, gained a space in the male-dominated literary world and created a new field of women's literature. In England and America, new women poets were also being sought by publishing houses and by leading journals.[2] At the same time, the principle of association generally became popular among liberal, middle-class women.[3] This principle motivated the professional association of female teachers, nurses, social workers, religious reformers, and feminist activists.

The dominant view held by society was that women's moral superiority should be used to save male culture from the evils of industrialism. If women led men to higher ways of living, this was according to God's plan. But if women led themselves to higher, cerebral ways of living, they were suspect. Women were, thus, supposed to be morally superior but intellectually inferior. Developing women's intellect was considered unnatural and perverse. The contradiction that surfaced for Dickinson and Rossetti in later life was a version of this dilemma: In becoming women poets and developing their intellectual selves to the fullest, had they disobeyed the omnipotent, patriarchal God? In the following sections, we explore each poet's answer to this problem according to how each one reconciled her nature as a woman with God's plan.

EMILY DICKINSON

Emily Dickinson felt herself to be very different from and sometimes better than most people, and she resisted outside definitions of herself, but at the price of intense isolation. What she seemed intent upon, through her poetic conversations with herself as primary audience, was a perfection of herself and an understanding of the ultimate authority of her being. In the process of this self-definition, her relationship to the definition of *women* played an essential part. According to her day, as well as to our own, she had first to confront herself through her sex. If she did not feel she fit the accepted mode of womanhood, she was willing to strike out on the icy frontiers of possibility! "I dwell in Possibility–" she wrote in 1862 (#657), the year she attempted to start her independent, unwomanly career as poet.

Many women probably dwelt in possibility. There is reason to believe Sue Gilbert Dickinson tried to evade the trap of *womanhood*, but she was not ready to pay Emily Dickinson's price. But of all the women who may have rebelled against their fetters, few left records Emily Dickinson found acceptable. Generally, she found herself offered two alternatives that were actually not alternatives for her.

Women's reproductive abilities almost completely defined the lives of women in the mid-nineteenth century. In response to a strong educational movement for women, conservatives promoted the ideology that studying and other intellectual pursuits robbed energy from women's wombs. Women's pubescent years were to be spent resting, eating bland foods, and thinking bland thoughts in an effort to "regulate their menses" in preparation for their lives as breeding animals.[4]

Women could only hope to have influence, as opposed to power, through their status as mothers, or at least as wives. To live outside the married state, as a spinster, was in some ways like being an outlaw, in the sense that wives were becoming increasingly protected by a series of Married Women's Property Acts beginning in 1839, but spinsters remained outside these legal gains.[5] Not to marry generally meant being perpetually without even a household of one's own to rule, to be always within the power of father or brothers. If a woman chose not to marry or was not chosen, she faced a future without status. The old maid was a scary, perpetual joke. However, for writing poetry, Dickinson found the daughter/spinster life less oppressive than the wife's.

Women such as Catherine Beecher and Mary Lyon postulated a solution for those who did not secure a wife's status–the only position really considered acceptable. They postulated the same set of characteristics for women that men did–pure, sexless, nobler than men in their moral standards– and they proposed to send these qualities into the world beyond the home to "civilize" male areas. Roles such as nurses or teachers of girls and the working-class were thought to be particularly appropriate for women, though opposition to women engaged in social work or some forms of teaching came when men either perceived women as a direct threat to their own jobs or as interfering with accepted public freedoms.[6]

Although Catherine Beecher and others argued that women might be most useful extending their maternal capabilities into the male spheres of commerce and western colonization, men, who had been upholding women as a great power for good, suddenly discovered that they wanted no part of that "good"–reforming schoolmarms interfering in the code of the west–in their happily wicked male domains. What most of the women who wanted to extend women's sphere had in common with one another was the belief that women were different from men, but that their difference gave them a special role in the larger society.

For a middle-class New England woman of Emily Dickinson's time, then, there were these two choices, both of which had at their basis the same fundamental view of woman's nature: She could either compete successfully in the marriage market or she could become a woman of good works. In either case, she would be an angel, whether in the house or in society-at-large.

As women of the day were helping make the church over in a fashion more suited to their needs, women in Emily Dickinson's poetry and letters emerged as both friends and enemies. Dickinson both does and does not want a "special place" sanctified for womanly virtue.

In remaining unpublished, whether choosing this or having it chosen for her, Emily Dickinson was able to argue with God, as we shall see in poems we discuss further on, more thoroughly than the women whose poetry was popular in the day. Published poetry for the most part echoed male sentiment. However, poem after poem by Emily Dickinson does not come to a pious conclusion. On the other hand, Emily Dickinson–as well as her more accepted sisters–considers how women are to fit into the kingdom of Heaven.

One tactic of the women within the various churches of England and

America was to make the Christian church live up to much of its rhetoric, particularly its rhetoric of meekness and poverty. Who could better know the life of the meek and the poor than women; for no matter what their husbands' standing, few women themselves possessed property. As for meekness, it, along with self-sacrificing love, were considered generic women's traits. Much of Emily Dickinson's poetry may be seen as an attempt, not always successful, to accommodate this approach to religion. With their echoes of Christina Rossetti's poems on the "lowest" room or "lowest" place, several of Dickinson's poems assimilate conventional religious attitudes in this way (#79, #486, and #964, for example), with #486 probably being the most frequently anthologized:

> I was the slightest in the House–
> I took the smallest Room–
> At night, my little Lamp, and Book–
> And one Geranium
>
> . . . .
>
> I never spoke–unless addressed–
> And then, 'twas brief and low–
> I could not bear to live–aloud–
> The Racket shamed me so–

In short, Dickinson exalts her poverty of person, both in her pride at small stature and her identification with small, unnoticed, weak objects.

Along with the renunciation of earthly power, and control, goes the renunciation of physical pleasure–very *explicit* physical pleasure. Poems #211 and #213 are tributes to abstinence and link again with such poems on heavenly, fleshless marriage as poem #625;

> Come slowly–Eden!
> Lips unused to Thee–
> Bashful–sip thy Jessamines–
> As the fainting Bee–
> Reaching late his flower,
> Round her chamber hums–
> Counts his nectars–
> Enters–and is lost in Balms.
>
> #211

Did the Harebell loose her girdle
To the lover Bee
Would the Bee the Harebell *hallow*
Much as formerly?

Did the "Paradise"—persuaded—
Yield her moat of pearl—
Would the Eden *be* an Eden,
Or the Earl—an *Earl?*

#213

'Twas a long Parting—but the time
For Interview—had Come—
Before the Judgment Seat of God—
The last—and second time

These Fleshless Lovers met—
A Heaven in a Gaze—
A Heaven of Heavens—the Privilege
Of one another's Eyes—

. . . .

Was Bridal—e'er like This?
A Paradise—the Host—
And Cherubim—and Seraphim—
The unobtrusive Guest—

#625

But there is another strain to this poetry which subverts the more conventional Christian morality, and that is the passionate and direct desire for ultimate power and reward. Almost superstitiously, women give up lesser prizes to attain greater triumph. Emily Dickinson addresses the rewards of such renunciation as well as the texture of the task of renunciation. Unlike the approved sentiment of the day, her expression in poem #528, for example, sends forth a triumphant trumpet blast of the rewards, couched in very earthly metaphors of power:

Mine—by the Right of the White Election!
Mine—by the Royal Seal!
Mine—by the Sign in the Scarlet prison—

Bars—cannot conceal!

Mine—there—in Vision—and in Veto!
Mine—by the Grave's Repeal—
Titled—Confirmed—
Delirious Charter!
Mine—along as Ages steal!

In answer to the poems of physical renunciation, poem #508 exalts the passion and power which follow death and, in its coy ending, gives us a glimpse of a place in which women may choose freely to be themselves first:

I'm ceded—I've stopped being Theirs—
The name They dropped upon my face
With water, in the country church
Is finished using now,
And They can put it with my Dolls,
My childhood, and the string of spools,
I've finished threading—too—

Baptized, before, without the choice,
But this time, consciously, of Grace—
Unto supremest name—
Called to my Full—The Crescent dropped—
Existence's whole Arc, filled up,
With one small Diadem.

My second Rank—too small the first—
Crowned—Crowing—on my Father's breast—
A Half unconscious Queen—
But this time—Adequate—Erect,
With Will to choose, or to reject,
And I choose, just a Crown—

These explicit fantasies of power would have been terrifying to male publishers and to women poets who found acceptance in the male world of writing by safely disguising or suppressing such longings. Indeed, Dickinson's closing line echoes Rossetti's closing in Sonnet 27 from "Later Life: A Double Sonnet of Sonnets": "While I supine with ears that cease to hear. . . / May miss the goal at last, may miss a crown." While Rossetti rather surprisingly expresses fear she will miss the crown,

Dickinson at the time of death boldly chooses it.

It is Dickinson's unease with the accepted women's way of dealing with passion and desire that may have led her to write poem #401.   Clearly she saw at least some other women as refusing to welcome any but the most ladylike religious, as well as earthly, experience.   And again, Emily Dickinson explores the conjunction of these two realms:

> What Soft—Cherubic Creatures—
> These Gentlewomen are—
> One would as soon assault a Plush—
> Or violate a Star—
>
> Such Dimity Convictions—
> A Horror so refined
> Of freckled Human Nature—
> Of Deity—ashamed—
>
> It's such a common—Glory—
> A Fisherman's—Degree—
> Redemption—Brittle Lady—
> Be so—ashamed of Thee—

For educated women, there was another choice, but it was a more threatening one to most people, men and women.   It was the choice of Margaret Fuller and other women intellectuals and professionals, the choice to compete with men on men's territory, especially the territory of the mind.   Though Margaret Fuller said in response to a question about what women should be allowed to become, "Let them become sea captains if they will," very few women were interested in becoming sea captains.[7]   There were many New England women, however, who, like Margaret Fuller, were interested in rigorous training in literature, science, languages, and philosophy and who were willing to defy convention and ridicule.

There were many examples of this type of woman to make possible a composite portrait, included in a memoir of Samuel Bowles by George Merriam:

> His closest intimacies were with women of a
> characteristic New England type. . . . fine intellect,
> an unsparing conscience, and a sensitive nervous
> organization; whose minds have a natural bent toward
> the problems of the soul and the universe; whose

energies, lacking the outlet which business and public
affairs give to their brothers, are constantly turned
back upon the interior life, and who are at once
stimulated and limited by a social environment which is
serious, virtuous, and deficient in gayety and
amusement. There is naturally developed in them high
mental power, and almost morbid conscientiousness,
while, especially in the many cases where they remain
unmarried, their fervor and charm of womanhood are
refined and sublimated from personal objects and
devoted to abstractions and ideals. They are platonic
in their attachments and speculative in their religion;
intense rather than tender, and not so much soothing as
stimulating.[8]

This rendering, with its emphasis on the pathological and the "natural,"
was probably intended to limn Maria Whitney, Bowles' closest friend, who
was at one time instructor of languages at Smith College. But it could
equally well have been intended for Emily Dickinson, particularly as she
was presented to her reading public for the first time after her death,
whereas Whitney was, according to Sewall, "well-traveled, scholarly" and
"cosmopolitan," hardly as "circumscribed" as Dickinson.[9] The
condescension drips from this piece in which every sentence emphasizes
the perversity of such women, a perversity which is out of their control,
since it is an innate characteristic.

The rendering makes understandable the hesitation of most women to
overstep their "natural" bounds, for when they did, as feminist lecturers,
for example, they found they elicited the anger of threatened males, like
John R. Clark, cited by Walker, who wrote for *Godey's Lady's Book*:

Oh, that women would be true to themselves, and
consider the exalted position they occupy! Consider
how far it transcends that of men! What an influence
they possess in controlling popular will! Then they
will not stoop to mingle in the strifes and petty
jealousies that clamor so loudly for "Women's Rights";
but, from their high station, frown upon everything so
repugnant to a high-minded and true-hearted woman.[10]

In light of such comments, the courage of feminists who did speak out
becomes much more clear, women like Elizabeth Oakes-Smith, who became a

lyceum lecturer after establishing her reputation as a poet.[11]

The perversity of Bowles' ideal woman also makes Emily Dickinson's decision to withdraw from conservative Amherst more understandable. She would not be defined by any man's desires. One quality, for example, which Bowles' imaginary bluestocking does not possess, which Emily Dickinson had in abundance, is humor. Of course, the strategy of stereotyping the intellectual woman as humorless has not lost its appeal or its effectiveness. Any woman, whether burdened with a "sensitive nervous organization" or not, thinks twice before becoming a figure of ridicule in public. One technique for maintaining one's right to levity may have been Sue Gilbert's—become a trend-setter, a securely married social climber, who reserves the ability to be brilliant at home. The other response is to construct one's own world at home, Dickinson's strategy, described by Adrienne Rich: "It was a life deliberately organized on her terms."[12]

What kind of world did she construct and organize from the privacy and control of home? If Emily Dickinson believed the unflattering portraits of her fellow American intellectuals, if she felt that within easy reach there was no one who could understand her, she could take as her models women she never saw, never would see. England had women poets who took the task of being a poet or a woman of letters seriously. In Emily Dickinson's room were the portraits of George Eliot and Elizabeth Barrett Browning. One poem specifically mentions Charlotte Brontë, but uses her androgynous pen name, Currer Bell. Dickinson read widely and, from our vantage point, somewhat indiscriminately. Her letters are larded with references to conventional women's poetry of the time. We have always assumed she did not *want* to write the conventional way; could she have felt unable to write this way? More than in any other terms, she defined herself as an admirer of poets. When she was revising "Safe in their Alabaster Chambers," she wrote to Sue, "Could I make you and Austin–proud–sometime–a great way off–'twould give me taller feet–."[13] Three poems from 1862 (#448, #544, and #569) and one poem from 1864 (#883) all define poets as those who encompass larger wholes than ordinary people. However, in none of these poems does she identify herself as a poet. Her pronouns are either "he," "they," "their," or "them." Where she places herself is in poem #250 (1861) as a singer, or in poem #505 (1862) as one who would *not* be a poet, though significantly, she places poet last in the list of artists she would not be.

Cheryl Walker makes the point that Dickinson followed many women poets who promoted their careers by associating with male literary leaders. "It was to Thomas Wentworth Higginson that Emily Dickinson thought to turn in 1862, rather than a woman poet or editor."[14] However, in this case, the more important points seem to be that despite Dickinson's misguided pursuit of Higginson, several key women pushed her career during her lifetime, and women created her public reputation after her death. Sewall, for example, acknowledged that Dickinson's pursuit of Higginson's approval was undeniably a mistake on her part: "Several times in her life Emily Dickinson showed poor judgment. She encouraged Austin's courtship of Sue, she sought literary help from Thomas Wentworth Higginson, and she tried to inject herself into the busy, utterly committed, and domestically complicated life of Samuel Bowles."[15]

The key women begin with Dickinson's actual sister Lavinia who, while omitted from the Emily-Austin dyad, nevertheless was a lifetime, loyal companion. Her friendship may have obviated Emily's need to seek friends elsewhere. In the most explicit of Emily's poems on sisterhood, #14 written in 1858, Emily described her sister possessively yet lovingly: "One Sister have I in our House"; she "came the road that I came– / And wore my last year's gown–." Lavinia saved Emily's poems and was the consistent force behind having them published.

Poem #14 extends the sisterhood to the sister-in-law, Sue Gilbert Dickinson, who "as a bird her nest, / Builded our hearts among." Dickinson asserts that she owns this sister too, "both belong to me;" and, in fact, she claims she has even selected her specially:

> I chose this single star
> From out the wide night's numbers–
> Sue–Forevermore!

A paean to Sue, to sisterhood, this poem was written when, according to Rebecca Patterson, Emily was just recovering from a "glum period" of four to five years that resulted after Sue and Austin married. However, it is also clear that Emily desired their marriage. As we have seen, their marriage was one way for Emily to have Sue permanently "belong" to her. Recall the intense letters Emily exchanged with Sue. Patterson commented: "Emily was left miserable without quite knowing why." However, "in late 1858," Rebecca Patterson continued,

> her sister-in-law introduced her to Elizabeth
> Browning's *Aurora Leigh*, a verse-novel about a
> successful woman poet, and this book revived her
> ambition and helped carry her poetry in a swelling
> triumph that crested in 1862-1863. Quite early in
> January 1859 an old school friend of Sue's, the

beautiful young widow Kate Scott Turner, began a first
visit which lasted two months and was followed by
several other visits over the next two years. Since
Kate was a lover of poetry and quite ready to fall in
love with Emily's, her admiration was another powerful
support.[16]

In her book *The Riddle of Emily Dickinson*, Patterson explored with more
depth the thesis that Emily Dickinson loved and was later rejected by Kate
Scott Anthon.[17]   Emily also felt rejected by Sue due to Sue's turbulent
relationship with Austin.   Emily sided with Austin in their fights over
Austin's affair with Mabel Loomis Todd, and, perhaps as a consequence, Sue
did not follow through on the publication of Emily's poems.   Why did
Austin's lover, Mabel Loomis Todd, commit herself to publishing Emily's
poems? Impressed by their quality, and perhaps fueled by the feud with
Sue, she remained true to a kind of literary sisterhood with Emily.

The theme of sisterhood elicited Dickinson's image of nature as
loving, transcendent, and bountiful. In the same year as poem #14, Emily
wrote another paean to sisterhood, #18. In this poem, summer is described
at season's end. The death of summer brings an ascension of spirit to the
poet's mind, and summer, portrayed as a dying "sister," becomes the
speaker's link between the natural and spiritual worlds:

> The Gentian weaves her fringes–
> The Maple's loom is red–
> My departing blossoms
>   Obviate parade.
> A brief, but patient illness–
> An hour to prepare,
> And one below this morning
> Is where angels are–
> It was a short procession,
> The Bobolink was there–
> An aged Bee addressed us–
> And then we knelt in prayer–
> We trust that she was willing–
> We ask that we may be.
> Summer–Sister–Seraph!
> Let us go with thee!

When nature and spirit are imaged as female and joined in "sisterhood," as in poem #18, Dickinson's "supposed person" expresses faith in the redemptive powers of the spiritual realm. However, when a patriarchal God is imaged as the arbiter, the delicate balance between nature and spirit is upset.

In echoes of that other female enfant terrible, Emily Brontë's Catherine Earnshaw, Dickinson extols the superiority of earth to a patriarchal heaven where "Father" is missing. She raises the possibility of Paradise not being enough, or at least not being suited to human life. This theme runs through poem #215, for example:

> What is-"Paradise"-
> Who live there-
> Are they "Farmers"-
> Do they "hoe"-
> Do they know that this is "Amherst"-
> And that I-am coming-too-
>
> . . . .
>
> You are sure there's such a person
> As "a Father"-in the sky-

This suspicion of the inadequacy of heaven opens a corollary worry. Is God adequate? Emily Dickinson first wrestled with the question of the size of God by paraphrasing a troublesome Bible story. In poem #59, the story of Jacob wrestling with the angel, the last two lines pose an interesting problem: "And the bewildered Gymnast / Found he had worsted God!" What kind of a God can be "worsted"? Beginning with this inquiry in 1859, Emily Dickinson wrote several poems that show her concern with God's adequacy, on a number of levels.

One of the dimensions of Dickinson's concern is the adequacy of God's compassion. Will God relieve distress? Is Jesus able to relieve distress? Poem #217 asks this question anxiously. In answer, poem #376, with its bird metaphor which calls up images of unheeded falling sparrows, seems to say "No," God is not compassionate. This poem, like many Dickinson poems, paints the picture of a bleak, deistic universe that uncaringly spins its way. It is more often Jesus, not God, who comprehends the female world of agony, particularly the agony of love denied or relationships sundered by death, again caused by God. This splitting of the aspects of God, in which Jesus becomes the powerless sufferer, fits well with a theology that assigns these feminine qualities to part of the Trinity. The "inhuman deist" of Harvard would have offered little to a woman intent on relief from women's suffering.

This "inhuman deist" is the God whom scientists such as Edward Hitchcock of Amherst were trying to assimilate with their new knowledge, but this God seemed foreign to the needs of Emily Dickinson. Could science threaten God himself? Was he strong enough to withstand it? Again, though she wrestled with the problem, she did not pretend it could be dismissed with pious exclamations. She treated it, instead, with humor in poems #70 and #168, or again, she mocked the savants' lack of trust in #185:

> "Faith" is a fine invention
> When Gentlemen can *see*—
> But *Microscopes* are prudent
> In an Emergency.

In defining her nature as a woman, Emily Dickinson struggled to find higher authority for the development of her intellectual and spiritual self. The bifurcated God/Jesus offered some solution, but to the end of the poems, Emily Dickinson is still questioning. She is expanding, but never serene. Her "Faith," in poem #1442 (1878), is "tattered," but she believes there "is a needle fair" to "mend" it. Again, she is able to achieve faith in the moral correctness of her controversial career when the agent of redemption is conceived as female, in this case a simple seamstress:

> To mend each tattered Faith
> There is a needle fair
> Though no appearance indicate—
> 'Tis threaded in the Air—
>
> And though it do not wear
> As if it never Tore
> 'Tis very comfortable indeed
> And spacious as before—

CHRISTINA ROSSETTI

Sisterhood was also Rossetti's way of linking the spiritual and social worlds. Themes of sisterhood abound in Rossetti's poetry during the 1850s and 1860s. They not only reflect her relationship to her mother, older sister, and female relatives and friends; they also express her assimilation of theoretical and political issues surrounding the development of all-female associations, such as the friendly societies, the charity schools, secondary schools, and colleges for women, and the Anglican Sisterhoods.

In 1965, Winston Weathers' article "The Sisterhood of Self" explored Rossetti's poems of sisterhood in Jungian terms. Weathers portrayed the sisters in Rossetti's poetry as conflicting aspects of her own personality—Dionysian and Apollonian elements—dividing her from herself.[18] But sisterhood is a social, historical, and literary as well as psychological and mythical metaphor in Rossetti's poetry, especially in her twenties and thirties when she was caught between the radical and the domestic feminist movements. On the one hand, she was active as a social worker and nurse in the evangelical, domestic reform movement which developed through exclusively female friendly societies and sisterhoods. In attempting to "reform" the poor, domestic feminists were proving their womanly capacity to be charitable, and they used their spiritual superiority to justify the idea of separate, more sanctified work for women. They did not challenge the division of the spheres by gender or initiate parliamentary reform.

Dante Gabriel encouraged Christina to focus less on her "legitimate exercise of anguish," and to take a more active role in the radical movement which was being led by Barbara Leigh Smith and Bessie Rayner Parkes.[19] Christina became acquainted with these feminist leaders. In contrast to the politics of renunciation and discipline developed by the sisterhoods, the radicals represented a platform of natural rights and privileges for women in a world where women had access to both public and private spheres.

The issue of how best to effect change for women was a concern of Rossetti's as early as 1851 when she worked in a day-school. In the poem "A Fair World Though Fallen" (1851), it is as if Rossetti's speaker is answering Dante Gabriel's criticisms:

> You tell me that the world is fair,
>   in spite
> Of the old Fall; and that I
>   should not turn
> So to the grave, and let my spirit
>   yearn
> After the quiet of the long last
>   night.
> Have I then shut mine eyes against

the light,
  Grief-deafened lest my spirit
    should discern?
  Yet how could I keep silence
    when I burn?
  And who can give me comfort?—
    Hear the right.
  Have patience with the weak and
    sick at heart:
    Bind up the wounded with a
      tender touch,
      Comfort the sad, tear-blinded
        as they go:—
  For, though I failed to choose the
    better part,
    Were it a less unutterable woe
  If we should come to love this
    world too much?[20]

Following her father's death in 1854, when Rossetti began working as a social worker, the sexual spoils of the market system must have become all too clear. "From the Antique" (1854) focused on women's invisibility and social uselessness—"doubly blank in a woman's lot"—and just the day before, in the sonnet "The World," she imagined the world as either a harlot house or as a "house of mercy," that is a sisterhood where prostitutes lived side-by-side with the Anglican Sisters:

  By day she woos me to the outer air,
    Ripe fruits, sweet flowers, and full satiety:
    But thro' the night, a beast she grins at me,
  A very monster void of love and prayer.[21]

At the sonnet's close, the key question is crystallized: Can women ever enter the world without giving up control of their sexuality? Is the world "a friend indeed"

      that I should sell
    My soul to her, give her my life and youth,
  Till my feet, cloven too, take hold on hell?

A central tenet of the all-female association, like the houses of mercy, the working-class women's schools, and the convent convalescent hospitals where Rossetti worked, was the special ability of women to be passionless, to renounce sexual impulse. As Nancy Cott explained:

> The belief that women lacked carnal motivation was the
> cornerstone of the argument for women's moral
> superiority, used to enhance women's status and widen
> their opportunities in the nineteenth century.
> Furthermore, acceptance of the idea of passionlessness
> created sexual solidarity among women; it allowed women
> to consider their love relationships with one another
> of higher character than heterosexual relationships
> because they excluded (male) carnal passion.[22]

All the Rossetti women were models of passionlessness. Epithets typically associated with the Polidori maiden aunts, included "good old soul" and "'constant and devoted' attendant."[23] In fact, Frances Lavinia's deepest conflicts with Gabriele revolved around their different approaches to sexuality, with Frances upholding staunch, evangelical passionlessness.

A realist, Frances Lavinia distrusted the idealization of the feminine that resulted from the Catholic practice of mariolatry, in which the figure of Mary is worshipped for her role as intercessor between man and God. In his work, Gabriele developed connections between Petrarch and Dante in terms of their paths for attaining spiritual enlightenment. He saw parallels between Dante's quest for spiritual truth, represented by Beatrice, and Petrarch's more romantic path toward ideal beauty, represented by Laura. For employing the female figure to represent an idealization, Gabriele considered Dante as writing in a courtly tradition of love poets. But to a High Church Anglican like Frances Lavinia, this was a blasphemous and heretical idea which falsely attributed an ideological pursuit of truth and beauty to courtly love's endorsement of sinful pleasure-seeking and physical love outside of marriage. Needless to say, conventional manner books of the day warned young middle-class ladies about men who harbored such false notions. Manner books advised young women never to enter such "platonic relationships."[24]

Following the evangelical tradition represented in the work of Hannah More and the development of charity schools, Frances Lavinia believed that women were made for God's purposes, not man's, and that, indeed, women had a higher calling than men to promote the moral good. Men could certainly be brilliant, as were her father, brother, husband, and sons, but they needed strongminded, evangelical women to keep them sane.

From Rossetti's point of view, her older sister Maria Francesca mastered passionlessness far better than she did. Maria was the more disciplined scholar who published a critical study of Dante, *A Shadow of Dante*, in 1872 and had a more formal relationship to the Anglican Sisterhoods. Maria joined All Saints' Sisterhood as a novice in 1873, and finally committed herself to God, through whose agency she strove for self-fulfillment. According to Packer, "Maria's new profession brought her unexpected happiness."[25] Maria translated the Day Hours of the Roman Breviary for the order, and this became, after revision, the standard volume. It was reissued in 1923 as *A Book of Day Hours for the Use of Religious Societies.* In a letter to Dante Gabriel, Maria Francesca explained how blessed convent life was because of the divine love existing among the members: "Human love is a figure of that which, being at once Divine and human, satisfies the soul as nothing else can. What that is in this most blessed life, when all is given up for it, cannot be expressed."[26] However, this divine love was attained through self-denial, not through the senses as her father's research and Dante Gabriel's painting and poetry proposed.

Since May 1873, Maria had known about an internal tumor, a condition which no doubt contributed to her decision to give up all and join All Saints' Sisterhood. She died in November 1876. The Rossettis and Polidoris who remained missed her hearty fortitude. It is clear we have insufficient information about Maria Francesca to formulate definitive conclusions about her relationship to Christina, but we do know that Christina admired Maria's way of handling a brief romance with John Ruskin.

John Ruskin's romantic interest in Maria, which she reciprocated, began a year after Ruskin's wife Effie annulled their marriage. The annulment was a blow to Ruskin. He escaped into his work, then left England. Ruskin's coolness raised doubts even among his supporters. Dante Gabriel, who later considered Ruskin "the best friend" he "ever had *out of*" his "*own family*," now wondered what to make of Ruskin's marital fiasco. He wrote to Ford Madox Brown:

> The "'Ruskin'" row seems to have grown into a roar in
> London. . . . Mrs. R will get a divorce it seems—her
> husband is—or *is not*—I know not what. There are other
> "'solitary habits'" besides those which you indulge in—
> more things in heaven and earth that are dreamt of in
> even Turner's philosophy. It seems Mrs. R's seven
> years of marriage have been passed like Rachel's seven

> marriageable years—in hope. I suppose it is more the
> right time to be in favour with her than with him. . . .[27]

When Ruskin returned, however, his friendship with Dante Gabriel became even closer. Ruskin was enthusiastic about Lizzy Sidall's talent as an artist and decided to become her patron. He also began to wonder about striking up a relationship with Dante Gabriel's older sister, Maria Francesca. "There, sir!" Dante Gabriel wrote to William Allingham (July 4, 1855), "R has asked to be introduced to my sister, who . . . will accompany Miss S and myself to dinner there on Friday."[28] Maria was close to thirty at this time, and her studious manner must have presented little threat to Ruskin.

Whatever fantasies Ruskin's interest generated in Maria, she eventually had to adjust to his rejection. Although Maria and Ruskin remained cordial friends, Maria began the painful process of sublimating her warm feelings toward him. Impressed by Maria's ability not to get carried away by this disappointing romantic distraction, Christina wrote about it in her entry for April 22 in her reading diary *Time Flies*: "One of the most genuine Christians I ever knew, once took lightly the dying out of a brief acquaintance which had engaged her warm heart, on the ground that such mere tastes and glimpses of congenial intercourse on earth wait for their development in heaven."[29]

From witnessing Maria's process, Christina gained a vision for dwelling in heaven with self-affirming power. Themes of abandonment run throughout Rossetti's repertoire, but it is first in the long, monodramatic narrative "From House to Home" (1858) that the fantasy of heavenly reunion with a male lover rings hollow and is superseded by a higher, spiritual vision of personal apotheosis, renewal, and growth. In the poem, a lover's rejection "destroyed" the speaker "like an avalanche." In tones reminiscent of Poe, the speaker cries:

> "My love no more," I muttered, stunned with pain:
>   I shed no tear, I wrung no passionate hand,
> Till something whispered: "You shall meet again,
>   Meet in a distant land."
>
> Then with a cry like famine I arose,
>   I lit my candle, searched from room to room,
> Searched up and down; a war of winds that froze
>   Swept thro' the blank of gloom.

I searched day after day, night after night;
   Scant change there came to me of night or day:
"No more," I wailed, "no more:" and trimmed my light,
   And gnashed but did not pray.

Until my heart broke and my spirit broke:
   Upon the frost-bound floor I stumbled, fell,
And moaned: "It is enough: withold the stroke.
   Farewell, O love, farewell."[30]

Letting go of dependency becomes a release. Healing "spheres and spirits" call out to her as "sister":

Then life swooned from me. And I heard the song
   Of spheres and spirits rejoicing over me:
One cried: "Our sister, she has suffered long"—
   One answered: "Make her see"—

One cried: "Oh blessed she who no more pain,
   Who no more disappointment shall receive"—
One answered: "Not so: she must live again;
   Strengthen thou her to live."

So while I lay entranced a curtain seemed
   To shrivel with crackling from before my face;
Across mine eyes a waxing radiance beamed
   And showed a certain place.

The "waxing radiance" gives rise to the speaker's apocalyptic vision of a majestic woman whose splendor derives from her linkage to heaven:

I saw a vision of a woman, where
   Night and new morning strive for domination:

   . . . .

Her eyes were like some fire-enshrining gem,
   Were stately like the stars, and yet were tender;
Her figure charmed me like a windy stem
   Quivering and drooped and slender.

> I stood upon the outer barren ground,
>   She stood on inner ground that budded flowers;
>
> . . . .
>
> Then marked I how a chain sustained her form,
>   A chain of living links not made nor riven:
> It stretched sheer up thro' lightning, wind, and storm,
>   And anchored fast in heaven.
>
> . . . .
>
> Therefore in patience I possess my soul;
>   Yea, therefore as a flint I set my face,
> To pluck down, to build up again the whole—
>   But in a distant place.
>
> . . . .
>
> My face is steadfast toward Jerusalem,
>   My heart remembers it.

Christina's vision presents a passionate, self-reliant woman. As a symbolic representation of womanhood, she stands in sharp contrast to the delicate, tremulous blessed damozel (1847) of Dante Gabriel's famous poem:

> The blessed Damozel leaned out
>   From the gold bar of Heaven:
> Her blue grave eyes were deeper much
>   Than a deep water, even.
> She had three lilies in her hand,
>   And the stars in her hair were seven.[31]

Like "From House to Home," many of Rossetti's poems of the late 1850s deal with a heroine's romantic/sexual tensions and the trauma consequent upon sexual confrontation. The heroines find relief, consolation and hope through variously conceived wish-fulfillment fantasies of heaven, like the self-accepting apocalyptic vision in "From House to Home."[32] These visions enable the speakers to face their lives as women alone by generating images of themselves as strong, enduring, and necessary links between the material and spiritual worlds.

If "From House to Home" is noteworthy for its woman-centered vision, "Goblin Market," Rossetti's masterpiece written just six months later, goes even further to posit, in the critic Jerome J. McGann's view, "an alternative, uncorrupted mode of social relations—the love of sisters."[33] Bonds of sisterhood compel Lizzie to redeem her "fallen" sister from the deceptive and sadistic commercial, male world which poisoned her. To do this, however, she must confront her own class pretensions to moral superiority, impeccable household propriety, and cleanliness as false values which have blinded her from her own potential to sin.

In manuscript, "Goblin Market" was inscribed "To M.F.R.," Christina's "dear only sister Maria Francesca Rossetti."[34] There is thus some validity to the traditional view that Lizzie is modeled on Maria. According to Packer, Maria "saved" Christina from being jealously obsessed about the notorious affairs of her would-be lover William Bell Scott. Around the time "Goblin Market" was written, Scott was having an affair with Alice Boyd.[35] Whether or not Christina was actually as focused on Scott as Packer contended, it does seem clear that Maria was a model of passionlessness that Christina tried to emulate. However, one-dimensional interpretations of passionless sisterhood are clearly inadequate for understanding the diversity of Rossetti's poetic treatments.

Two other poems which also appeared in the *Goblin Market* volume are highly critical of sisterhood—the ironically titled "Noble Sisters," written several months after "Goblin Market," and "Sister Maude," date of composition unknown. In "Noble Sisters," a passionless sister with high moral standards thwarts a more passionate sister's romance because the suitor is from a lower class and would "shame our father's name." The irony is that while the sisters are highborn, one's treatment of the other is less than noble or sisterly. In "Sister Maude," two sisters compete sexually for the same comely man. The loser informs their parents. When the poem opens, the man is dead:

> You might have spared his soul, sister,
>   Have spared my soul, your own soul too
> Though I had not been born at all,
>   He'd never have looked at you.[36]

Christina Rossetti was the "other" woman in several different romantic triangles. The first triangle was composed of her, Letitia Norquoy, and Norquoy's husband, William Bell Scott. According to Packer, Rossetti began her romantic life as the potential lover of William Bell Scott. Scott, however, did not immediately inform Christina or her family that he was a married man. Christina would not have sex outside of marriage, much less with a married man, and therefore could never fulfill Scott's physical needs for a lover. Though Scott was attracted to Christina, he looked to other women, like Alice Boyd, for physical intimacy. Sara Teasdale's incompleted biography, however, suggests Christina stopped the potential affair with Scott mainly because of her growing friendship with Scott's wife, Letitia Norquoy. Despite the paucity of Christina's extant correspondence, there are warm and lively references to Mr. and Mrs. Scott, as well as to Alice Boyd, throughout Christina's *Family Letters*. Often, Christina spent time together with the Scotts and Alice Boyd, sometimes in London, other times at Boyd's home, Penkill Castle, in Scotland. Sometimes they composed a ménage à trois; at other times they formed a ménage à quatre.[37]

Although Christina Rossetti always maintained unusually close family ties with her brothers, she became, at the same time, secondary to them once they developed intimate, romantic involvements with other women. For instance, Dante Gabriel's lover and later wife Elizabeth Siddall tested Christina's practice of sisterhood, not because of any intrinsic competitive spirit in either of their natures, but because of the position Dante Gabriel put them in, in relationship to each other. This, of course, recalls the thwarted sisterhood between Sue Gilbert and Emily Dickinson once Sue and Austin married. In this case, however, Dante Gabriel inadvertently played an active role in keeping Lizzy and Christina apart. He allowed Lizzy to usurp Christina's position within the Pre-Raphaelite Brotherhood, and he began to promote Lizzy's career as an artist and poet at precisely the same time Christina was developing her skills in these areas. Moreover, Christina observed Lizzy developing dependent patterns of behavior and accepting poor treatment from her brother and the other Pre-Raphaelites.

We have seen Dante Gabriel's excitement over Lizzy's golden-haired beauty, an excitement he communicated to Christina. But within the Pre-Raphaelite Brotherhood, he was careless with Lizzy, sometimes even crude. His letter to William Michael of September 3, 1850, condemns an insensitive game involving Lizzy, not because it objectified Lizzy, but because it may have offended Dante Gabriel's friend Jack: "Hunt and Stephens have been playing off a disgraceful hoax on poor Jack Tupper, by passing Miss Siddall upon him as Hunt's wife. . . . As soon as I heard of it, however, I made the Mad (Hunt) write a note of apology to Jack."[38] No word of his apology to Lizzy. Then, in 1852, a fiasco occurred which had a lingering effect on Lizzy's health. She was modeling for Millais' Ophelia. According to the *Life and Letters of Sir John Everett Millais*:

In order that the artist might get the proper set of
the garments in water and the right atmosphere and
aquous effects, she had to lie in a large bath filled
with water, which was kept at an even temperature by
lamps placed beneath. One day, just as the picture was
nearly finished, the lamps went out unnoticed by the
artist, who was so intensely absorbed in his work that
he thought of nothing else, and the poor lady was kept
floating in the cold water till she was quite benumbed.
She herself never complained of this, but the result
was that she contracted a severe cold.[39]

The editors of Dante Gabriel's letters, Doughty and Wahl, make the point: "D.G.R. does not appear to have borne any malice" for Millais' carelessness. However, we learn that just a few weeks later, Dante Gabriel joined Lizzy at Hastings where she had gone to cure her bad health.[40]

A greater interaction between Christina and Lizzy as writers would have undoubtedly improved Lizzy's poetry. At one point, Christina thought she would publish some of Lizzy's verses in her second volume, *The Prince's Progress*, but she decided against this because the poems were too full of despair.

Lack of faith was Rossetti's major criticism of women who were friends of the Pre-Raphaelites and involved in the radical movement. However, Rossetti did see the need for women to enter the political sphere. She even entered the political sphere herself by petitioning on issues of antivivisection and minors' protection. Rossetti thought women might need the right to vote in order to gain full equality, and she was willing to differ from other domestic reformers on this issue. Mackenzie Bell published Rossetti's correspondence to her suffragist friend, Augusta Webster: "'If female rights are sure to be overborne for lack of female voting influence, then I confess I feel disposed to shoot ahead of my instructresses, and to assert that female M.P.'s are only right and reasonable.'"[41] Other issues were brewing among feminists at this time. They took stands against the inherent male privilege of the illegitimacy laws and against slavery in the American South. "A Royal Princess" was published in a poetry volume devoted to the antislavery cause. The princess realized connections between her own redundancy and the peasants' complaints. She saw the need to join with other classes to upset feudal patriarchy. The patriarchy is also the target of criticism in "'The Iniquity of the Fathers Upon the Children.'" In this case, fathers are blamed for not assuming responsibility for children born out of wedlock.

Rossetti continued doing church work until she became too ill. Her end was due to a long, slow illness, "cancer . . . along her left shoulder and arm." Yet, "until her last illness," which became serious a year before her death in 1894, "she was present at nearly all the weekly services at Christ Church, and received Holy Communion every Sunday and Thursday," according to Reverend Glendinning Nash:

> "She took" he says, "the deepest interest in Christ
> Church, its schools, and its district. She subscribed
> generously, and nearly every Sunday during her illness
> sent money for the offertory."[42]

Lucy Brown, who was an agnostic raised in the free-thinking atmosphere of the Madox Brown household, found the doggedness of Christina's faith irritating. Her lack of comprehension for Christina's religious concerns was one reason Christina and her mother moved to a separate residence after having lived with William Michael and Lucy for two years.

Rossetti took care of her mother and maiden aunts in their old age and received admiring visitors. Yet a canker of doubt plagued her. Had she become too smug? Why had she been so intolerant of her sister-in-law Lucy's agnosticism? After all, hadn't she lived with the agnosticism of William Michael and Dante Gabriel all these years? For solace, she turned to a fastidious faith. The world needed conversion, a return to heartfelt feeling and compassion as bases for social interaction; but the class structure of society was becoming more, not less, rigid. Rossetti's vision was of an alternative female culture–a solid circle of female relatives and a work-oriented sisterhood. Part of her doubt, in the end, resulted from the contradiction between this vision and the patriarchal hierarchy of Anglicanism.

After Christina died, William Michael wrote to her biographer Mackenzie Bell,

> "Assuredly my sister did to the last continue believing
> in the promises of the Gospel, as interpreted by
> Theologians; but her sense of its threatenings was very
> lively, and at the end more operative on her personal
> feelings. . . . She remained firmly convinced that her
> mother and sister are saints in heaven, and I
> endeavored to show her that according to her own
> theories, she was just as safe as they: but this–such

was her humility of self-estimate–did not relieve her
from troubles of soul."[43]

Another way of looking at William Michael's disclosure is that Christina
Rossetti did not think God, the ultimate God she had imagined and of whom
she was taught, would accept her. Why? She told her nurse Mrs. Read,
"This illness has humbled me. I was so proud before."[44] As a published
woman poet, she had been more than proud, if one used an orthodox
yardstick. In her poems, her poets are singers who enjoy earthy lushness.
One early singer is "Eleanor" (1847):

> Cherry-red her mouth was
>
> . . . .
>
> Sometimes she spoke, sometimes she
>   sang;
> And evermore the sound
>   Floated, a dreamy melody,
> Upon the air around;
>   As though a wind were singing
> Far up beside the sun,
>   Till sound and warmth and glory
> Were blended all in one.[45]

Another appears in "Song" (1848):

> She sat and sang alway
>   By the green margin of a stream,
> Watching the fishes leap and play
>   Beneath the glad sunbeam.[46]

She worried lest she become like the social climber in her poem "Is and
Was" (1850):

> Now she is a noble lady
> With calm voice not over loud;
> Very courteous in her action,
> Yet you think her proud;
> Much too haughty to affect;
> Too indifferent to direct

Or be angry or suspect;
Doing all from self-respect.[47]

Like Emily Dickinson, Christina Rossetti called on Jesus, more than on God, for salvation. One of Rossetti's famous, passionate appeals to Jesus is "A Better Resurrection" (1857):

I have no wit, no words, no tears;
　My heart within me like a stone
Is numbed too much for hopes or fears;
　Look right, look left, I dwell alone;
I lift mine eyes, but dimmed with grief
　No everlasting hills I see;
My life is in the falling leaf:
　O Jesus, quicken me.[48]

For Rossetti, Christ reaches out even to sinners who cannot "will" their recoveries; that is, Christ provides the will and the way. "A Bruised Reed Shall He Not Break" illustrates the sinner's struggle and Christ's compassionate response:

I will accept thy will to do and be,
　Thy hatred and intolerance of sin,
　Thy will at least to love, that burns within
　　And thirsteth after Me:
So will I render fruitful, blessing still
　The germs and small beginnings in thy heart,
　Because thy will cleaves to the better part.–
　　Alas, I cannot will.

. . . .

What, neither choose nor wish to choose? and yet
　I still must strive to win thee and constrain:
　For thee I hung upon the cross in pain,
　　How then can I forget?
If thou as yet dost neither love, nor hate,
　Nor choose, nor wish,–resign thyself, be still
　Till I infuse love, hatred, longing, will.–
　　I do not deprecate.[49]

In a previously unpublished holograph titled "Eve," now located in the J.C. Troxell Collection of Rossetti manuscripts at Princeton University, Rossetti reconstructed the story of the fall to exonerate Eve from blame for original sin.[50] She developed a fascinating argument by quoting St. Paul, who said it was in Adam all die, not in Eve. Further, she simply used logic: "Eve herself was derived from Adam: he therefore was, she was not, the exclusive head and stock of mankind." This may seem like a problematic spot for women, with Man so clearly at the Head. But with Man/Adam as the "originator" of sin, Eve is freed to be only a "channel." Thus, "it seems to ensue that all we inherit and all spiritual corruption entailed on the human family the Fall, descend to us thro' Eve indeed but from Adam." Another woman is the vehicle of redemption. Through the Virgin Mary, "the entail of sin" is "broken." Her son Jesus is born sinless, "without a human father." For Rossetti, the virgin birth signified a challenge to the ideas that women were innately inferior and naturally subordinate.

Invoking Jesus to support the redemptive power of women was a clever way to turn religion in women's favor. No less of a feminist than Sojourner Truth used such logic to sway an entire audience at an Akron, Ohio convention to believe that women were not the weaker sex and that male supremacy was not a Christian principle: "That little man in black there, he says women can't have as much rights as men, because Christ wasn't a woman! Where did Christ come from? Where did your Christ come from? From God and a woman! Man had nothing to do with Him."[51] Till the end, Christina Rossetti was asking: Does inheriting the richness of heaven compensate for the struggle of woman's lot? One of her last devotional poems, "Heaven Overarches," asks: "What though to-night wrecks you and me / If so to-morrow saves?"[52] Like other women of her day, she had learned to suffer, to be still, and to hope for self-perfection, if not for a better world on earth. Whereas Dickinson's "Faith," though "tattered," is as "spacious as before," Rossetti's is diminished. In the end, "Herself" was her last and only frontier:

> Therefore myself is that one only
>   thing
> I hold to use or waste, to keep or
>   give;
> My sole possession every day I
>   live,
> And still mine own despite Time's
>   winnowing.[53]

In this chapter, we have discussed the attempts of these two well-educated women poets to reconcile the ways of God and woman. They both worried lest their pursuit of intellectual enlightenment and artistic perfection mar their moral characters and cause them to miss the heavenly goal. They assimilated conventional attitudes about the meek nature of woman only to reject them in favor of an image of woman as powerfully connected to other women in sisterhood and as a transcendental link between the natural and spiritual worlds. This precarious vision sustained Dickinson till the end of her life, but Rossetti questioned if she had gone too far.

It is time for us to assess the legacy these two poets have left. We move to consider their place as poets in their age and in our own.

PART IV

CONCLUSION

Emily Dickinson.
Retouched daguerrotype by permission
of the Houghton Library.

Chapter 8

Women Poets, Literary Influence, and the Canon

Finally, we examine the place of Dickinson and Rossetti in literary history, their influence, and their placement in the literary canon. We show that Dickinson and Rossetti were part of a continuum of women writers who were challenging the convention of romantic love and the limitations on subject matter which restricted women writers. They extended bold precedents set by their influential literary foremothers, including Letitia Landon, Emily Brontë, and Elizabeth Barrett Browning, by addressing subversive subjects in highly original ways. Their innovative styles and radical content won them places in the canon when their contemporaries have faded from it: the Langham Place poets in London, like Bessie Rayner Parkes and Adelaide Procter, and the activist Helen Hunt Jackson in America.

The poet's place in literary history and her influence are inextricably linked to the image of the artist held by the dominant culture. In an inhospitable climate, the image of the artist is constantly in revision. In the 1830s, the role the male poet would play in the coming industrial age was unclear. Followers of Byron and Shelley bemoaned the loss of poets as legislators of the world. Even as young men, Robert Browning and Tennyson began expressing the poet's responsibility for soothing the ills of industrial society. In America, Emerson sought to find appropriate moral values to guide the nation as it moved from an agrarian to an industrial society, while Whitman celebrated the uncontrolled energy of the new age. The alienated romantic individualist who was the popular male poet in the early nineteenth century, and often the voice of revolution, was becoming more and more peripheral as the captain of industry and the scientist determined major economic and political developments.

The problem of the artist's image and role is particularly acute for the woman artist who lacks the male authority to mold opinion. In establishing the role of the woman poet, she confronts not only the hostile reactions her own generation poses to her chosen identity, but also the constricting images of preceding generations of women writers. Dickinson and Rossetti struggled in diverse ways to forge their own identities as women writers by confronting the influential images of their literary foremothers.

Both poets used the controversial public figure of Elizabeth Barrett Browning as a starting point for their treatments of women as artists. A privileged education and aptitude for the "manly" enterprise of classical translation trained Elizabeth Barrett Browning as a poet. Once appreciated for her expression of feminine sentiment, she paved the way for women poets after her to write on social and political issues. She contributed to the humanitarian movement by treating subjects in her poems, such as child labor, aimed at remedying social evils created by "progress." Both before and after her marriage to Robert Browning, she was a well-known woman who, if she had been an invalid and reclusive earlier, was never reclusive in her efforts to put her views before the world. Her idealization of heterosexual love and of woman's responsibility to correct social injustice were the acts of a public woman poet. She was, in this respect, following the Tennysonian "public bard" model for poets, a model which had previously been assumed in England only by men.

That Emily Dickinson admired Elizabeth Barrett Browning greatly and thought of her poetry as an ideal she had no hope of reaching, is evinced not only in her poem to Elizabeth Barrett Browning which credits her writing with a power which transformed Emily Dickinson's life, but also in the personal grief she exhibits to her friends at Browning's death. There is also much evidence that Dickinson's poetry was inspired by Browning's, particularly by Browning's long feminist poem *Aurora Leigh.*[1]

For Rossetti, Elizabeth Barrett Browning was a reality as well as an ideal. The Brownings were personal friends of Rossetti's brother, Dante Gabriel. While Christina marveled at Elizabeth's ability to versify a wide range of political and personal subjects, Dante Gabriel pressured her to divert from Elizabeth's style which he considered too masculine, "falsetto muscularity."[2] Nevertheless, Rossetti continued to use poetry for the "masculine" purpose of social criticism, especially in the 1850s and 1860s. Her first published volumes, as we have seen, established her more as a social poet than as the religious poet we know her as today, and they marked her as Elizabeth Barrett Browning's successor, Victorian England's second leading woman poet.

One significant way Rossetti did differ from Browning, though, was in her treatment of romantic love. Whereas Browning's "Sonnets From the Portuguese" (1850), idealized traditional romantic love, Rossetti's sonnet series, "Monna Innominata" (1866-1870) stressed the pain women experience in traditional romantic relationships. Sonnet One sets the dominant tone:

> "Love, with how great a stress dost thou vanquish me
> to-day!"
>
> Petrarca.

> Come back to me, who wait and watch for you:–
>   Or come not yet, for it is over then,
>   And long it is before you còme again,
> So far between my pleasures are and few.
>
>   . . . .
>
>   Howbeit, to meet you grows almost a pang
>   Because the pang of parting comes so soon.[3]

In her epigraph to "Monna Innominata," Rossetti objected to the "fancy" in Browning's love sonnets, their lack of authentic frustration. Indeed, Browning's love sonnets fulfilled a dominant, romantic myth, and they never engendered the sexist critiques that her political poems elicited.

Novelists were also targets of these double standards. Since the matter of novels—manners and social customs—were viewed as appropriate women's topics, women were in one sense encouraged to write them. On the other hand, women were not taken seriously as thinkers and were expected to write and think in a preconceived feminine mode. When fictional heroines challenged dominant assumptions about female intelligence and passivity, their authors either had difficulty being accepted, like the Brontës, or like George Eliot, had difficulty overcoming the deep-seated fear of rejection.

Dickinson's potential publisher, Thomas Wentworth Higginson, encouraged Dickinson to follow the model set by the more conventional American writer Helen Hunt Jackson, whose poetry was highly popular in the day. Jackson wrote conventional verse on motherhood, death, and nature, but later in the century, when poetry reflected more of an art-for-art's-sake movement, she espoused the rights of Native Americans through essays and novels to express her indignation. *Ramona* is still read and enjoyed, but little of her verse survives today.

Charlotte Brontë and George Eliot both objected strongly to these double standards and, therefore, found it convenient to adopt male pseudonyms in order to be innovative in their writing and to be taken seriously. Indeed, Emily Dickinson, in the elegiac poem #148, comments on Currer Bell's anguish and the final self-emergence of Charlotte Brontë in heaven:

> All overgrown by cunning moss,
> All interspersed with weed,
> The little cage of "Currer Bell"
> In quiet "Haworth" laid.
>
> Gathered from many wanderings–
> Gethsemane can tell
> Thro' what transporting anguish
> She reached the Asphodel!
>
> Soft fall the sounds of Eden
> Upon her puzzled ear–
> Oh what an afternoon for Heaven,
> When "Bronte" entered there.

By the 1860s, when Dickinson and Rossetti attempted most vigorously to publish, women novelists and poets were by no means novelties. However, women writers were still evaluated according to aesthetic codes that were different from those by which men were evaluated. Poetry was a more established genre than the novel and had more rigid rules of form. As a result, when women poets attempted to express their political ideologies in poetic form, they felt compelled to follow the conventional structure for political poetry–the iambic pentameter couplet–which had been extremely popular for satiric verse in the eighteenth century.

One example is a poem about the need for divorce in the *English Woman's Journal* of 1858, "Lines Suggested By More Than One Domestic History":

> Yet, surely, she may fly an unloved mate,
> And find relief in undisturbed retreat?
> Not so–the law its powerless victim cites
> To forced communion and unwilling rites.

Which sting with insult; whilst the loathed caress
But desecrates the couch it may not bless.[4]

Despite their advanced positions politically, the poets who published in the *English Woman's Journal* did not try to develop new poetic forms, nor did they challenge women's role in popular love poetry. They treated themes in conventional lyric and narrative verse which romantic poets had abandoned thirty years earlier: grief as a common state of mind redeemable only by faith in oneself through faith in God; fidelity as a virtue more naturally attainable by women than by men; and the beauty and pathos of unrequited love. For example, "The Old Chateau" by the Langham reformer Bessie Rayner Parkes uses the loyal love of a woman to stress the theme of love's eternity and contrasts this with the passing glory of male warlike heroism:

Clash and clang of swords
Soon dies away,
Shrined apart in a people's heart
Love lives alway:
France will not forget this name,
Gabrielle D'Estree![5]

Such themes reinforced dominant ideas about women as spiritually superior and, thereby, more capable than men of renouncing the material world. These poets—whose themes were often reformist, but whose poetic forms were conventional and who did not challenge conventional romantic imagery and patterns—have been lost from today's canon in poetry: Isa Craig, Adelaide Procter, Dora Greenwell, and Bessie Rayner Parkes.

More innovative poets, like Rossetti, Dickinson, and their subversive predecessors, took the theme of heterosexual love transcending the grave and turned it upside down. Emily Brontë was one of these mavericks, although like Dickinson, her contemporaries did not know her for her poetry. An enduring poem, "Remembrance" (1845), shows how Brontë undercut the dominant use of women as symbols for eternal love. The senselessness of the tradition is highlighted by the female speaker's candid denial of her ability to be forever loyal:

Cold in the earth—and fifteen wild Decembers,
From those brown hills, have melted into spring:
Faithful, indeed, is the spirit that remembers
After such years of change and suffering!

> Sweet Love of youth, forgive, if I forget thee,
> While the world's tide is bearing me along;
> Other desires and other hopes beset me,
> Hopes which obscure, but cannot do thee wrong![6]

Rossetti inherited Brontë's ironic approach to conventional romantic themes. She turned the conventions of elegiac poetry on their heads with an important shift in persona. Compare her "Song" of December 12, 1848, with Brontë's poem. Rossetti's speaker is the dead woman, directing the lover who is still alive with an irony that recalls and deepens Brontë's realism and is, perhaps, a comment on a woman's more realistic assessment of the male inability for faithfulness:

> When I am dead, my dearest,
>   Sing no sad songs for me;
> Plant thou no roses at my head,
>   Nor shady cypress tree:
> Be the green grass above me
>   With showers and dewdrops wet:
> And if thou wilt, remember,
>   And if thou wilt, forget.[7]

Another role open to women in the arts was, of course, the muse. The improvisatrice, exemplified by Madame de Staël and her English translator, Letitia Elizabeth Landon, was a new, muse-like female character in poetry in the generation before Dickinson and Rossetti. The improvisatrice was a highly talented, magnetic personality who could inspire, like a muse, through spontaneous, verse speech making. Of course, like all improvisation, such an art form is largely ephemeral, dependent on the presence of the author who is herself part of the performance.[8]

In a lyric monologue addressed to Letitia Landon as a poetic foremother, Rossetti captured instead of the excitement of a brilliant performance, a lonely, despairing woman who finds no satisfaction in her art:

> Downstairs I laugh, I sport and jest with all:
>   But in my solitary room above
> I turn my face in silence to the wall:
>   My heart is breaking for a little love.

. . . .

I deck myself with silks and jewelry,
   I plume myself like any mated dove:
They praise my rustling show, and never see
   My heart is breaking for a little love.[9]

By Rossetti's time, the public taste demanded only "rustling show" from women poets—decorative and refined sentiment—rather than passion or rigorous intellectual creation. The woman poet is an essentially frivolous entertainer whose deepest needs are not met by the audience she serves.

Rossetti's poem, "In an Artist's Studio," shows the female muse as she was used in the visual arts:

One face looks out from all his canvases,
One selfsame figure sits or walks or leans:
We found her hidden just behind those screens,

. . . .

A nameless girl in freshest summer-greens,
A saint, an angel—every canvas means
The same one meaning, neither more nor less.
He feeds upon her face by day and night,
And she with true kind eyes looks back on him,

. . . .

Not as she is, but was when hope shone bright;
Not as she is, but as she fills his dream.[10]

The muse knows what her fate would be if she exposed her real thoughts, therefore the emphasis is on the woman as unknown and reclusive, though public.

The woman artists in Dickinson's poetry possess the freedom of expression Rossetti's muses lack. The ballerina in Dickinson's poem #326 can dance "a Prima mad," but only when the male guide and audience are absent. Two themes are present. First, she has no "Ballet knowledge" because "no Man" instructed her. Thus, she can not shape her "Glee" into the traditional, stylized, and rigid form. Secondly, despite the fact that no one is watching, she does not lack. She is "full as Opera," full of words:

> I cannot dance upon my Toes—
> No Man instructed me—
> But oftentimes, among my mind,
> A Glee possesseth me.
>
> That had I Ballet knowledge—
> Would put itself abroad
> In Pirouette to blanch a Troupe—
> Or lay a Prima, mad,
>
> And though I had no Gown of Gauze—
> No Ringlet, to my Hair,
> Nor hopped for Audiences—like Birds,
> One Claw upon the Air,
>
> Nor tossed my shape in Eider Balls,
> Nor rolled on wheels of snow
> Till I was out of sight in sound,
> The House encore me so—
>
> Nor any know I know the Art
> I mention—easy—Here—
> Nor any Placard boast me—
> It's full as Opera—

The ballet metaphor provides the key to this poem's unusual form. Far from formless, the lines evoke the dancer's leaps because they alternate between three and four beats to each line, and each line is arranged in rhythmic, staccato iambs:

> Nor ány knów I knów the Árt
> I méntion-éasy-Hére-
> Nor ány Plácard boást mé-
> It's fúll as Óperá-

The first critical response to Emily Dickinson and Christina Rossetti during their lifetimes was concerned primarily with inability—the woman's lack of poetic organization. Earliest criticism of both poets deplored their lack of artistic control. This, along with the accusation of eccentricity, persisted to the turn of the century. Even Christina Rossetti, who looks more than disciplined to a modern audience, was considered, according to Allan R. Life, "at best a spontaneous and at worst a naive technician."[11] Though evidence of their creative process was available in the form of drafts of poems and worksheets, the image of the inspired child/woman who does not labor over her production was more congenial to male critics.

Victorian women poets, particularly those who depended on sales of their work for their living, had little interest in challenging this image. Whether to reconcile within themselves the discrepancy between the genteel woman and the woman intensely involved in her work, or because it was important to promote themselves as unsoiled creatures in order to advance professionally, many women writers of this era stressed the little effort they put into their writing, how the words flowed, as if from a higher source. A woman must be childlike, a pre-pubescent at play.

In America, even other myths of innocence were used. Early critics of Emily Dickinson, particularly those anxious to promote her work, such as Higginson, persistently used metaphors to link the poet with natural forces, like flowers. Conrad Aiken noted, for example, that four years after Dickinson's death, Higginson said that Dickinson's "verses will seem to the reader" upon publication "'like poetry torn up by the roots.'"[12]

Mabel Loomis Todd, the person really responsible for Emily Dickinson's success, had the commercial sense to sell this version of the innocent child/woman to the American public. Emily Dickinson as the madcap, merry gamin was further promoted by Dickinson's niece, Martha Dickinson Bianchi. Bianchi competed with Todd and Todd's daughter, Millicent Todd Bingham, in the publication of Emily Dickinson's poems. Both parties had not only a poetic reputation to promote, but also a family reputation to preserve.

Both considerations led to censorship and distortion as some poems and memories were "regularized" to conform to current taste and others were suppressed. Emily Dickinson, dressed perpetually in white, became a patron saint of children and nature, the woman who renounced men and the world, the New England nun of poetry. It was not until 1958 that all of Emily Dickinson's known work was published as she wrote it.

Christina Rossetti has not been as fortunate. As a young woman, she was cast as the Virgin Mary by her brother, Dante Gabriel, and by other young painters in the revolutionary Pre-Raphaelite Brotherhood. She sat as a model for such well-known paintings as Dante Gabriel's *Girlhood of Mary Virgin* (1849) and *Ecce Ancilla Domini* (*The Annunciation*, 1849-50), and, with her mother as chaperone, for Holman Hunt's *Light of the World* (1852). Criticism proceeded to confuse the woman with the image, viewing her poetry as an extension and proof of a moral superiority based on sexual renunciation. Hunt, for example, commented that Rossetti was "exactly the pure and docile hearted damsel that her brother portrayed God's Virgin pre-elect to be."[13]

As her literary executor, editor, and biographer, Christina's other brother, William Michael, assigned importance to only two incidents in his sister's life, two engagements to be married—which she broke. He also kept many of her poems from publication. In his hallmark "Memoir," published along with Christina Rossetti's first posthumous collection of poetry in 1904, we find that despite William Michael's mention of Christina's involvement with day-schools, Florence Nightingale's Crimean War campaign, foreign travel, religious controversy and revolutionary and aesthetic theory, he made the counterclaim that she "had no politics" and "little fundamental opinion of her own and no connoisseurship."[14]

Until this bias was challenged by feminist scholars, Rossetti's image remained that of an unusually reticent, pious, repressed personality. The spiritualized eroticism frequently cited as the distinguishing characteristic of her verse was attributed to deep frustrations of her inner life, open guilt wounds that never healed. This was the view put forward earlier, in 1898, by Rossetti's first biographer, Mackenzie Bell. William Michael had been Bell's major source of information, and Bell found no reason to challenge William Michael's view. The men Bell identified in Rossetti's life served mainly to further emphasize the extent of her renunciation. She is the "blessed damozel" grown to passive, sexless maturity, inspired or inspiring, never alive.

In spite of these patronizing portraits of Dickinson and Rossetti by biographers committed to upholding conventional womanhood, the impact of Dickinson and Rossetti on modern poetry was quickly visible. In experimenting with the relationship between form and content, both Dickinson and Rossetti were precursors of the symbolists of the next generation and the later modernists. Symbolists incorporated epigrammatic elements into their verse as well as different kinds of rhythm. Yeats, for example, employed the same metaphor as Dickinson—the dancer and the dance—to signify the individual's relationship to the life process. His well-known poem of 1927, "Among School Children," which is a metaphysical speculation on the significance of the aging process to generations of men and women, closes with the speaker addressing nature, symbolized by the "chestnut tree":

> O chestnut tree, great-rooted blossomer,
> Are you the leaf, the blossom or the bole?

O body swayed to music, O brightening glance,
How can we know the dancer from the dance?[15]

Gerard Manly Hopkins, a religious symbolist poet, acknowledged his debt to Christina Rossetti in his letters. He was impressed by several of her poetic devices, including her use of eye-rhymes and assonance.[16] Hopkins was actually Rossetti's contemporary, having met her in 1864, but his own poetry was not published until 1918, twenty-nine years after his death. Like Algernon Charles Swinburne, Hopkins had the highest respect for Christina Rossetti as a poetic innovator.

Thus, some turn-of-the-century writers, like Swinburne, Hopkins, and, later, Virginia Woolf, acknowledged Christina Rossetti's influence. Dickinson, on the other hand, was only then just beginning to become popular. Louise Bogan and Babette Deutsch reviewed Dickinson's "new" books in their journal *Poetry* in 1920.

Dickinson and Rossetti both gained their staying power through their poetic originality. According to Jeanne Kammer, Dickinson's syntactic compression; her unusual juxtaposition of images; and her unconventional use of punctuation, capitalization, space, and line all contributed to her aesthetics of silence.[17] This aesthetic was inherited by such modernist poets as Sylvia Plath, Elizabeth Bishop, Denise Levertov, Anne Sexton and Adrienne Rich.

By the second half of the nineteenth century, therefore, these two women whose works later survived to become part of the literary canon had made some important decisions concerning the protection of their poetry. Rejecting the protection of male pseudonyms and yet desiring to explore and innovate in style and themes, these two poets changed and extended the subversive language women poets permitted themselves and were permitted. Our readings of their poetry depend not only on deciphering their language, but also on our determining how much our views have been colored by changing responses to their lives and work.

As the twentieth century matured, and the public became reassured about the normality of sexual impulses, the missing sexuality in the lives of these poets began to be filled in. In the absence of verifiable heterosexual lovers, like Elizabeth Barrett Browning's Robert or George Eliot's G.H. Lewes, private myths ran rampant. Working women poets were clearly concerned about the straitjacket the Victorian ideals had put them in. They needed to create foremothers, not saints. Louise Bogan, in particular, did much to dispel the myth of the inspired writer at play by concentrating on Emily Dickinson's craft, but, for most critics, the new source of inspiration for both women was to be found in the men in their lives.

The series of biographies written in the 1920s and 1930s about Dickinson and Rossetti all had one thing in common, the *cherchez l'homme* theme. To these critics, Emily Dickinson and Christina Rossetti went on a wild, adolescent dating spree. They all read more like detective romances than biographies of literary figures, each biographer choosing that part of their canon which could be interpreted as substantiation for the identity of the missing man and, in one case, missing woman. The excuse for these exercises is that the discovery of the missing lover will provide insight into the poems, which, it is assumed, could not have been created without a male muse. The common theme of the biographies is thwarted love caused by the marriage of the man, Puritan codes of respectability, class difference, or the intervening Wimpole Street father.

The biographies of Christina Rossetti which celebrated her centenary stressed different reasons for her continued single state. Some recall the conventional reasons for rejecting a suitor that had been applied to Dickinson: the intervening brothers this time, instead of the Wimpole Street father, and class differences. However, overriding these is the theme of a woman whose first love is her church. In the biography of Christina Rossetti begun by Sara Teasdale in the early 1930s but left unfinished, the "married man as the missing lover" theory was put forward for the first time and set the tone for the majority of subsequent biographies.

In the 1950s and 1960s, the lives of Rossetti and Dickinson were still viewed as oddities, women poets and spinsters isolated from other women, special in their strangeness. Both Thomas H. Johnson and Lona Mosk Packer standardized the impression of these two women. Johnson's portrait of Dickinson was completed in 1958 with his edition of her letters. Three years earlier, he had published both an interpretive biography and an edition of her poetry and prose. The predominant image of Dickinson he painted was of a frail, ethereal, upper middle-class, womanly woman. As a properly socialized lady, her physical and emotional disabilities were integral parts of her identity. According to Johnson, the search for a "Master" that characterized Dickinson's entire life did not provide her with the guidance or leadership she needed to play an active, social role. Recalling William Michael's description of Christina Rossetti fifty years earlier, Johnson wrote: "She did not live in history and held no view of it, past or current."[18]

To Johnson, Dickinson's poetry was fetishistic. It expressed her way of compensating for a lack in, or block to, her sexual/emotional development. That she circulated her cryptic and terse unpublished poetry to friends and acquaintances through letters only highlighted for him Dickinson's contradictory situation, described twenty years later by Adrienne Rich as "Vesuvius At Home." Dickinson's language is volcanic, explosive. For Rich, this reveals Dickinson's remarkably powerful mind; for Johnson, it reveals her pathology: "Such intensity of feeling was a handicap that she bore as one who lives with a disability, and her friends must have increased the burden by often making her aware that they felt sympathy for a pathetic situation."[19]

In 1963, Lona Mosk Packer generated research for what was, until 1981, the most complete biography of Rossetti. Mainly, Packer extended Teasdale's insight, by providing vast circumstantial evidence–from manuscripts of poems to diary entries–to prove the identity of Rossetti's missing male lover. Rossetti's love for a freethinking, married man remains unconsummated, according to Packer, because of her devotion to a patriarchal god who promises spiritual salvation. She matures in frustration and bitterness. All the poetry, even the dramatic monologues, are read as confessional testimony of this erotic/spiritual conflict. Georgina Battiscombe's newer biography (1981) corrects Packer's traditional, romantic bias and retells the story of Rossetti's life until young womanhood with convincing realism. Yet, the presentation of Rossetti's adult sexuality is still skewed. The secular nun is substituted for the frustrated, other woman.

It is but a step from these frail, obsessed Eminent Victorians with their secret sexuality to the later formulations which presented the modern, poetic problem of the poet as madwoman. By the early 1970s, with Sylvia Plath and Anne Sexton known in many circles more for their lives (and deaths) than their poetry, and the recent publication of Alfred Alvarez's *The Savage God*, John Cody, a psychoanalyst, offered the culmination of these views in his biography of Emily Dickinson published in 1971.[20] It traces what he imagined to be the etiology of her schizophrenia in much the same way earlier biographers had identified her lover, with imaginary scenes to fill in the blanks in her life created from a portion of her letters and poetry and Cody's own, clinical experience. A new hero emerges, a kindly, understanding family psychoanalyst, called in by Emily Dickinson's concerned and loving father. This patriarchal duo restores Emily Dickinson to partial health, though not to the full poetic powers Cody regards as symptomatic of her illness.

From the high hysteria of these psychoanalytic critics, it was only possible to move in one direction–down to a more reasoned, balanced picture of both poets. It was bound to occur to someone that women this out of control would have difficulty putting pen to paper, let alone writing masterpieces.

For Emily Dickinson, the rescue began with an exhaustive work, *The Years and Hours of Emily Dickinson* by Jay Leyda, a compendium of material by her and by her contemporaries about her and her family.[21] This was followed by Richard Sewall's definitive biography, which excuses some of her verbal excesses as Dickinson's style. He does what Amy Lowell proposed to do: analyze her life in relationship to her family. However, when he departs from using family members as reference points, he organizes his work around the supposed important man in her life; hence, chapters entitled "Samuel Bowles," "Charles Wadsworth," and so on. Unfortunately, in his even-handed treatment, it is also possible to forget that he is writing about a woman who was first a poet. This is a deficiency which feminist criticism addresses, although it does not always challenge Sewall's assumptions.

Even feminist critics like Susan Gubar, Sandra Gilbert, and Adrienne Rich mimic Sewall in the way they all portray the workings of Dickinson's mind, life, and art as essentially inscrutable enigmas, onions with infinite layers. Sewall's Dickinson is a child/woman who never ceased playing games. In her few relationships with people and events, she adopted different masks, none of which disclosed the core of her true, private self. Gilbert and Gubar transformed and developed Sewall's insight into an elaborate explanation of how Dickinson, as woman and poet, maintained emotional stability in a culture that did not allow women to be serious artists. Dickinson expressed her real angers and anxieties by living her life as though it were a series of theatrical performances, requiring different, dramatic postures or masks. Dickinson's different masks or voices composed the persona she developed for herself, her "supposed person," a kind of alter ego that allowed the real Dickinson to express herself without fear of censure:

> Dickinson's life itself, in other words, became a
> kind of novel or narrative poem in which, through an
> extraordinarily complete series of maneuvers, aided by
> costumes that came inevitably to hand, this inventive
> poet enacted and eventually resolved both her anxieties
> about her art and her anger at female subordination. .
> . . We will argue here, however, that Dickinson's
> posing was not an accident of but essential to her
> poetic self-achievement, specifically because–as we
> have suggested–the verse drama into which she
> transformed her life enabled her to transcend what

> Suzanne Juhasz has called the "double bind" of the
> woman poet: on the one hand the impossibility of
> self-assertion for a woman, on the other hand the
> necessity of self-assertion for the poet. In the
> context of a dramatic fiction, Dickinson could
> metamorphose from a real person (to whom aggressive
> speech is forbidden) into a series of characters or
> supposed persons (for whom assertive speeches must be
> supplied).[22]

While Gilbert and Gubar bring us closer to an understanding of the conception behind Dickinson's "supposed person," they do not greatly expand our understanding of the self Dickinson took responsibility for being–the active agent in her own experience. This continued lack of information has generated rich speculation about Dickinson which expresses fantasies and myths about women common in our culture. The hidden and withdrawn woman who harbors a secret transgression or weakness and who poses in order to escape facing reality expresses a fantasy that transcends the particularity of Dickinson's or Rossetti's lives. This fantasy has, for example, most recently been embodied in Pinter's film version of John Fowles' *The French Lieutenant's Woman*.

Any truth about these women is hard to discover. The image critics present of the enigma, the many-layered woman, is as much a result of critical overpainting as it is of their lives. Why, then, have these women endured in a male-dominated canon when their contemporaries have been discarded? One reason may be the tantalizing blankness of the canvas which invites these critical contradictions. In the absence of hard, factual events, it is easy to invent anything to account for the power of their work.

Another is that the ingredients for producing powerful work were present. Both women came from positions of relative privilege, with Emily Dickinson clearly the more affluent. She at least did not have to write to live and so had more freedom than the women who needed to please the public taste. Both were well-educated for their day and both had access to male sources of power through fathers and brothers, Christina Rossetti most obviously through the Pre-Raphaelite Movement and Emily Dickinson through her father's and brother's friends in publishing. It is chilling to remember, however, that despite her privilege, had it not been for a woman, Emily Dickinson would be totally unknown today.

They also were able to gain for themselves the most important gift for any author–leisure. That they had more opportunity for their writing was due partly to economic position, but they also chose to fight for it. Rossetti refused a position as head director of a House of Charity and many opportunities to governess to ensure that she had leisure after her manifold family and domestic responsibilities were fulfilled. Wealthy though Dickinson's family was, she also battled with the conflict between domestic responsibilities and time for her writing.

Perhaps the most telling reason for their staying power was their ability to choose what was correct for them. Paradoxically, though they had access to male power, they often appeared to undercut this privilege by their poetic choices. Yet their flouting of Victorian conventions led to the very strengths which made them appeal to a twentieth century audience: the unconventional subject matter and experimental prosody.

What, then, were the costs of their poetry? For these women had little power over anything beyond their interior vision. They lived in a time which forbade any but a very narrow slice of the world to women. Following their own vision cost them friends, family, common human warmth, and even denied them their identity while they lived and left them vulnerable to the worst excesses on their memories after they were dead. All the very real pain incurred, even by these relatively privileged women, must not be minimized in an attempt to present the power of the woman poet. Poetry does not proceed in a vacuum. The woman poet has been transformed in each age to conform to dominant societies' notions of the correct woman poet, and these images have often had a chilling force on women attempting to follow their paths. Perhaps more injurious, they deny to the women who wish to follow them full, real, struggling women, caught in a complex web of will and restriction.

Notes

PREFACE

1. Mary Ellmann, *Thinking About Women* (New York: Harcourt, Brace & World, 1968).
2. Kate Millet, *Sexual Politics* (Garden City: Doubleday, 1970).
3. Ellen Moers, *Literary Women: The Great Writers* (Garden City: Doubleday, 1976).
4. Elaine Showalter, *A Literature of Their Own: British Women Novelists from Brontë to Lessing* (Princeton: Princeton University Press, 1977).
5. Elaine Showalter, *The New Feminist Criticism: Essays on Women, Literature and Theory* (New York: Pantheon, 1985).
6. Shira Wolosky, *Emily Dickinson: A Voice of War* (New Haven: Yale University Press, 1984).
7. Dolores Rosenblum, "Christina Rossetti's Religious Poetry: Watching, Looking, Keeping Vigil," *Victorian Poetry*, 20.1 (1982): 33-50; Sandra Gilbert and Susan Gubar, *The Madwoman in the Attic* (New Haven: Yale University Press, 1979).
8. Margaret Homans, "'Syllables of Velvet': Dickinson, Rossetti and the Rhetorics of Sexuality," *Signs*, 11.3 (1985): 569-93.
9. Lillian Robinson, "Working/Women/Writing," *Sex, Class, and Culture* (Bloomington: Indiana University Press, 1978)

CHAPTER 1: OVERVIEW

1. Christina Rossetti, "From the Antique," *The Poetical Works of Christina Georgina Rossetti,* ed. William Michael Rossetti (London: Macmillan, 1904) 312-13.

2. Emily Dickinson, poem #435, *The Poems of Emily Dickinson,* ed. Thomas H. Johnson, 3 vols. (Cambridge, MA: The Belknap Press of Harvard University Press, 1955) 1: 337. Dickinson's poems will be cited in the text by number from these volumes.

3. For Dickinson and Rossetti as neurotic, see especially John Cody, *After Great Pain: The Inner Life of Emily Dickinson* (Cambridge, MA: Harvard University Press, 1971), and Georgina Battiscombe, *Christina Rossetti: A Divided Life* (London: Constable, 1981). Feminist "rescuers" include Shira Wolosky, *Emily Dickinson: A Voice of War* (New Haven: Yale University Press, 1984); Wendy Martin, *An American Triptych: Anne Bradstreet, Emily Dickinson, Adrienne Rich* (Chapel Hill: University of North Carolina Press, 1984); Suzanne Juhasz, *The Undiscovered Continent: Emily Dickinson and the Space of the Mind* (Bloomington: Indiana University Press, 1983); Barbara Antonina Clarke Mossberg, *Emily Dickinson: When a Writer Is a Daughter* (Bloomington: Indiana University Press, 1982); Cheryl Walker, *The Nightingale's Burden* (Bloomington: Indiana University Press, 1982); Dolores Rosenblum, "Christina Rossetti's Religious Poetry: Watching, Looking, Keeping Vigil," *Victorian Poetry,* 20.1 (1982): 33-50; Allan R. Life, "The Pre-Raphaelites," *Victorian Poetry,* 19.3 (1981): 276-87; Jerome J. McGann, "Christina Rossetti's Poems: A New Edition and a Revaluation," *Victorian Studies,* 23 (1980): 237-54, among others.

4. Richard B. Sewall, *The Life of Emily Dickinson,* 2 vols. (New York: Farrar, Straus and Giroux, 1974) 2: 713-14.

5. R. W. Franklin, ed. *The Manuscript Books of Emily Dickinson,* 2 vols. (Cambridge, MA: The Belknap Press of Harvard University Press, 1981) 1: 533-60.

6. Carroll Smith-Rosenberg, "The Female World of Love and Ritual: Relations Between Women in Nineteenth Century America," *Signs,* 1.1 (1975): 1-29; Nancy F. Cott, *The Bonds of Womanhood: Woman's Sphere in New England,* 1780-1835 (New Haven: Yale University Press, 1977).

7. Sewall 2: 363, 466, 598, 607, 671.

8. "From Missouri," *The Springfield Republican,* 1 January 1862: 4.

9. "Proclamation of a Fighting General," *The Springfield Republican,* 1

January 1862: 2.

10. "The Progress of the War," *The Springfield Republican*, 3 January 1862: 4.

11. "The Upper Potomac," *The Springfield Republican*, 3 January 1862: 4.

12. Marilyn L. Williamson, "Toward a Feminist Literary Theory," *Signs*, 10.1 (1984): 136-47.

13. Ray Strachey, *The Cause* (1928; London: Virago, 1978) 17.

14. "Queen Bees Or Working Bees?" *Saturday Review of Politics, Literature, Science, and Art*, 12 November 1859: 576.

15. Martha Vicinus, *Independent Women* (Chicago: University of Chicago Press, 1985); Lee Chambers-Schiller, *Liberty, A Better Husband* (New Haven: Yale University Press, 1984).

16. Christina Rossetti, "The Lowest Room," *The Complete Poems of Christina Rossetti*, ed. R. W. Crump, 2 vols. to date (Baton Rouge: Louisiana State University Press, 1979-) 1: 200-7.

17. William Michael Rossetti, ed. *Ruskin: Rossetti: Preraphaelitism, Papers 1854 to 1862* (London: Allen, 1899) 258-59.

18. Christina Rossetti, *Goblin Market, and Other Poems* (London: Macmillan, 1862), *The Prince's Progress, and Other Poems* (London: Macmillan, 1866). The difference between English rhyme and French feminine rhyme consists in whether accented or unaccented syllables are paired for sound. In English rhyme, the echoing of sounds usually occurs between accented syllables in the last two words of consecutive or nearby lines. Four lines from "Goblin Market" illustrate English rhyme:

> One had a cat's face,
> One whisked a tail,
> One tramped at a rat's pace,
> One crawled like a snail.

However, in French feminine rhyme, the rhyming words at the ends of lines contain unstressed syllables, as in the next two lines of "Goblin Market": "One like a wombat prowled obtuse and furry, / One like a ratel tumbled hurry skurry."

19. #268, *The Letters of Emily Dickinson*, ed. Thomas H. Johnson, 3 vols. (Cambridge, MA: The Belknap Press of Harvard University Press, 1958) 2: 412.

20. Rebecca Patterson, "Emily Dickinson Feminist," *Amazon Expedition* (New York: Times Change Press, 1973) 33-42.

21. #261, #265, and #271, *The Letters of Emily Dickinson* 2: 404, 409,

414.

22. Sewall 1: 5-6, 220-22.
23. Sewall 475-76.
24. See, for example, Adrienne Rich, "Vesuvius at Home: The Power of Emily Dickinson," *Shakespeare's Sisters: Feminist Essays on Women Poets,* eds. Sandra Gilbert and Susan Gubar (Bloomington: Indiana University Press, 1979) 99-121.
25. Eleanor Walter Thomas, *Christina Georgina Rossetti* (1931; New York: Ams Press, 1966) 45.
26. Nina Auerbach, *Communities of Women: An Idea in Fiction* (Cambridge, MA: Harvard University Press, 1978).
27. Allen Tate, "Emily Dickinson," *Emily Dickinson: A Collection of Critical Essays,* ed. Richard B. Sewall (Englewood Cliffs: Prentice Hall, 1963) 19.
28. Lona Mosk Packer, *Christina Rossetti* (Berkeley: University of California Press, 1963); William H. Shurr, *The Marriage of Emily Dickinson: A Study of the Fascicles* (Lexington: University of Kentucky Press, 1983).
29. Conrad Aiken, "Emily Dickinson," *Emily Dickinson: A Collection of Critical Essays,* 10.
30. Tate 19.

CHAPTER 2: PARALLEL SKETCHES

1. *The Complete Poems of Christina Rossetti* 2: 119.
2. Packer 1-2.
3. *The Complete Poems of Christina Rossetti* 1: 56-57.
4. Sewall 1: 67.
5. #94, *The Letters of Emily Dickinson* 1: 212.
6. #36, *The Letters of Emily Dickinson* 1: 99.
7. #30, *The Letters of Emily Dickinson* 1: 82.
8. Sewall 2: 678-79.
9. Martha Dickinson Bianchi, *Life and Letters of Emily Dickinson* (Boston: Houghton Mifflin, 1924) 26-27, 384.
10. Jackson's letter to Dickinson included in #476a, *The Letters of Emily Dickinson* 2: 563-64.
11. Jackson's letter to Dickinson included in #573a, *The Letters of Emily Dickinson* 2: 624-25.
12. Letter to William Michael Rossetti, December 6, 1890, *The Family Letters of Christina Georgina Rossetti,* ed. William Michael Rossetti (London: Brown, Langham & Co., 1908) 176-77.

13. *The Poetical Works of Christina Georgina Rossetti* 378.

CHAPTER 3: EMILY DICKINSON

1. #330, *The Letters of Emily Dickinson* 2: 460.
2. Mary E. Wilkins (Freeman), *A New England Nun and Other Stories* (New York: Harper & Bros., 1905), *Short Fiction of Sarah Orne Jewett and Mary Wilkins Freeman*, ed. Barbara H. Solomon (New York: New American Library, 1979).
3. *The Scarlet Letter* was published when Dickinson was twenty; *The House of Seven Gables* was published the year after.
4. Frank Prentice Rand, *The Village of Amherst: A Landmark of Light* (Amherst: The Amherst Historical Society, 1958) 61-115.
5. David F. Allmendinger, Jr., "Mt. Holyoke Students Encounter the Need For Life Planning 1837-1850," *History of Education Quarterly* 19.1 (1979): 27-46.
6. Sewall 1: 81.
7. #123, *The Letters of Emily Dickinson* 1: 249.
8. Quoted in Sewall 1: 153. Quoted with permission from the Emily Dickinson Collection, Clifton Waller Barrett Library, University of Virginia Library.
9. #1, *The Letters of Emily Dickinson* 1: 3.
10. #16, *The Letters of Emily Dickinson* 1: 47-49.
11. #110, *The Letters of Emily Dickinson* 1: 235.
12. #96, *The Letters of Emily Dickinson* 1: 215.
13. #103, *The Letters of Emily Dickinson* 1: 222-23.
14. #18, *The Letters of Emily Dickinson* 1: 53-56.
15. Katherine M. Kearns, "Farmers' Daughters: The Education of Women at Alfred Academy and University Before the Civil War," unpublished paper delivered at "Collaborations and Connections in Women's Studies," University of Pennsylvania, March 15-16, 1985.
16. Poems using scientific metaphors include #66, #168, #290, #630, #954, #1002, among many others. They can be found by using the helpful Subject Index in *The Poems of Emily Dickinson* 3: 1214-1226.
17. Anne Firor Scott, "The Ever Widening Circle: The Diffusion of Feminine Values from the Troy Female Seminary, 1822-1872," *History of Education Quarterly* 19.1 (1979): 3-25.
18. Sewall 2: 338-39.
19. #10, *The Letters of Emily Dickinson* 1: 27-28.
20. #35, *The Letters of Emily Dickinson* 1: 94.
21. #23, *The Letters of Emily Dickinson* 1: 66.

22. Martha Dickinson Bianchi, *Emily Dickinson Face to Face: Unpublished Letters With Notes and Reminiscences* (Boston: Houghton Mifflin, 1932) 46.
23. See Bianchi and Clark Griffith *The Long Shadow: Emily Dickinson's Tragic Poetry* (Princeton: Princeton University Press, 1964); Thomas H. Johnson, *Emily Dickinson: An Interpretive Biography* (Cambridge, MA: The Belknap Press of Harvard University Press, 1955) and George Frisbie Wicher, *This Was A Poet: A Critical Biography of Emily Dickinson* (New York: Scribner's, 1938).
24. Sewall 1: 189-94.
25. Alfred Tennyson, *The Poetic Dramatic Works of Alfred Lord Tennyson* (Boston: Houghton Mifflin, 1898) 135-36.
26. Patterson 39.
27. #223, *The Letters of Emily Dickinson* 2: 366.
28. Vicinus, *Independent Women* 11, 46.
29. Vicinus, *Independent Women* 10-13.
30. #234, *The Letters of Emily Dickinson* 2: 376.
31. Sue's response to Emily included in #238, *The Letters of Emily Dickinson* 2: 380.
32. *The Poems of Emily Dickinson* 1: 154.
33. *The Letters of Emily Dickinson,* vol. 3.
34. Karl Keller, *The Only Kangaroo Among the Beauty; Emily Dickinson and America* (Baltimore and London: Johns Hopkins University Press, 1979) 206-13.
35. #792, *The Letters of Emily Dickinson* 3: 754-55.

CHAPTER 4: CHRISTINA ROSSETTI

1. Packer 5.
2. Nina Auerbach, *The Woman And The Demon* (Cambridge, MA: Harvard University Press, 1982) 128.
3. Edmund Gosse, *Critical Kit-Kats* (New York: Charles Scribner's Sons, 1914) 140.
4. William Michael Rossetti, "Memoir," *The Poetical Works of Christina Georgina Rossetti* lxvi-lxvii.
5. Packer 1, 10-11; Thomas 14-17.
6. William Michael Rossetti, "Memoir," *The Poetical Works of Christina Georgina Rossetti* xlix; Thomas 18.
7. Gosse 140.
8. Mackenzie Bell, *Christina Rossetti* (London: Thomas Burleigh, 1898) 11.
9. Thomas 21; Battiscombe 35.

10. As quoted in Battiscombe 35; taken from James A. Kohl, "A Medical Note on Christina Rossetti," *Notes And Queries,* 15 (1968): 423-24.

11. Barbara Ehrenreich and Deirdre English, *Complaints and Disorders: The Sexual Politics of Sickness* (Old Westbury: The Feminist Press, 1973) 22, 25, 42-43.

12. Rossetti's first recorded poem, "To My Mother on the Anniversary of Her Birth," was written when she was twelve, *The Poetical Works of Christina Georgina Rossetti* 82.

13. *Letters of Dante Gabriel Rossetti,* eds. Oswald Doughty and John Robert Wahl, 4 vols. (Oxford: Clarendon Press, 1965) 1: 109.

14. As quoted in Thomas 29.

15. William Michael Rossetti, "Memoir," *The Poetical Works of Christina Georgina Rossetti* xlviii.

16. Battiscombe 22.

17. Battiscombe 23.

18. Packer 12.

19. William Michael Rossetti, "Memoir," *The Poetical Works of Christina Georgina Rossetti* lvi.

20. *The Complete Poems of Christina Rossetti* 1: 223-24.

21. Kinuko Craft, "Goblin Market," *Playboy* 20 (1973) 119.

22. Sandra Gilbert and Susan Gubar, *The Madwoman In The Attic* (New Haven: Yale University Press, 1979) 539-580; Rich, "Vesuvius at Home: The Power of Emily Dickinson": 110.

23. "Repining," *The Poetical Works of Christina Georgina Rossetti* 9-12, 460. This poem is discussed at length in chapter three, "War Poems." "Behold, I Stand at the Door and Knock," *The Poetical Works of Christina Georgina Rossetti* 147, 470.

24. William Michael Rossetti, "Notes," *The Poetical Works of Christina Georgina Rossetti* 470.

25. As quoted in Battiscombe 54.

26. Both published in *The Athenaeum,* 14 and 21 October 1848, respectively.

27. Cott 15-16.

28. William Michael Rossetti, "Notes," *The Poetical Works of Christina Georgina Rossetti* 467.

29. Battiscombe 26.

30. *The Family Letters of Christina Georgina Rossetti* 2-14.

31. Thomas 28; Walker traces the image of the melancholy woman poet back to the classical myth of Philomela as nightingale, especially in chapter 2, "Founding the Tradition: The Poetess at Large," 21-58.

32. Christina Georgina Rossetti, *Maude: Prose and Verse,* ed. R. W. Crump (Hamden: Archon, 1976) 29-30.

33. *Maude* 69.

34. *Maude* 53.

35. Diane D'Amico, "Christina Rossetti's *Maude:* A Reconsideration," *University of Dayton Review,* 15.1 (1981): 136.

36. "Biographical Notice" to *Wuthering Heights,* 19 September 1850, contains this description of Emily Brontë by Charlotte Brontë: "The awful point was, that while full of ruth for others, on herself she had no pity."

37. *The Complete Poems of Christina Rossetti* 1: 122.

38. Doughty and Wahl 1: 45.

39. Dr. C. Willett Cunnington, *Feminine Attitudes in the Nineteenth Century* (1935; New York: Haskell House, 1973) 139-42.

40. M. Jeanne Peterson, "The Victorian Governess: Status Incongruence in Family and Society," *Suffer and Be Still,* ed. Martha Vicinus (Bloomington: Indiana University Press, 1973) 6.

41. *National Review,* 15 (1862); reprinted in 1869 as a separate pamphlet, then again in *Literary and Social Judgments* (Boston: James R. Osgood, 1873).

42. Helene E. Roberts, "Marriage, Redundancy or Sin: The Painter's View of Women in the First Twenty-Five Years of Victoria's Reign," *Suffer and Be Still* 57.

43. As quoted by A. James Hammerton in "Feminism and Female Emigration, 1861-1886," *A Widening Sphere,* ed. Martha Vicinus (Bloomington: Indiana University Press, 1977) 53.

44. Roberts 57.

45. Roberts 57.

46. Roberts 63.

47. Auerbach, *The Woman And The Demon* 124.

48. Cunnington 143-44.

49. Packer 55.

50. Desmond Morse-Boycott, *The Secret Story of The Oxford Movement* (London: Skeffington and Son, 1933) 98.

51. Auerbach, *The Woman And The Demon* 124.

52. As quoted in Packer 21.

53. Cunnington 150-51.

54. Thomas 57.

55. Thomas 21.

56. Battiscombe 72.

57. *Letters of Dante Gabriel Rossetti* 1: 108-9.

58. Packer 99.

59. Barbara Charlesworth Gelpi, "The Feminization of D. G. Rossetti,"

The Victorian Experience: The Poets, ed. Richard A. Levine (Athens: Ohio University Press, 1982) 94-114.

60. *The Family Letters of Christina Georgina Rossetti* 23.
61. *Letters of Dante Gabriel Rossetti* 1: 156.
62. Ford Madox Hueffer, *Rossetti: A Critical Essay on His Art* (London: Duckworth, 1902) 30-32.
63. *Letters of Dante Gabriel Rossetti* 1: 170.
64. Thomas 40-41.
65. This summary of acquaintances is a compendium from William Michael Rossetti's "Memoir" and the biographies of Rossetti by Bell, Thomas, Packer, and Battiscombe.
66. Bell 36-37, 161-62.
67. *Letters of Dante Gabriel Rossetti* 1: 163.
68. *The Family Letters of Christina Georgina Rossetti* 110.
69. Barbara Taylor, *Eve and the New Jerusalem: Socialism and Feminism in the Nineteenth Century* (New York: Pantheon, 1983) 279-81; Bessie Rayner Parkes, "A Year's Experience in Woman's Work," *English Woman's Journal,* 1 September 1860: 117; Lee Holcombe, *Victorian Ladies at Work* (Hamden: Archon, 1973) 5-22, 73.
70. Taylor 27.
71. Battiscombe 25.
72. Bell 54.
73. Taylor 275-79.
74. "The Disputed Question," *English Woman's Journal,* 1 August 1858: 364-65.
75. Taylor 279.
76. *The Complete Poems of Christina Rossetti* 1: 149.
77. *The Complete Poems of Christina Rossetti* 1: 176.
78. See "A Portrait," *The Complete Poems of Christina Rossetti* 1: 122; "Repining," "The Dead City," "Three Stages," "Seeking Rest," and "Three Moments," *The Poetical Works of Christina Georgina Rossetti* 9-12, 99-103, 288-300, 296.
79. 1881 *A Pageant and Other Poems* includes mainly new poems; 1875 *Goblin Market, The Prince's Progress and Other Poems* combines *Goblin Market* with *The Prince's Progress,* omits five previously published poems, and adds thirty-seven new ones; 1893 *Verses* merely collects the poetry scattered through her previous volumes published by the Society for Promoting Christian Knowledge.
80. See notes for "A Ballad of Boding" by William Michael Rossetti, *The Poetical Works of Christina Georgina Rossetti* 462.
81. Packer 232-35, 359-64.

82. Rosalie Glynn Grylls, *Portrait of Rossetti* (London: Macdonald, 1964); "Extracts from a Diary kept by Christina Rossetti on behalf of her Mother, 1881-6," *The Family Letters of Christina Georgina Rossetti* 222-33.

83. Ellen A. Proctor, *A Brief Memoir of Christina G. Rossetti* (London: S.P.C.K., 1895) 66-68.

84. Cristina G. Rossetti, *The Face of the Deep: A Devotional Commentary on the Apocalypse* 5th ed. (1892; London: S.P.C.K., 1907) 422.

85. Bell 110-11.

86. Bell 111-12.

87. *The Complete Poems of Christina Rossetti* 2: 149-50.

88. "Notes," *The Poetical Works of Christina Georgina Rossetti* 463.

89. Bell 176-77.

CHAPTER 5: WAR POEMS

1. Examples of women's war poetry and descriptions of it can be found in: *The Atlantic Monthly,* 1858-1866; *English Woman's Journal,* 1858-1862; Christopher Hibbert, *The Destruction of Lord Raglan* (Boston: Little, Brown, 1961); Florence Nightingale, *Cassandra* (New York: Feminist Press, 1979); Adelaide A. Procter, *The Poems of Adelaide A. Procter* (New York: Thomas Y. Crowell, 1880); Philip Warner, *The Crimean War* (New York: Laplinger, 1973).

2. Bell 112.

3. William Michael Rossetti, "Notes," *The Poetical Works of Christina Georgina Rossetti* (London: Macmillan, 1904) 461. William Michael's defensive interpretation of his sister's poem is just one example of the way political poetry by women has been hidden.

4. Helen Rossetti Angeli, *Dante Gabriel Rossetti* (London: Hamish Hamilton, 1949).

5. *The Poetical Works of Christina Georgina Rossetti* 82-83, 464-65.

6. Dwight A. Culler, "Monodrama and the Dramatic Monologue," *PMLA,* 90 (May, 1975): 366-85.

7. *The Poetical Works of Christina Georgina Rossetti* 9.

8. *The Poetical Works of Christina Georgina Rossetti* 12.

9. Packer 93. Packer attributed Rossetti's writing block to "illness."

10. Procter 145-47.

11. Procter 147-51.

12. *The Complete Poems of Christina Rossetti* 1: 200-207.

13. William Michael Rossetti, "Notes," *The Poetical Works of Christina Georgina Rossetti* 460-61; *The Family Letters of Christina Georgina*

Rossetti 55.

14. Packer 153.
15. "Memoir," *The Poetical Works of Christina Georgina Rossetti* lxx.
16. William Michael Rossetti, "English Opinion on the American War," *The Atlantic Monthly,* 17, No. C (February, 1866): 129-49.
17. "Textual Notes," *The Complete Poems of Christina Rossetti* 1:   284; "Notes," *The Poetical Works of Christina Georgina Rossetti* 461.
18. Robert Langbaum, *The Poetry of Experience* (London: Chatto and Windus, 1957).
19. *The Complete Poems of Christina Rossetti* 1:   149-152.
20. *The Complete Poems of Christina Rossetti* 1:   95-110.
21. Janet Camp Troxell, ed. *Three Rossettis: Unpublished Letters to and from Dante Gabriel, Christina, William* (Cambridge, MA: Harvard University Press, 1937) 141.
22. *The Complete Poems of Christina Rossetti* 1:   214-16.
23. Wolosky xviii, xiii, 95.
24. #30, *The Letters of Emily Dickinson* 1:   84.
25. #280, *The Letters of Emily Dickinson* 2:   423.
26. Sewall 2:   536.
27. #234, *The Letters of Emily Dickinson* 2:   375-76.

CHAPTER 6:   THE MARKET IS FOR BANKERS, BURGLARS, AND GOBLINS

1. June Sochen, *Herstory* (Palo Alto: Mayfield, 1982) 77-101.
2. Strachey 91-92.
3. McGann and Auerbach have been previously cited.   Also Bonnie Zimmerman, "The New Tradition," *Sinister Wisdom,* 1.2 (1976):   34-41.
4. Strachey 89.
5. *The Complete Poems of Christina Rossetti* 1:   41.
6. McGann 245.
7. Packer 106.
8. Packer 106.
9. *The Complete Poems of Christina Rossetti* 1:   30.
10. *The Complete Poems of Christina Rossetti* 1:   43-44.
11. *The Complete Poems of Christina Rossetti* 1:   44-46.
12. Martha Vicinus, "The Study of Nineteenth-Century British Working-Class Poetry," *The Politics of Literature* (New York: Vintage, 1973) 330.
13 *The Complete Poems of Christina Rossetti* 1:   32.
14. *The Complete Poems of Christina Rossetti* 1:   191-92; "Notes," *The*

Poetical Works of Christina Georgina Rossetti 485.

15. Packer 153-54.
16. *The Complete Poems of Christina Rossetti* 1: 164-78.
17. Troxell 143.
18. *The Complete Poems of Christina Rossetti* 1: 11-26.
19. McGann 244-45.
20. Karl Marx, *Grundrisse,* trans. Martin Nicolaus (1857; New York: Penguin, 1972) 145.
21. McGann 250.
22. McGann 245-50.
23. McGann 251.
24. Ellen Dubois, "The Nineteenth-Century Women Suffrage Movement and the Analysis of Women's Oppression," *Capitalist Patriarchy and the Case for Socialist Feminism,* ed. Zillah Eisenstein (New York: Monthly Review Press, 1979) 139.
25. Quoted in Susan P. Conrad, *Perish the Thought: Intellectual Women in Romantic America,* 1830-1860 (New York: Oxford University Press, 1976) 143.
26. Shurr, note 26, 234.
27. #39, *The Letters of Emily Dickinson* 1: 102-05.
28. Herbert G. Gutman, "Work, Culture and Society in Industrializing America, 1815-1919," *Work, Culture and Society in Industrializing America: Essays in American Working-Class and Social History.* (New York: Knopf, 1976) 3-78.
29. Sewall, note 8, 2: 476.
30. #127, *Letters of Emily Dickinson* 1: 253-55.

CHAPTER 7: WOMAN'S PLACE/WOMAN'S NATURE

1. Tillie Olsen, "Biographical Interpretation," *Life in the Iron Mills* by Rebecca Harding Davis (Old Westbury: The Feminist Press, 1972) 82, 162-63.
2. The story behind the publication of Christina Rossetti's "Goblin Market" illustrates how women poets became an active part of British cultural life in the working and middle classes. Before deciding to publish "Goblin Market" as the title poem in a complete volume, Alexander Macmillan gave the poem a "test reading" at a "small working-man's society" in Cambridge. "They seemed at first to wonder whether I was making fun of them; by degrees they got as still as death, and when I finished there was a tremendous burst of applause. I wish Miss Rossetti could have heard it." George Macmillan, ed.

Letters of Alexander Macmillan (Glasgow: privately printed, 1908) 94-95. As cited in Lona Mosk Packer, ed., *The Rossetti-Macmillan Letters* (Berkeley: University of California Press) 7. According to most critics, Emily Dickinson's attempt to publish was influenced by Thomas Wentworth Higginson's invitation to young women writers, "Letter to a Young Contributor," *Atlantic Monthly,* April 1862. See Sewall 2: 538-40.

3. Strachey 86-87.
4. Barbara Ehrenreich and Deirdre English, *For Her Own Good* (New York: Doubleday, 1978), especially Chapter Four, "The Sexual Politics of Sickness."
5. Barbara Sinclair Deckard, *The Women's Movement* (New York: Harper and Row, 1983) 155.
6. Vicinus, *Independent Women.* See, for example, Chapter six, "Settlement Houses: A Community Ideal for the Poor," 214-16.
7. Quoted in Keller 237.
8. As quoted in Sewall 2: 471.
9. Sewall 2: 471-72.
10. Walker 32-33.
11. Walker 31, 81.
12. Rich, 102.
13. #238, *The Letters of Emily Dickinson* 2: 380.
14. Walker 80.
15. Sewall 2: 473.
16. Patterson 37.
17. Patterson, *The Riddle of Emily Dickinson* (Boston: Houghton Mifflin, 1951).
18. Winston Weathers, "The Sisterhood of Self," *Victorian Poetry* 3 (1965): 81-91.
19. *Letters of Dante Gabriel Rossetti* 1: 162-63.
20. *The Poetical Works of Christina Georgina Rossetti* 302, 303.
21. *The Complete Poems of Christina Rossetti* 1: 76-77.
22. Nancy F. Cott, "Passionlessness: An Interpretation of Victorian Sexual Ideology, 1790-1850," *Signs,* 4.2 (winter 1978): 233.
23. *Letters of Dante Gabriel Rossetti* 1: 1-2 n.1, 5.
24. Cunnington 161.
25. Packer 305.
26. Packer 305.
27. *Letters of Dante Gabriel Rossetti* 1: 200, 250.
28. *Letters of Dante Gabriel Rossetti* 1: 257.
29. Christina Rossetti, *Time Flies: A Reading Diary* (1885; Boston:

Roberts Brothers, 1886) 97; see also Packer 418 n.5.

30. *The Complete Poems of Christina Rossetti* 1: 82-88.

31. *The Germ* (1850; New York: Ams Press, 1965) 80.

32. See "Look on This Picture and on This," *The Poetical Works of Christina Georgina Rossetti* 323-25; "Memory, II," *The Complete Poems of Christina Rossetti* 1: 148 and "The Convent Threshold," *The Complete Poems of Christina Rossetti* 1: 61-65.

33. McGann 250.

34. William Michael Rossetti, "Notes," *The Poetical Works of Christina Georgina Rossetti* 459; Bell 207.

35. Packer 138-41.

36. *The Complete Poems of Christina Rossetti* 1: 59-60.

37. See Packer 120-23, 124, 126, 132, 174, 180.

38. *Letters of Dante Gabriel Rossetti* 1: 92.

39. *Life and Letters of Sir John Everett Millais*, ed. John Guille Millais, 2 vols. (New York: Frederick A. Stokes, 1899) 1: 144.

40. *Letters of Dante Gabriel Rossetti* 1: 107 n.5, 109 n.4.

41. Bell 112.

42. Bell 168-69.

43. Bell 177.

44. Bell 176.

45. *The Poetical Works of Christina Georgina Rossetti* 105.

46. *The Complete Poems of Christina Rossetti* 1: 58.

47. *The Poetical Works of Christina Rossetti* 300.

48. *The Complete Poems of Christina Rossetti* 1: 68.

49. *The Complete Poems of Christina Rossetti* 1: 67-68.

50. Christina Rossetti, "Eve," Box 1, No. 5, J. C. Troxell Collection, Princeton University.

51. Sojourner Truth, "Ain't I a Woman," *Women And The Politics of Culture*, eds. Michele Wender Zak and Patricia A. Moots (New York and London: Longman, 1983) 153.

52. *The Poetical Works of Christina Georgina Rossetti* 286.

53. "The Thread of Life," *The Complete Poems of Christina Rossetti* 2: 123.

CHAPTER 8: WOMEN POETS, LITERARY INFLUENCE, AND THE CANON

1. This connection was first established by Moers 84-95.

2. "Notes" for "The Lowest Room," *The Poetical Works of Christina Georgina Rossetti* 460-61.

3. The translation from Petrarch is from William Michael Rossetti's "Notes" for "Monna Innominata," *The Poetical Works of Christina Georgina Rossetti* 462. *The Complete Poems of Christina Georgina Rossetti* 2: 86.
4. H. G., "Lines Suggested By More Than One Domestic History," *English Woman's Journal,* June 1858: 244.
5. Bessie Rayner Parkes, "The Old Chateau," *English Woman's Journal,* March 1859: 26.
6. *Poems of Charlotte, Emily & Anne Brontë with Cottage Poems by Patrick Brontë* (London: J. M. Dent, 1893) 83.
7. *The Complete Poems of Christina Rossetti* 1: 58.
8. Moers 275-90.
9. *The Complete Poems of Christina Rossetti* 1: 153-54.
10. *The Poetical Works of Christina Georgina Rossetti* 330.
11. Life 276.
12. Aiken 10.
13. W. Holman Hunt, *Pre-Raphaelitism and the Pre-Raphaelite Brotherhood* 2 vols. (New York: Macmillan, 1905) 1: 154.
14. William Michael Rossetti, "Memoir," *The Poetical Works of Christina Georgina Rossetti* lxx.
15. William Butler Yeats, "Among School Children," *The Poems: A New Edition,* ed. Richard J. Finneran (New York: Macmillan, 1983) 217.
16. Humphry House, ed. *The Journals and Papers of Gerard Manly Hopkins* (London: Oxford University Press, 1959) 287; Packer 185.
17. Jeanne Kammer, "The Art of Silence and the Forms of Women's Poetry," *Shakespeare's Sisters* 153-64.
18. Thomas H. Johnson, "Introduction," *The Letters of Emily Dickinson* 1: xx.
19. Thomas H. Johnson, "Introduction," *The Letters of Emily Dickinson* 1: xv.
20. Alfred Alvarez, *The Savage God: A Study of Suicide* (Harmondsworth: Penguin, 1974).
21. Jay Leyda, *The Years and Hours of Emily Dickinson* (New Haven: Yale University Press, 1960).
22. Gilbert and Gubar 583-84.

Selected Bibliography

Aiken, Conrad. "Emily Dickinson," in Richard B. Sewall, ed. *Emily Dickinson: A Collection of Critical Essays.* Englewood Cliffs: Prentice-Hall, 1963. 9-15.

Allmendinger, Jr., David F. "Mount Holyoke Students Encounter the Need For Life Planning 1837-1850." *History of Education Quarterly* 19.1 (1979): 27-46.

Alvarez, Alfred. *The Savage God: A Study of Suicide.* Harmondsworth: Penguin, 1974.

Angeli, Helen Rossetti. *Dante Gabriel Rossetti.* London: Hamish Hamilton, 1949.

The Atlantic Monthly. 1858-1866.

Auerbach, Nina. *Communities of Women: An Idea in Fiction.* Cambridge, MA: Harvard University Press, 1978.

____. *The Woman and the Demon: The Life of a Victorian Myth.* Cambridge, MA: Harvard University Press, 1982.

Battiscombe, Georgina. *Christina Rossetti: A Divided Life.* London: Constable, 1981.

Bell, Mackenzie. *Christina Rossetti.* London: Thomas Burleigh, 1898.

Bianchi, Martha Dickinson. *Emily Dickinson Face to Face: Unpublished Letters with Notes and Reminiscences.* Boston: Houghton Mifflin, 1932.

____. *Life and Letters of Emily Dickinson.* Boston: Houghton Mifflin, 1924.

Brontë, Charlotte. Biographical Notice. *Wuthering Heights.* By Emily Brontë. 1847. New York: Random House, 1943. v-x.

Chambers-Schiller, Lee. *Liberty, A Better Husband.* New Haven: Yale

University Press, 1984.

Cody, John. *After Great Pain: The Inner Life of Emily Dickinson*. Cambridge, MA: Harvard University Press, 1971.

Conrad, Susan P. *Perish the Thought: Intellectual Women in Romantic America, 1830-1860*. New York: Oxford University Press, 1976.

Cott, Nancy F. *The Bonds of Womanhood: Woman's Sphere in New England, 1780-1835*. New Haven: Yale University Press, 1977.

____. "Passionlessness: An Interpretation of Victorian Sexual Ideology, 1790-1850." *Signs* 4.2 (Winter, 1978): 219-36.

Culler, Dwight A. "Monodrama and the Dramatic Monologue." *PMLA* 90 (May 1975): 366-85.

Cunnington, Dr. C. Willett. *Feminine Attitudes in the Nineteenth Century*. 1935. New York: Haskell House, 1973.

D'Amico, Diane. "Christina Rossetti's *Maude*: A Reconsideration." *University of Dayton Review* 15.1 (1981):129-142.

Deckard, Barbara Sinclair. *The Women's Movement*. New York: Harper and Row, 1983.

Dickinson, Emily. *The Poems of Emily Dickinson*. Ed. Thomas H. Johnson. 3 vols. Cambridge, MA: The Belknap Press of Harvard University Press, 1955.

"The Disputed Question." *English Woman's Journal* (1 August 1858): 364-65.

Doughty, Oswald and John Robert Wahl, eds. *Letters of Dante Gabriel Rossetti*. 4 vols. Oxford: Clarendon Press, 1965.

Dubois, Ellen. "The Nineteenth-Century Woman Suffrage Movement and the Analysis of Women's Oppression." *Capitalist Patriarchy and the Case for Socialist Feminism*. Ed. Zillah Eisenstein. New York: Monthly Review Press. 137-50.

Ehrenreich, Barbara and Deirdre English. *Complaints and Disorders: The Sexual Politics of Sickness*. Old Westbury, NY: The Feminist Press, 1973.

____. *For Her Own Good*. New York: Doubleday, 1978.

Ellmann, Mary. *Thinking About Women*. New York: Harcourt Brace & World, 1968.

English Woman's Journal. 1858-1862.

Franklin, R.W. *The Manuscript Books of Emily Dickinson*. 2 vols. Cambridge, MA: The Belknap Press of Harvard University Press, 1981.

"From Missouri." *The Springfield Republican* (1 January 1862): 4.

H.G. "Lines Suggested By More Than One Domestic History." *English Woman's Journal* (June 1858): 244.

Gelpi, Barbara Charlesworth. "The Feminization of D. G. Rossetti." *The*

Victorian Experience: The Poets. Ed. Richard A. Levine. Athens: Ohio University Press, 1982. 94-114.

The Germ. 1850. New York: Ams Press, 1965.

Gilbert, Sandra and Susan Gubar. *The Madwoman in the Attic: The Woman Writer and the Nineteenth-Century Literary Imagination.* New Haven: Yale University Press, 1979.

_____, eds. *Shakespeare's Sisters: Feminist Essays on Women Poets.* Bloomington: Indiana University Press, 1979.

Griffith, Clark. *The Long Shadow: Emily Dickinson's Tragic Poetry.* Princeton: Princeton University Press, 1964.

Grylls, Rosalie Glynn. *Portrait of Rossetti.* London: Macdonald, 1964.

Gutman, Herbert G. *Work, Culture and Society in Industrializing America: Essays in American Working-Class and Social History.* New York: Knopf, 1976.

Hammerton, A. James. "Feminism and Female Emigration, 1861-1886." Vicinus, *A Widening Sphere.* 52-71.

Hawthorne, Nathaniel. *The Scarlet Letter.* 1850. 2nd ed. New York: Norton, 1978.

_____. *The House of Seven Gables.* New York: A. L. Burt, 1851.

Hibbert, Christopher. *The Destruction of Lord Raglan.* Boston: Little, Brown, 1961.

Holcombe, Lee. *Victorian Ladies at Work.* Hamden: Archon, 1973.

Homans, Margaret. "'Syllables of Velvet': Dickinson, Rossetti and the Rhetorics of Sexuality." *Signs* 11.3 (1985): 569-93.

House, Humphry, ed. *The Journals and Papers of Gerard Manly Hopkins.* London: Oxford University Press, 1959.

Hueffer, Ford Madox. *Rossetti: A Critical Essay on His Art.* London: Duckworth, 1902.

Hunt, W. Holman. *Pre-Raphaelitism and the Pre-Raphaelite Brotherhood.* 2 vols. New York: Macmillan, 1905.

Johnson, Thomas H. *Emily Dickinson: An Interpretive Biography.* Cambridge, MA: The Belknap Press of Harvard University Press, 1955.

_____, ed. *The Letters of Emily Dickinson.* 3 vols. Cambridge, MA: The Belknap Press of Harvard University Press, 1958.

Juhasz, Suzanne. *The Undiscovered Continent: Emily Dickinson and the Space of the Mind.* Bloomington: Indiana University Press, 1983.

Kammer, Jeanne. "The Art of Silence and the Forms of Women's Poetry." Gilbert and Gubar, *Shakespeare's Sisters.* 153-64.

Kearns, Katherine M. "Farmers' Daughters: The Education of Women at Alfred Academy and University Before the Civil War." Collaborations and Connections in Women's Studies. University of Pennsylvania, 15-16

March 1985.

Keller, Karl. *The Only Kangaroo Among the Beauty: Emily Dickinson and America.* Baltimore: Johns Hopkins University Press, 1979.

Kohl, James A. *"A Medical Note on Christina Rossetti." Notes and Queries* 15 (1968): 423-24.

Langbaum, Robert. *The Poetry of Experience.* London: Chatto and Windus, 1957.

Leyda, Jay. *The Years and Hours of Emily Dickinson.* New Haven: Yale University Press, 1960.

Life, Allan R. *"The Pre-Raphaelites," Victorian Poetry* 19.3 (1981): 276-87.

Martin, Wendy. *An American Triptych: Anne Bradstreet, Emily Dickinson, Adrienne Rich.* Chapel Hill: University of North Carolina Press, 1984.

Marx, Karl. *Grundrisse.* Trans. Martin Nicolaus. 1857. New York: Penguin, 1972.

McGann, Jerome J. *"Christina Rossetti's Poems: A New Edition and a Revaluation." Victorian Studies* 23 (1980): 237-54.

Millett, Kate. *Sexual Politics.* Garden City: Doubleday, 1970.

Moers, Ellen. *Literary Women: The Great Writers.* Garden City: Doubleday, 1976.

Morse-Boycott, Desmond. *The Secret Story of the Oxford Movement.* London: Skeffington and Son, 1933.

Mossberg, Barbara Antonina Clarke. *Emily Dickinson: When a Writer Is A Daughter.* Bloomington: Indiana University Press, 1982.

Nightingale, Florence. *Cassandra.* New York: The Feminist Press, 1979.

Olsen, Tillie. Biographical Interpretation. *Life in the Iron Mills.* By Rebecca Harding Davis. 1861. Old Westbury: The Feminist Press, 1972.

Packer, Lona Mosk. *Christina Rossetti.* Berkeley: University of California Press, 1963.

____, ed. *The Rossetti-Macmillan Letters.* Berkeley: University of California Press, 1963.

Parkes, Bessie Rayner. *"The Old Chateau." English Woman's Journal* (March 1859): 26.

____. *"A Year's Experience in Woman's Work." English Woman's Journal* (1 September 1860): 117.

Patterson, Rebecca. *"Emily Dickinson Feminist." Amazon Expedition.* New York: Times Change Press, 1973. 33-42.

____. *The Riddle of Emily Dickinson.* Boston: Houghton Mifflin, 1951.

Peterson, M. Jeanne. *"The Victorian Governess: Status Incongruence in Family and Society."* Vicinus, *Suffer and Be Still.* 3-19.

Poems of Charlotte, Emily & Anne Brontë with Cottage Poems by Patrick

Brontë. London: J. M. Dent, 1893.

"Proclamation of a Fighting General." *The Springfield Republican* (1 January 1862): 2.

Procter, Adelaide A. *The Poems of Adelaide A. Procter*. New York: Thomas Y. Crowell, 1880.

Proctor, Ellen A. *A Brief Memoir of Christina G. Rossetti*. London: S. P. C. K., 1907.

"The Progress of the War." *The Springfield Republican* (3 January 1862): 4.

Rand, Frank Prentice. *The Village of Amherst: A Landmark of Light*. Amherst: The Amherst Historical Society, 1958.

Rich, Adrienne. "Vesuvius at Home: The Power of Emily Dickinson." Gilbert and Gubar, *Shakespeare's Sisters*. 99-121.

Roberts, Helene E. "Marriage, Redundancy or Sin: The Painter's View of Women in the First Twenty-Five Years of Victoria's Reign." Vicinus, *Suffer and Be Still*. 45-76.

Robinson, Lillian. *Sex, Class and Culture*. Bloomington: Indiana University Press, 1978.

Rosenblum, Dolores. "Christina Rossetti's Religious Poetry: Watching, Looking, Keeping Vigil." *Victorian Poetry* 20.1 (1982): 33-50.

Rossetti, Christina Georgina. *The Complete Poems of Christina Rossetti*. Ed. R.W. Crump. 2 vols. to date. Baton Rouge: Louisiana University Press, 1979- .

____. *The Face of the Deep: A Devotional Commentary on the Apocalypse*. 5th ed. 1892. London: S. P. C. K., 1907.

____. *Goblin Market, and Other Poems*. London: Macmillan, 1862.

____. "Eve," ms. Box 1, No. 5, J. C. Troxell Collection. Princeton University: Princeton.

____. *Maude: Prose and Verse*. Ed. R. W. Crump. 1897. Hamden: Archon, 1976.

____. *The Poetical Works of Christina Georgina Rossetti*. Ed. William Michael Rossetti. London: Macmillan, 1904.

____. *Time Flies: A Reading Diary*. 1885. Boston: Roberts Brothers, 1886.

Rossetti, William Michael. "English Opinion on the American War." *The Atlantic Monthly* 17, No. C (February, 1866): 129-49.

____, ed. *The Family Letters of Christina Georgina Rossetti*. London: Brown, Langham & Co., 1908.

____. *Ruskin: Rossetti: Pre-Raphaelitism, Papers 1854 to 1862*. London: Allen, 1899.

Saturday Review of Politics, Literature, Science, and Art. 1855-1860.

Scott, Anne Firor. "The Ever Widening Circle: The Diffusion of Feminine Values from the Troy Female Seminary, 1822-1872." *History of Education*

Quarterly 19.1 (1979): 3-25.

Sewall, Richard B., ed. *Emily Dickinson: A Collection of Critical Essays.* Englewood Cliffs: Prentice Hall, 1963.

———. *The Life of Emily Dickinson.* 2 vols. New York: Farrar, Straus and Giroux, 1974.

Short Fiction of Sarah Orne Jewett and Mary Wilkins Freeman, ed. Barbara Solomon. New York: New American Library, 1979.

Showalter, Elaine. *A Literature of Their Own: British Women Novelists from Brontë to Lessing.* Princeton: Princeton University Press, 1977.

———, ed. *The New Feminist Criticism: Essays on Women, Literature and Theory.* New York: Pantheon, 1985.

Shurr, William H. *The Marriage of Emily Dickinson: A Study of the Fascicles.* Lexington: University of Kentucky Press, 1983.

Smith-Rosenberg, Carroll. "The Female World of Love and Ritual: Relations Between Women in Nineteenth Century America." *Signs* 1.1 (1975): 1-29.

Sochen, June. *Herstory.* Palo Alto: Mayfield, 1982.

The Springfield Republican (January 1862).

Strachey, Ray. *The Cause.* 1928. London: Virago, 1978.

Tate, Allen. "Emily Dickinson." Sewall, *Emily Dickinson: A Collection of Critical Essays.* 16-27.

Taylor, Barbara. *Eve and the New Jerusalem: Socialism and Feminism in the Nineteenth Century.* New York: Pantheon, 1983.

Tennyson, Alfred. *The Poetic Dramatic Works of Alfred Lord.* Boston: Houghton Mifflin, 1898.

Thomas, Eleanor Walter. *Christina Georgina Rossetti.* 1931. New York: Ams Press, 1966.

Troxell, Janet Camp, ed. *Three Rossettis: Unpublished Letters to and from Dante Gabriel, Christina, William.* Cambridge, MA.: Harvard University Press, 1937.

Truth, Sojourner. "Ain't I a Woman." *Women and the Politics of Culture.* Eds. MicheleWenderZakandPatriciaA.Moots.NewYork:Longman,1983. 153.

"The Upper Potomac." *The Springfield Republican* (3 January 1862): 4.

Vicinus, Martha. *Independent Women.* Chicago: University of Chicago Press, 1985.

———. "The Study of Nineteenth-Century British Working-Class Poetry." *The Politics of Literature.* Eds. Louis Kampf and Paul Lauter. New York: Vintage, 1973. 322-53.

———, ed. *Suffer and Be Still.* Bloomington: Indiana University Press, 1973.

———, ed. *A Widening Sphere.* Bloomington: Indiana University Press, 1977.

Walker, Cheryl. *The Nightingale's Burden.* Bloomington: Indiana University Press, 1982.

Walsh, Walter. *The Secret History of the Oxford Movement.* London: Swan Sonnenschein, 1898.

Warner, Philip. *The Crimean War.* New York: Laplinger, 1973.

Weathers, Winston. "The Sisterhood of Self". *Victorian Poetry* 3 (1965): 81-91.

Whicher, George Frisbie. *This Was A Poet: A Critical Biography of Emily Dickinson.* New York: Scribner's, 1938.

Wilkins (Freeman), Mary E. *A New England Nun and Other Stories.* New York: Harper & Bros., 1905.

Williamson, Marilyn L. "Toward a Feminist Literary Theory." *Signs* 10.1 (1984): 136-47.

Wolosky, Shira. *Emily Dickinson: A Voice of War.* New Haven: Yale University Press, 1984.

Yeats, William Butler. *The Poems: A New Edition.* Ed. Richard J. Finneran. New York: Macmillan, 1983.

Zimmerman, Bonnie. "The New Tradition." *Sinister Wisdom* 1.2 (1976): 34-41.

Index to Dickinson's Poems Cited in Text

Index to Rossetti's Poems Cited in Text

Index